Illustrated Dictionary of Pottery Decoration

Illustrated Dictionary of Pottery Decoration

Robert Fournier

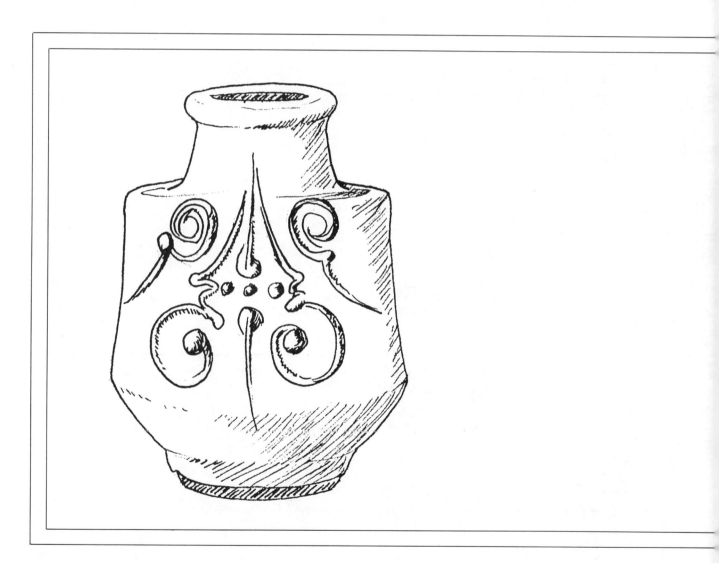

PRENTICE HALL PRESS • NEW YORK

Published by Prentice Hall Press
A Division of Simon & Schuster, Inc.
Gulf + Western Building
One Gulf + Western Plaza
New York, NY   10023

PRENTICE HALL PRESS is a trademark of Simon & Schuster, Inc.

Library of Congress Cataloging in Publication Data

Fournier, Robert.
   Illustrated dictionary of pottery decoration.

   Bibliography: p.
   1. Pottery craft.   2. Decoration and ornament.
3. Glazes.   I. Title.
TT920.F677   1986   738′.03′21   86-534
ISBN 0-671-61376-6

Manufactured in the United States of America

10 9 8 7 6 5 4 3 2 1

First Edition

Dedicated to my wife, Sheila, for her patient help with the many drawings for my books and for her imaginative ceramics, which have provided many photographs.

Acknowledgments

I have many people to thank for help in compiling this dictionary. Foremost, Mike Seaborne for advice and for his splendid and patient processing and printing of some 600 pictures. Grateful thanks also to Cleo Witt of the Bristol Museum for making available ceramics to photograph, for reading the text to check for historical accuracy, and for giving advice in this field.

For allowing me to photograph their rich collections: the British Museum, the Stoke-on-Trent Museum, and Sudbury Hall; and personally to Kathy Niblett of Stoke and Cherry Ann Knott of Sudbury Hall for their time and advice. To Eileen Lewenstein and Emmanuel Cooper of *Ceramic Review* for making available their archives and other material, and to John Anderson for processing slides into prints and allowing the use of some of his photographs.

To Bob Broughton at the Central School of Art, London, for setting up silkscreen printing and allied techniques for three valuable picture series, and to Siddig El'Nigoumi for his time and help. To Jon and Kate Catleugh, Mary Ball, May and Leslie Savage, Sybil Houldsworth, and Lord David Eccles. To the Beaux Arts and St. James Galleries in Bath, and to Barley Roscoe at the Crafts Study Centre. To the Craftsmen Potters Shop, British Crafts Centre, and Five Dials Gallery in London, the Chestnut Gallery, Bourton-on-the-Water, and the Katherine House Gallery, Marlborough, Wiltshire.

To Sutton Taylor, Alan Caiger-Smith, Joan Hepworth, and other friends who have lent slides, pictures, or pots. Finally, but by no means least, to the authors of the many books in the Bibliography for their specialized information and out-of-the-way techniques.

Introduction

I have attempted in this book to survey the basic and important techniques—together with some minor ones—for the enhancement of clay forms, and to give an idea of their development through the years they have been practiced. The emphasis is on nonindustrial work, though some repetition methods are also mentioned, and on modern variants of familiar historical techniques.

While the styles of pottery have varied widely over the 8,000 years of ceramic history, the underlying materials and methods have remained relatively constant, evolving in technology but not necessarily in aesthetics; the design values at the very dawn of clay work were as high then as they have ever been since. A few systems are wholly of our day, such as photoceramics. Countless pots were, of course, without decoration other than the placing of a lug or the form of a rim or spout, but all potters have felt the need to emphasize or embellish with overt decoration. This, in fact, became the priority attraction in many cultures, especially among the Greeks, the Islamic peoples, and the luster and tin-glaze potters of Europe. The necessarily brief historical introductions in this dictionary are intended to give the potter a sense of belonging to a long period of development and design, to give a broad view, and perhaps to find modern inspiration in the work of great craftsmen of the past as well as in contemporary work.

While the book does not deal specifically with the aesthetic problems of design and pattern, the illustrations have been chosen to suggest the wide scope and varied applications of techniques. It is hoped that these will speak to each reader according to his or her own preferences and style of work, suggesting fresh applications and ideas. Many writers have tried to articulate design rules and theories, but one of the wisest, Dora Billington, advises reference to "principles of decoration" only if and when a design appears to be going wrong. Nevertheless, scale, balance, contrast, and tension are fundamental to successful work. The only real enemies of good design are flabbiness, monotony, and imitation without understanding.

One of the aspects of much pottery decoration not often shared by other arts is repetition: ceramics is still to a degree a quantity craft. There are, however, two kinds of repetition: the mechanical and precise reproduction of industrial ceramics, and the evolving and subtly varied repetition of painting and other hand techniques. Thus we find a basic idea being developed and altered over many years: Hamada's storm-tossed grasses, Colin Pearson's wing handles, and Rudolf Staffel's "Light-Gatherers" are but a few examples. The student beginning to decorate pots cannot have the fluency that only time can bring, and he must be prepared to work on a lot of pots, learning from the failures and concentrating on the development of a style. Ideas come from work more often than work comes from ideas. The teaching method, which involves drawing from nature and adapting the sketches to pottery forms, has much to recommend it as a starting point, but it can lead to "applied" motifs that are not necessarily in harmony with the contour, style, or three-dimensional form of the ceramic. Modern approaches involving textures, combing, scratching, adding clay, grog, and rough color, or pouring and flicking on slip and glaze, while often hit-and-miss, can establish a sense of unity with the clay and the form. At the other extreme are deliberately disparate images applied to shiny glazed surfaces; photographic technology applied to raku-like textures; or shapes broken into geometric, graphic patterns. Here the object is to set up a conflict of impressions in the eye of the beholder, sometimes to agitate, sometimes to amuse, or sometimes with wider psychological pretensions in view. This is not unique to modern times; potters have traditionally played tricks and made visual puns in their work. Shock without satisfaction is, however, liable to the law of diminishing returns. The intelligent approach is not to set the often superbly virile and controlled skill of much decoration against the slap-happy and the iconoclastic but to consider all as comprising a great and continuing panorama of ceramic effort. I hope that this is the impression that this book will give.

Illustrated Dictionary of Pottery Decoration

Agate Ware

In true or solid agate ware, colored clays are laminated and the colors therefore go right through the wall of the piece. The partial blending of colored clays to resemble agate or marble dates back at least to first-century Roman pottery, for example, marbled **Samian ware.** Marbled pieces, sometimes with additional stamped or cut decoration, in the form of cups, headrests, vases, or bowls, were made in T'ang China. Some of these appear to have been made by a method similar to that known in Japan as **neriage**, which keeps the pattern under firmer control. In the eighteenth and nineteenth centuries, country potters in the west of England and many Staffordshire potteries made agate ware. Staffs solid agate mixed white with blue-and-brown-stained clays. A yellow and brown agate ware from Yorkshire was known as "snail horn." With the classical revival, copies of Roman and Egyptian artifacts in glass and stone were imitated by Wedgwood and others in ceramic, often coming very close in texture and appearance to natural stone. Agate was called "scroddled ware" in the United States. Modern potters—Lucie Rie, Joanna Constantinidis, Robin Hopper, Michael Bayley, and others—have used the technique, often with great subtlety and reserve, in earthenware, stoneware, and porcelain bodies.

A

Four examples of agate ware with the sharply defined color separation that is typical of this technique through the last 1,000 years. A. An early Chinese bowl, probably Song (Sung) period, made by the **neriage** *technique. B. A nineteenth-century cat model with a curious white "mask." C. A bowl by Sheila Fournier with a spiral from a single layer of darker clay, thrown, turned, and polished. D. An agate bowl by Mary Rogers. Hand-built.*

B

C

D

A bowl and a pot with the more subtle gradations of color that are favored by some modern potters. By Lucie Rie.

For Ewen Henderson, anything goes in his laminations of porcelain, stoneware, and coarsely stained bodies, as in this lively hand-built bowl with its striking variety of surface.

A cylinder has been thrown in mixed clays, the top section smeared over by the action of throwing, and the agate colors exposed only by turning.

Agate ware can be made in a mold, in which case the pattern will remain relatively sharp, or it may be thrown. The latter process involves turning the whole surface when the clay is fairly stiff to produce the necessary definition. The main technical problem arises from variations in shrinkage between the different colored clays, especially if natural clays are used—for example, a fusible red clay and a buff stoneware body— but this can be obviated to a degree by using one basic, light-colored clay stained with various oxides to produce the required hues. Even with this method, large additions of manganese, for instance, will alter the behavior of the clay and can cause it to bubble and bloat. This is true of porcelain with cobalt carbonate. An even consistency throughout a layered block can be encouraged by wrapping it in plastic sheeting for a day or two before use. It is always advisable to make tests before mixing clays in any quantity.

It is not necessary to use a large number of layers. One or two thinner colored slabs between blocks of neutral clay will give interesting swirling gradations in a thrown bowl or pot. In molded agate, Michael Bayley contrasts fine lines with open spaces in his very controlled work. *Ceramic Review 68* illustrates David Greaves' "geological fault" formations. Paul Philp uses a form of agate inlay: grooves are turned into the walls of pots, slightly undercut, and strips of agate clay are set with slip into the bands and trimmed. All these remarks apply to solid agate where the color permeates the body. Details of special techniques can be found under **Inlay, Lamination, Marquetry,** and **Neriage.** Surface decoration with effects similar to agate but using colored slips or glazes is discussed under **Marbled ware.** The agate stone itself—agata—is used in South America for burnishing.

Ailes de Mouche _____

See **Crackle** and **Enamel.**

Airbrush, Airograph _____

See **Spraying** for discussion of types of airbrushes and their use.

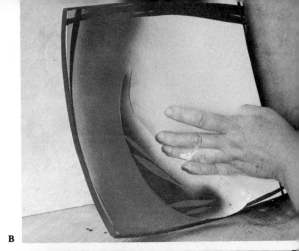

B

C

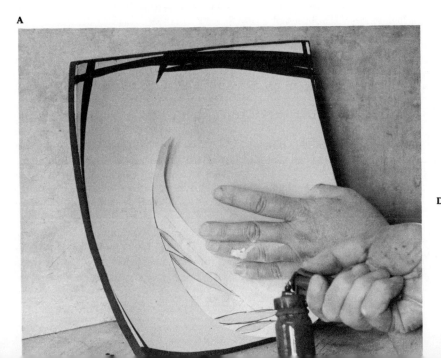

A

D

Using stiff paper cutouts in conjunction with an airbrush.
A. Holding the template in first position with spray-gun ready.
B. One side of the dish has been sprayed in a single color. (Brushwork lines have previously been laid on to contain the design.) C. The shapes cut from the original template are now used with a different pigment to add complexity and color to the design. D. Only one motif has been used but in sprayed and resisted variations. See also **Spraying**.

Albany Slip

A rich, fusible clay found near Albany, New York, which has been used for some 200 years to give a dark, smooth glaze at stoneware temperatures. It was used by New England potters of the northern tradition from around 1800, was well established by 1840, and continued in use through most of the nineteenth century. Although it was decorative in itself, the early potters generally confined it to the interiors of vessels to give an easily cleaned surface. Today it is used alone or as part of a recipe to produce a dark, unctuous, earthy glaze.

Alkaline Glazes

Alkaline, low-alumina glazes originated in Egypt and the Near East at least 2000 B.C. In one particular form, now known as **Egyptian paste**, soda and copper will migrate from the body onto the surface during drying, where they combine with the silica in the body at about 900° C. to form a thin, integrated glaze of bright turquoise. The same color can be induced in more traditionally applied alkaline glazes, often over a white slip to increase brilliance and occasionally on a semitranslucent frit/clay body. Applied alkaline glazes reached their supreme period between the ninth and twelfth centuries A.D. in Persia and Egypt.

Other oxides can be used in alkaline glazes to give bright colors at comparatively low temperatures. The great disadvantage is their tendency to craze, due to the high coefficient of expansion of soda and potash. A third alkali, lithia, is more adaptable, but the minerals which contain it—lepidolite, spodumene, etc.—have their own problems, such as the bubbling of the fluorine in lepidolite. Most alkaline glazes have a short firing range, and some are slightly soluble in water and even more so in weak acids such as fruit juices, which can lead to a dulling of the surface. Additions of alumina or the alkaline earths can steady the glaze, but only with a loss of some of its character. Crazing and solubility thus restrict the use of alkaline glazes mainly to decorative pieces. They are popular in **raku**.

Ammonium Metavanadate

A yellow pigment that will stand a fairly high temperature, 1,200° C. (Seger cone 6) or higher. See **Vanadium** and **Yellow**.

Anatase

One of the three oxide ores of titanium and the source of white titania.

Antimony, Antimoniate of Lead

Antimony will combine in various ways with glaze materials, modifying and opacifying, but its main decorative value is that, in combination with lead, it forms yellow tints. It will color a high-lead glaze but is more often used as a pigment, compounded with lead oxide. This is called antimoniate of lead or Naples yellow. It has been used as a yellow color for at least 3,000 years and in quantity since the fifteenth century, especially on **Italian maiolica**.

Antimony holds an ambiguous position as a metaloid, behaving both as a metal and as a nonmetal. In painting, its yellow form can assume a rather unpleasant quality like dried mustard, and it is useful to dilute it with some of the base glaze or with a soft lead frit. One percent of the oxide or up to 5 percent of Naples yellow are required to color a lead glaze, and 8–12 percent is required in a slip to be covered by a high-lead glaze. At 1,200° C., antimony compounds will begin to volatilize. All forms are toxic. Owing to its refractory nature the yellow color will often fail to migrate through an opaque glaze and may even cause local crawling if used as an underglaze pigment.

Applied Decoration

This covers a wide field, from the simple boss or strip to elaborately modeled sprigs, and has been used on every type of pottery from primitive earthenwares to sophisticated porcelains. The early Japanese Haniwa culture, for instance, used strips and more detailed additions to their simple but powerful figures; the Lung Shan tripod jugs of the first millennium B.C. are decorated with strips and bosses; Colombian tomb figure-pots show applied features and vestigial limbs; Roman and East European pottery has scales formed from overlaid pressed-out balls of clay, a style which carried over into medieval times. Applied clay is sometimes in imitation of metalwork, though this type of relief was more often molded. Although the Roman **barbotine** was apparently applied as slip, it is sufficiently three-dimensional to come almost into the category of applied decoration. Patterns of applied lengths of rolled clay resembling or imitating rope have spanned millennia: they concealed the coil joins in the enormous Cretan storage jars, they feature on the Hungarian Great Plain double-handled pots, and they appear in many forms through the ages and even occasionally on modern studio pieces. See also **Rope decoration**. The development of **salt-glaze** and stoneware in Europe with attendant increase in hardness of material and definition of form, combined with thin glazes, encouraged the use of applied and molded ornament, as on fifteenth- and sixteenth-century Siegburg wares and on many later pieces. The technique can lead to excess, and many potters, even those of the normally well-controlled Song (Sung) Chinese period, have taken applied ornament to fantastic lengths. Some European pots are submerged beneath surface excrescences.

Strips of clay, providing ribs and feet, majestically transform a simple spherical shape. Ninth-century Japanese.

Snakes and other creatures realistically portrayed on dishes and pots culminated in the work of Palissy (see **Trompe l'oeil**). This curious piece was probably used in the worship of the goddess Astoreth and is from prehistoric Bethshan, Palestine.

Detail of applied decoration on the side of a medieval jug found in London. Probably freehand modeling in very shallow relief. Small scale-like pads of clay have been pressed down the front and back of the beast. The form is emphasized by painting the surround with red slip or iron oxide.

Crude stamped, slip-trailed, and roughly modeled white clay (pipe clay) surface decoration on Wrotham (Kent, England) ware of 1697. A strange combination of techniques.

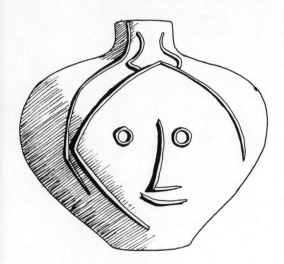

In modern craft pottery, Anita Scott uses the rope motif. Other styles include the tiny, cup-like "flowers" applied to simple spherical forms, building up elaborate textures, by Mary Keepax. She also uses an older method of pushing clay through a course sieve and delicately applying the "spaghetti" to the surface of her pieces. Rudolf Staffel applies thin slabs and strips to his porcelain "Light Gatherers" to give darker shapes by transmitted light. Similar additions, apparently very casual but with telling effect, by Robert Turner, are reminiscent of the Haniwa style. Betty Wooman is another American potter who covers her simple shapes almost completely with extruded, combed, and pressed ribbons and **bosses**. Potters of the Vanguard school of Japan apply rough fragments and slabs to their pots, while at the other extreme Michael Casson achieves vigorous patterns with his clean-edged flattened coils and balls of clay on stoneware and porcelain. A strange and original pot by Bruce Nuske is partly covered with tiny squares of colored clay set in at an angle (see illustrations in Lane, 1980).

Telling and amusing strips of clay on a pot designed by Picasso.

A

B

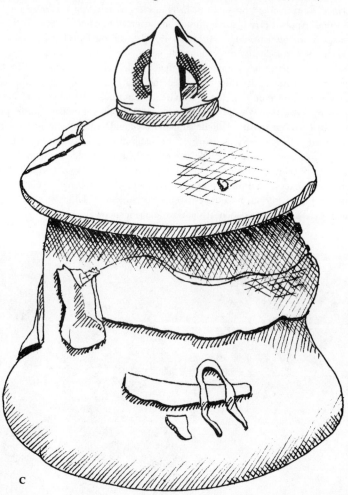

C

Three modern styles of clay additions. A. Pressed and modeled wafers of clay stuck to the surface of a simple form give variety of weight and interest and break the otherwise severe contour. By Irene Vonck. B. A hand-built bowl by Ewen Henderson has circular fragments of contrasting clay. C. The application of roughly formed pads and strings of clay is typical of the 1970s antitradition, especially in America, although it harks back to some early Japanese and other work. This example is by Robert Turner.

A boldly conceived platter by Peter Smith, the very construction constituting the major decorative elements, with stamping and trailing added in a free asymmetric style.

Sheila Fournier prefers the term "added clay" to describe applied layers that constitute part of the form itself.

In direct contrast to the platter is this geometric, angular, applied decoration in colored clays on a bowl by Penny Fowler.

A series showing the use of thrown spirals of clay as applied decoration. A slab pot is used here but other forms including thrown shapes may be found to be suitable.
A. Deeply grooved thumb or finger spirals thrown on discs.
B. A selection of various patterns of spiral. Larger-scale and more extreme styles are possible.

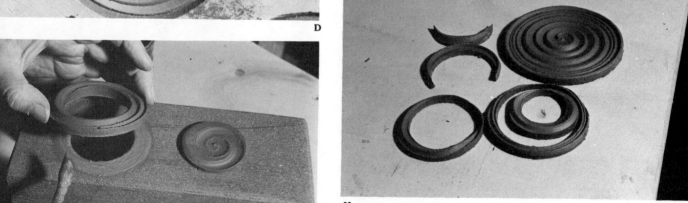

C and D. Cutting the center from a leather-hard disc. The cut circle and the ring can be used as seen in E and F, adhered with a minimum of slip and integrated into the surface with a tool. G. and H. Showing variations on the sphere; others will occur to potters.

Applied clay can be further enhanced by pinching, stabbing, rouletting, stamping, or impressing. Color contrasts are also useful. With animal and bird additions to lids, handles, etc., we are in the rather different sphere of modeling and form. A particular wave effect from applied strips of clay has been used on pottery as dissimilar as Song porcelain and unglazed European peasant ware and is described under **Frilled cordon**. **Pate-sur-pate** is a laborious form of applied decoration by means of layers of painted slip.

Technically applied decoration is not difficult so long as the pieces to be attached are reasonably similar to the body clay in both material and condition. Small elements can be applied directly with a minimum of water or slip; larger pieces need slipping and careful pressing from the center outwards. Many potters score the surface, but I have never found this necessary. Billington recommends a merely damp surface without the use of slip for sprigging "with no disturbance of the surface of the pot around it." This careful, clean approach is in direct contrast to the rapid slapped and slashed work of many modern potters where "disturbance" is part of the game, though even here, in the best work, there is much art concealing art, as in the cunning spontaneities of Paul Soldner. There is room in the ever-widening spectrum of modern ceramics for all styles. See also **Shavings**.

For the beginner, the very simplicity of the method can lead to overloading the form. Tony Birks (1974) recommends confining early work to simple straps and whorls, and he warns against striving after natural forms that will rarely relate to the shape to which they are applied. He also suggests that the profile of a pot can be spoiled by "excrescences," but a profile can, in many cases, be given extra interest and significance by carefully planned breaks in its smooth flow.

Arabian Luster

A name given to the Hispano-Moresque type of luster. An ochrous clay can be mixed with copper and silver sulphides to give a golden hue, or copper oxide can be used alone with china clay which has been previously calcined to 1,000° C. (cone 06) or above. The base glaze is normally a tin-glaze matured at about 1,050° C. Alkali/lead glazes are reputed to give better results than pure lead glazes. Hamer recommends a small proportion of titania in the glaze. The luster is, of course, reduced at the top temperature of 650–700° C. (cone 020). See also **Luster**.

Arabesque

Decoration derived from or resembling Arabian work. It was a feature of fifteenth- to seventeenth-century Hispano-Moresque luster ware. The term is used especially to describe the intricate interlacing of lines in a design. It was incorporated into the classical styles of the sixteenth and seventeenth centuries and evolved into scroll work with fanciful heads, flowers, armor, etc., in Mannerist and Baroque decoration.

Asbolite

An olive-colored pebble containing 10–30 percent of cobalt. See **Gosu**.

These drawings show stages in the formalization of the arabesque. The first is from a small bowl from twelfth-century Rayy (Persia), free and lively in character, a background to the figure; the second still has movement but is tending toward a more stylized, geometric form (from a Manises plate of the fifeenth century); the later European arabesque became more rigid and eventually changed its character entirely.

A great deal of work went into Victorian backstamps, and this is a characteristic example from John Ridgeway of Shelton, ca. 1830, although it conveys little information other than the pretensions of the potter.

Three very different styles of banding: on a Greek Geometric Period bottle, applied with unbelievable precision and on several planes; the restrained "push-banding" of the pottery industry, where the brush is rolled over before lifting off to give a darker outside edge to the stroke (from Gray's of Staffordshire); and the free and varied brushwork on a bowl by Murray Fieldhouse, where both the initial loading of the brush and the textured surface have been turned to advantage.

Aventurine Glazes

Aventurine is a mineral, a feldspar with small shining crystals of hematite. An aventurine glaze is, therefore, one with an overall sparkle, often derived from an excess of coloring oxide. It can occur on any glaze, earthenware or stoneware, but it is often associated with low-alumina lead glazes. The effect can be lost through too little or too much of the oxide—often this is iron, as in the mineral hematite. A thickish glaze with slow firing and cooling will help. It can occur accidentally on stoneware as a sparkle, but the effect is seldom an attractive one. Up to 20 percent of iron or chrome oxides can be used, as can zinc silicates. Parmalee recommends using elements with low atomic weights: calcium, magnesium, iron, and lithium. Titanium, phospherous, uranium, and bismuth have been mentioned. Boron is of doubtful value. The small crystals can be of varied and sometimes brilliant colors. See also **Crystalline glazes**.

Backstamp

A printed or impressed indication of the maker and other information about a pot that is found under the base. Type of body, decorator, date, and similar details are found under nineteenth-century pottery. The stamps may often be ornate or charming, with scenes and motifs surrounding or accompanying the information.

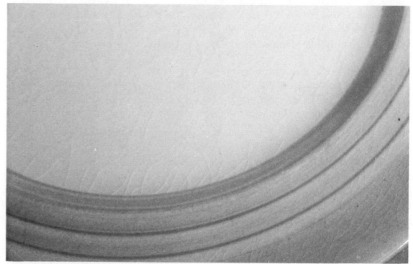

Banding

A term applied to the painting of lines of pigment on a pot as it rotates on the wheel. Normally the hand is held steady to produce a horizontal band, but variations are possible if the brush is moved during application. Slips can be trailed on in a similar manner.

In the true sense of a single spun line, banding has been used since the dawn of ceramics to delineate and contain geometric or free design; as an emphasis on rim, shoulder, or foot; or to form a block by close repetition, as on the early Greek Geometric designs in the centuries around 1000 B.C. Leach, in *A Potter's Book*, sums up in his usual succinct manner: "The curvature of a pot . . . is usually divided up by natural emphasis into constructive movements. Potters of all ages have been inclined to add further emphasis to the slight but life-giving angles by banding. This can be regular and precise or free and of varying thickness according to the nature of the potter and the pot." Even on the otherwise freely decorated Japanese Oribe ceramics, fine double banding on plates and pots often helps to contain and connect asymmetric designs, though the banding is, admittedly, also fairly free. Industrial banding before the early nineteenth century was reputed to have been freehand: "one finger . . . was used as a guide to regulate the distance of the band from the edge of the article" (Hughes). When banding on the wheel, the positions of the hands and arms are important, steadying them against one another, on a batten of wood, a block, a brick, or another firm support. Rim banding, either to replace scraped-away glaze with pigment or over the glaze itself, needs very careful application and even more careful subsequent handling if it is not to appear smudged and irregular.

The freer spinning of lines is virtually another technique. The thickness can vary, and spiral and crossed lines can roam up and down the pot. It can be effective if weight and variety of line and mass are considered, but dull and chaotic if applied without skill. Using a fairly large brush, spun lines can be merged to cover a surface over resist or as a basis for further brushwork. Practice and quick reflexes are needed for effective and lively free banding. The dishes of John Parker are good examples. The painting of circular pots is also discussed under **Spun color.**

Spinning color onto small cylinders on a banding wheel.

Barbotine

A late-nineteenth-century term derived from the French word for "slip" and applied to a form of slip trailing in high relief, especially the Rhenish and Romano-British

These two Romano-British beakers and the detail of a stag show the skill in formation and the high relief of the barbotine slip ware of 1,800 years ago. Liveliness and speed are conveyed in a brilliantly simple manner. Note the modeled haunch and muscle of the front leg of the stag; even the rib cage is suggested. The right-hand beaker shows a curious stylized "duck" design, again in continuous motion. The roulette is also in evidence in the stag detail.

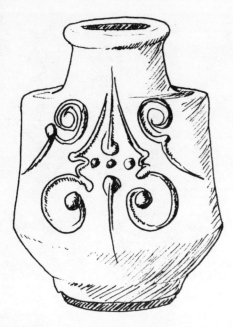

Slip trailing very much in the barbotine style but by the Japanese potter Kanjiro Kawai, ca. 1955.

While without the high-relief effect of the Roman examples, this dish by Bernard Leach exhibits more solidarity of slip than is usual today and suggests muscular and three-dimensional aspects.

second- and third-century trailed imitations of Arrentine ware. The term is still used in many books on antiques. The earlier Rhenish pottery was decorated with small flowers on dish rims, but the later British hunting and other motifs on Castor ware are in such bold and sculptured relief that simple trailing can hardly account for them. A distinct term is therefore useful. The vital movement and remarkable skill in detailing form and muscle on some of these pots is rarely given sufficient consideration today. Clays also had to be found that allowed such thick applications without scaling off— this has sometimes happened, but only after 2,000 years! On sprigged Samian pieces from the same period the stems of plants were sometimes trailed on.

In the nineteenth century, a method of painting with liquid slip mixtures of pigment oxides and clay (now generally called **engobes**) was developed by Chaplet and introduced into the United States, especially at Rookwood Pottery in Cincinnati. The clay additions helped to stabilize and give body to the brushstrokes, and, probably because of the slight relief imparted, the style was known as "procès barbotine." The results were "rich, Rembrantesque underglaze surfaces in brown, ochre, and blue" (Clark and Hughto). Some nineteenth-century tiles, handpainted with slip, were also known as barbotine tiles.

Basalt Ware

The name given by Wedgwood to an imitation in ceramic of basalt, a dense, black, fine-grained igneous rock. The pottery material consisted of around 50 percent clay, with ironstone and manganese making up the balance. Similar bodies—for example, Egyptian black—had been produced in Staffordshire earlier in the eighteenth century and were known as "dry body wares." Wedgwood refined the texture and produced a group of unglazed stonewares. Hughes (1966) quotes from a contemporary source describing the ware as "refined ball clay, calcined ochre, and a glassy slag from puddled ironstone, with the addition of 10 percent manganese dioxide. This was fired twice . . .

coated with potter's varnish and refired to a red heat." There is no indication as to what potter's varnish may have been, not to mention the puddled ironstone.

An approximately similar material can be achieved with 20 percent of iron and manganese in a red and ball clay body, perhaps with a small amount of fluxing material such as nepheline. Colin Pearson, in his winged forms, and some other modern potters have used the material to give an unglazed but permanent finish to hand-built or thrown and altered pots.

Basketwork

Many historians assert that the earliest ceramics were pressed into baskets, which formed simple molds, and they quote basket-weave patterns on the outside of early pots. It is, however, difficult to find specimens or even photographs of these primeval bowls or pots. Some 4000 B.C. Danubian pottery is incised with basketry designs, and there is Arizonian Indian decoration which appears to be derived from basketwork, although it is rendered in an angular and abstract manner. Potters have always imitated other materials, and basketry patterns have been copied or suggested on many pieces from Neolithic impressed rings to the sophisticated Italian pierced ware of the sixteenth century. Simple Japanese basket forms, the osier pattern on Meissen porcelain, and the all-too-realistic Victorian trinkets are but a few examples. As well as the surface imitation of cane weave, strands of clay have actually been woven into a lattice as in the Beleek (Irish) ware in the nineteenth century and in some modern studio ware. The plaiting of clay strips or coils is practiced in the United States by Rina Peleg and others.

Bat

See **Beater.**

Bat Printing

Also called "stipple engraving," bat printing is a system of transferring prints onto ceramic surfaces from flexible glue sheets instead of paper, with the advantage that a degree of curvature can be accommodated. It was first used by W. Baddeley in 1777. The impressions—from stipple engravings, according to Boger (1971)—are taken in oil and the transferred designs dusted with enamels. Synthetic resin can also be used. The method continued until the end of the nineteenth century, and the idea is now incorporated in the Murray-Curvex machine. The dusting of color onto gum in this way is little used by studio potters but some photoceramic processes include it.

Bead Decoration

In a curious use of glaze, occurring in Song China, beads of glaze were fired onto the neck of a globular pot, itself a copy of an earlier, hand-built form. Forms of applied beadwork also appear on Worcester porcelain of the 1860s and on other wares. Today a similar use of viscous glaze would be possible, resembling the jeweled effect on slipware, but a recent use of beads, as illustrated, is much less integrated; they are simply wired through holes onto the piece.

Beaded Rim

Although to an archeologist a bead rim is distinctively rounded in section, a beaded rim

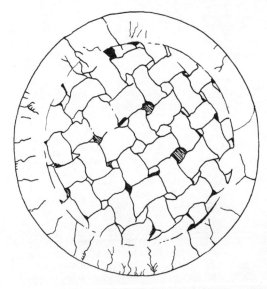

A "woven" open basket work plate by Ann Mortimer.

Glaze "beads" on a later Chinese imitation of a primitive form: a rare use of an obviously highly viscous glaze.

A less integrated example of the use of beads on ceramics, wired on through holes. By Ian Byers.

A large thrown pot by Janet Leach which has been beaten and deformed in the plastic clay state. Although this type of work must be free and direct, it can easily be taken too far and considerable discipline must be exercised as to when to stop.

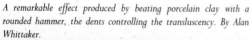

A remarkable effect produced by beating porcelain clay with a rounded hammer, the dents controlling the transluscency. By Alan Whittaker.

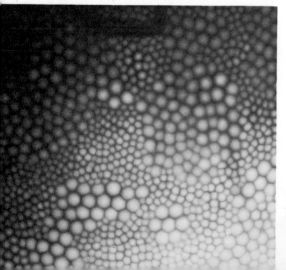

A

B

Four stages in a beaten pattern on a slab pot using only the slightly rounded edge of a beater.
A. Roughly formed strips of clay have been applied to the surface and beaten with the edge of a wooden bat.
B. Showing the effect of beating halfway along the strip.
C. The beaten pattern can be left sharp or planed down to give a more varied and subtle effect.
D. On the next page, the finished pot.

C

has a close series of small bosses or beads, probably formed with a roulette. Found on Nottingham salt-glaze and other industrial wares.

Beaten Patterns _____

Many hand-built pots are beaten at some time during their making, and this alone can leave textured traces. It is a small step to make these more conscious and explicit by using the contour or edge of the beater itself, or by binding it with string, rope, or cloth to impress the soft surface. Many Jomon pieces, possibly as early as the 7th millennium B.C., are decorated all over with elaborate cord impressions, even on the highly modeled handles and rims. Some of the strips of clay appear to have been pre-beaten before attachment. Later and modern Japanese potters have developed a battery of carved and bound paddles for decorating surfaces. Some **cord impressions** are rolled on rather than beaten. Beaten patterns are widespread in West African and other cultures.

There is a difference in character between beaten and impressed patterns. The former is more spontaneous, sometimes violent, and is often ragged and irregular. A good deal can be done with a single tool such as a heavy ruler, beating lines close together to build up a texture. Sun rays and other designs can be beaten on separate slabs of clay for applying as sprigs on slab pots and other pieces (see Fournier, 1977 for method illustrations). Where edges have become sharp, Leach recommends softening with a finger, leather, or sponge, but with some modern ceramics a certain pain in the holding of a piece seems to be part of the potter's intention. See also **Beater** and **Paddled decoration.**

Beater, Bat, Paddle _____

Throughout the history of ceramics, various textures have been beaten into clay. As mentioned under **Beaten patterns**, probably the greatest variety emanates from Japan, where the simple wooden beater is bound, wound, or cut, patterned, and

D

Using a string-wound paddle to beat a patterned texture into a faceted cylinder.

Designs of cut-faced wooden paddles used by Hamada (from Sanders). More ornate and specific patterns were also used

An eighteenth-century Bristol plate with flower and pineapple design and a detail showing the bianco-sopra-bianco more clearly. The chinoiserie-cum-pastoral brushwork, charming though it is, seems a little weighty for the delicacy of the rim.

shaped. The illustration shows only three out of an incredibly wide range. A degree of weight in a beater makes control easier. The butter pat has its uses but is usually too light.

Berettino

Opaque white painting on a blue ground, also called "bianco-sopra-azzuro," possibly first practiced in Faenza in the late fifteenth century and on later Venetian and other tin-glazed wares. The ground color was always of a darker hue than for **bianco-sopra-bianco**. Variations on the technique, such as the use of engobes on colored glazes, have been practiced elsewhere, generally in a broader style. Bleu Persan was an opaque white decoration on a dark blue ground from Nevers (mid-seventeenth century), which was imitated in Rouen, Delft, and Lambeth.

Bianco-Sopra-Bianco

A method of painting in opaque white (tin oxide and fluxes) onto an off-white (bluish or pale gray) tin-glaze ground. It was used at Faenza, Castel Durante, and other centers from the early sixteenth century and was taken up by Nevers and Marieberg. In the eighteenth century, probably via Sweden, it was practiced at Bristol, Lambeth, and Liverpool. The character of bianco-sopra-bianco fits well with the prevailing pale colors and lightness of Rococo styles. It was widely used on Delftware from 1750–1770. While often limited to a border, it also appears on very wide rims and in intricate patterns.

Hamer states that it was originally developed because of a degeneration of the tin-glaze from white to a "dirty color" through the introduction of cheaper materials, but the early date does not suggest this and Caiger-Smith (1973) does not mention it. The Bristol bianco stands more assertively from the surface than others. The earliest known English date is 1747. Petals and leaf sprays, flattened spirals, flowers, and pineapples were painted at Liverpool, Lambeth, Bristol, and elsewhere.

The technique is of limited value in modern ceramics, though it is still used in modified forms. At its best it is mysterious and delicate.

Bib

The rounded shoulder of a pot or the side of a bowl may be dipped in slip or glaze to form a "bib" of contrasting color. This can then be treated as a panel for **sgraffito** or other decoration, if required. One advantage of a bib is that its contours will automatically reflect the shape of the pot. Bibs are found on medieval pots and have been popular among country potters. Sam Haile has used them in a modern context.

A glaze-over-glaze bib on a flattened thrown pot by Rosemary Wren. The dip covers more of the form than is usual but still gives enhancement to the shape.

A unique style of slip trailing developed by Sam Haile in the 1940s. In this case the side of the jug has been dipped into black slip to form a bib. The whole decoration was done with liquid slip, as can be seen by the feathering.

Bismuth

A thin layer of bismuth deposited on a glaze by reduction gives the so-called mother of pearl luster, characterized as "slimy" by Honey. It was reputedly used at Beleek (Ireland) and in U.S. potteries late in the nineteenth century.

Parmalee says that bismuth can give "interesting results" in neutral or basic crystalline glazes. It can modify colors and can be used as a carrier for other lusters (see Hamer).

Black

Black can cover a number of very dark colors in ceramics. The light absorption necessary for a good black can be developed in a shiny glaze, in a vitrified body, or by burnishing and firing in a reducing and carbonizing fire.

The third type has been common since the earliest times; for instance, in South America and in the pottery of the La Tene cultures and other early peoples in Europe. It is common in African ware using clamps, bonfires, and other primitive, smoky kilns. The necessary shine, which can turn a deep gray to a true black, has also been achieved in African pots by beating them while they are hot with certain plants (see **Nonceramic surfaces**). Raku reduction and sawdust or clamp firing will turn a body black, but Sanders warns that swift cooling is necessary if the black is not to revert to red-brown or gray.

One of the best examples of a shiny black glaze, the **mirror black** of the K'ang Hsi period of China, is reputed to have been colored with iron together with "a cobaltiferous ore of manganese" (Boger, 1971), and this is the classic mixture—cobalt, iron, and manganese—used to produce black stains and pigments. Iron alone has produced a shiny black in a laurel ash glaze (12 percent of iron oxide). The Japanese Seto black is an iron glaze, and many tenmoku glazes are a dense black. Large additions of manganese can give black in an oxidized stoneware glaze. Any opacifier in a glaze is likely to limit the color to a deep gray. In the nineteenth century a dark cobalt glaze on a red body, fired in a "smother kiln," gave a lustrous black.

An example of the vitrified body is the early industrial Egyptian black, which was, according to Hughes, stained with iron oxide and "fired to a temperature barely sufficient to produce a vitreous stoneware." Other recipes are known (see also **Basalt ware**).

When used as a pigment for painting, the iron/cobalt/manganese mixture may separate out to some degree (though quite pleasantly) and may run. Replacing the cobalt with copper will give a gun-metal appearance, which is really a deep gray. Nickel and chrome are also used in prepared industrial colors where the oxides are sintered together and may be combined with a flux, alumina, and other materials. Iron/chrome/nickel/cobalt/alumina is the combination quoted by Dodd as "standard black."

An excess of copper (used as a pigment or in a glaze) will fire black, but of a cindery quality, and brownish on biscuit. Black slip is normally made of red clay with 8–10 percent of manganese dioxide, though this will tend toward a deep brown. A small addition of cobalt can be made to intensify the color. The chrome present in many prepared blacks can cause trouble if used in conjunction with tin glazes. Iridium has been quoted as a fine black but is hard to obtain. Manganese can act as a powerful flux in slip or color if the biscuit firing is taken above about 1,050° C. (cone 05), and this can pose problems through inhibiting glaze-water aborption and giving uneven coatings of glaze.

Three unencumbered Greek joggers. "Black-figure" slip painting on a light terra-cotta ground with details cut through in sgraffito. See **Red-figure ware** *for illustrations of this technique.*

Black- and Red-Figure Painting

These are the two principle styles of Classic Greek pottery decoration. They are self-explanatory. In the first, the design—usually of figures and animals, occasionally birds, together with scrolls and symbols and suggestions of architecture—was painted in a black slip on a terra-cotta ground. Details of garment folds, faces, muscles, etc., were cut through the black to the red beneath and, for female flesh, white was added. A few pieces have a white ground. The main period for black-figure was 650–520 B.C.

During the latter half of the sixth century B.C. a reversal took place, and pottery painters started to use black for the background with the design in reserve on the red body. Details were then painted in, rather than scratched away. The "invention" of red-figure is said to have been made by an assistant to the potter Andokides. Touches of purple are found, but white becomes very rare. In the final decadent phase, designs became more three-dimensional and a good deal of a rather friable white was used. The overall impression of Greek ware is rather drab and monotonous in color, but the strength of the drawing is remarkable—"lines like coiled springs." It is obvious that the "fine art" of the period had a high concentration in ceramics, a rare phenomenon.

There have been a number of explanations of the technique employed, not simply the use of red and black slips but involving reduction and reoxidation methods, which, if true, show a very considerable firing skill and sophistication of kiln design. There are comparatively few "seconds" as regards color, at least in the great Attic output. The slight surface shine is attributed to a very fine-grain slip (see **Burnishing** and **Gloss ware**).

Blacksmith's Scale

See **Ilmentite** and **Magnetic iron.**

Black-Topped Pots

A typical beautifully shaped Egyptian black-top pot, the form a forerunner of the amphora.

There are many pots extant from pre-Dynastic Egypt (Naquada, *ca.* 3500 B.C.) where the firing method has produced a decorative red and black finish. The burnished red clay pots, some with symbols in relief, appear to have been fired standing on their rims. As the fire died down, the top quarter or so remained in the ashes and was "reduced" to black, often glossier than the main form. A similar effect was achieved in the Iron Age Indus Valley. The system, which must have been a simple one, could be reproduced today, but there is no evidence that it has been achieved in quite the same well-defined way.

Bleed-Through

A colloquial term for the breaking through of impurities in the body—generally iron compounds such as pyrites—to speckle and color the glaze. It is most pronounced in reduced stonewares, although special bodies can be mixed to produce speckle in oxidation using iron spangles or coarse pigment additions. Other coarse minerals could be tried. Fireclays are often incorporated to produce speckle in reduction. Rhodes (1969) illustrates a rather excessive degree of spotting, which has become decoration in its own right.

Decorative and varied bleed-through on a pot by Michael Casson. Reduction firing on a well-grogged body.

Extreme bleed-through has all but destroyed the natural surface of the glaze, but in its place there have developed an overall pattern and texture that are very suitable to the form. By John Webber.

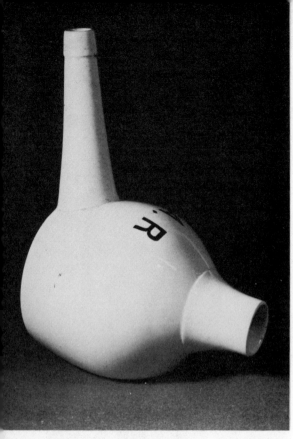

This strange form was used in nineteenth-century Stoke-on-Trent to produce industrial slip trailing, probably on pots turning on a lathe. A cork with a nozzle would have been fitted into the lower aperture. The slip must have been fairly viscous.

In another sense some pigments, notably copper oxide, will permeate a body to appear on the opposite side of the wall to that on which it was applied. In *Ceramic Review 69* an interesting note on Robin Welch states that he "sometimes uses copper oxide on the outside of a thinly thrown rim over the glaze so that the copper migrates through the clay to appear as a pink blush on the inside. This often fails to appear in the normal reduction firing but refiring in a bisque kiln produces the pink." See also **Transmutation of color.**

Bleu Persan

See **Berettino.**

Blistering

Of all the glaze faults this is the most unpleasant, leaving dangerous, sharp edges. Nevertheless it is the basis for modern so-called **volcanic** or **crater glazes**. Gases from many materials, which disassociate at various times during a firing, send bubbles of gas through a glaze to burst on the surface. If used as a decorative effect the firing should be taken to the point where the glaze craters begin to collapse and lose their sharp edges.

Blow Bottle

A form of slip trailer once commonly used in the pottery industry. It consisted of a glass or ceramic bottle fitted with a trailer nozzle through a hole in the side. The operator blows through the neck so that a stream of slip is forced from the nozzle. It was used to trail bands onto a horizontally revolving pot immediately after turning on a lathe. There are examples dating back at least to the early nineteenth century, and a Stoke-on-Trent stoneware blow bottle is illustrated. There is a short article on the subject in the Harrison-Meyer (pottery suppliers) Leaflet Number 23. A similar modern system using a flexible blow-tube for greater freedom is illustrated in Fournier (1977).

Blown Slip

A layered effect can be obtained by blowing onto a newly slipped surface. This could be used as a surface for trailing or painting on.

Blue

Cobalt blue, as distinct from the turquoise obtained from copper, is found in early Egyptian glazes. It was used sparingly on T'ang multicolored earthenware, but it was from the tenth century A.D. in the Near East and in the Orient that this blue pigment began to dominate pottery and porcelain decoration. See **Cobalt** for a more detailed discussion of this material. Copper in an alkaline glaze or in a stoneware glaze with barium and dolomite can give an almost true blue, as also can iron in reduction, especially on Chun ware and occasional celadons such as some by Richard Batterham and a never-to-be-repeated black-currant ash glaze by Geoffrey Whiting. A modern and very dependable blue stain is compounded industrially from vanadium and zircon.

Blue-Dash Charger

Slanting, blue-painted strokes appear on the rims of a group of late-seventeenth- and early-eighteenth-century Lambeth and Bristol tin-glazed plates, which have become known as blue-dash chargers. Manganese was also used. In the twentieth century, Picasso stabbed away at the edges of dishes, and the style has been imitated to good effect by a few modern potters.

Blush

Both copper and chrome can cause pinkish areas on glazed pots through vaporization from one pot to another or from one side of a pot wall to another (see also **Bleed-through**). My most spectacular "blush" kiln resulted from a flashlight being left inside during an earthenware firing following a somewhat merry Christmas party! The delicate purplish patches on some pale blue Chinese Qing (Ch'ing) pieces are known as "clair de lune" flush. Occasionally the iron from a body will break through as a rosy area. See also **Flashing.**

Bole

An Eastern Mediterranean clay that by reason of its composition—mainly kaolinite with iron oxide—can produce a good red. The Armenian bole used by potters of Isnik in the sixteenth century is a case in point. Bole is also used in compounding enamels.

Boss

A simple and age-old decoration formed by pressing a ball of clay onto a pot to form a spherical hump. On Early Bronze Age "grape cups," the bosses still retain the appearance of squashed spheres. On Chinese pottery, from the 2000 B.C Lung Shan jugs

Two contrasting bosses on early pottery: the first pushed out from the inside to form rough chevrons on a first-century Romano-British pot, a style known as "repoussé" among archeologists; and the second a powerful 1000 B.C. German form with pointed bosses set into recessed circles.

Modeled bosses were common on this type of shallow dish from Ming China. They are usually referred to as "bulb bowls."

Stamped, modeled bosses, partially pushed out from the inside. By John Huggins.

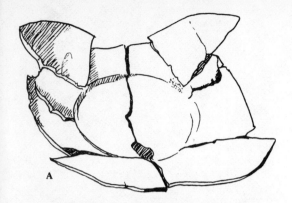

A

B

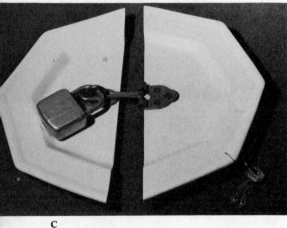

C

Three modern approaches to the broken pot. A. A torn and reassembled thrown dish by Peter Voulkos. B. A raku bowl by Rick Dillingham that has been broken after firing, each piece decorated separately and without reference to one another. These are refired in a raku kiln and then glued together. The colors are reddish, black, and gold. C. A plate by Ingeborg Strobl that is not only cut through but held apart. The philosophical content, with its suggestions of the state of marriage and other human relationships, is typical of much modern ceramic work, the making of statements (often enigmatic) beyond the visual-tactile impressions.

to the narcissus bowls of 3,000 years later, the bosses are prominent but more fully integrated with the surface, especially so in the Chun wares because of the thick, unctuous glaze. In some pots, notably the Belgic Iron Age "buckleurnen" and some Roman Empire pots, the bosses were pressed from the inside, possibly in distant imitation of metalwork, while the clay was still soft. Among modern potters Dan Arbeid has made bossed pots of this type, although smaller applied bosses are more common.

Brass

See **Metals**.

Bright or Liquid Gold

This is a solution of gold sulphoresinate with other metal resinates and a flux such as bismuth. In its raw state it looks like thin brown treacle. When fired to 750° C. (cone 017), with plenty of ventilation up to 400° C., it becomes a shiny gold that needs no burnishing but lacks the more subtle sheen of **burnish gold**. Because of its expense it is sold in packs as small as 5 grams, less than ¼ ounce. It can be thinned with precious metal essence but not with turpentine. Like all gold pigments it needs precise firing if applied thinly: overfiring may turn it a purplish red on tin-glaze. Brushed on more generously, however, on stoneware or porcelain it will often stand a higher temperature, around 1,000° C. (cone 06).

Broken Pottery

It was difficult to invent a heading for a highly individual approach to the decorative appearance of a pot as described in *Ceramic Review 76*. Rick Dillingham of New Mexico breaks his hand-built pots into a number of pieces, decorates and raku fires them separately, and then glues the whole together again. The result, says Dave Roberts, is "marvelously articulated . . . by sensitve juxtaposition of subtly different surfaces." Another presentation of broken pottery is also shown in the illustration. See also **Cracked ware.**

Described as "clipped" rather than broken, the breaks in the rim of this bowl by Stephanie LaLange have the appearance of cuts with pinking scissors.

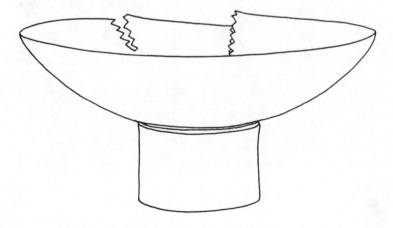

Bronze Luster

This can be obtained by using chromium and lead compounds in reduction, but experiment along these lines is not recommended and use should be made of an industrially made luster. A bronze-like finish is also possible with manganese or copper/manganese mixtures—see also **Copper** and **Copper/Manganese.**

Brookite

A natural titanium dioxide—the source of white titanium.

Brown

Most red clays fire to orange-brown, rust, terra-cotta, and other brown hues, the iron reacting with other ingredients. The iron will be bleached if calcium is present, especially in reduction and at high temperatures. Iron oxide is responsible for most brown colors; it can be deepened by the addition of manganese, which on its own also gives browns tending to purple. Nickel and zinc oxide additions will alter the behavior of these metals. The iron "café au lait" brown used on Chinese porcelains, at Meissen, and on some faience might have been treated in this way. A slightly mottled brown/cream can result from the addition of tin oxide to iron oxide. Alkalis "cool" the color, compared to the effect in a lead glaze. Rutile gives broken cream/browns; ilmentite darker colors; and nickel brown to gray. Albany slip gives a dark brown glaze.

Brown Mouth

A normally buff body can become brown on the rim of a pot under certain glazes, even though these themselves may be of a pale color. Fusible glazes may run from the rim to leave a thinner, darker coating, especially in reduction. Certain celadons and similar glazes show this tendency. It can be decorative in contrast with the thicker glaze but only when glazing has been done perfectly. It is possible to wipe most of the glaze away from a rim to give the effect deliberately, or to scrape the glaze away and to apply pigment, though this lacks the subtlety of the genuine article.

Brush-Applied Glaze

While it is difficult to detect how early glazes were applied, it is doubtful whether many of them were brushed on. There is evidence that some American/German New England slip dishes had the glaze spun on with a brush, and the cuenco and cuerda seca designs probably had their small pockets of colored glaze laid in with a brush. Among modern potters Otto Natzler, an Austrian-born American, brushes his distinctive glazes onto biscuited pots. When one glaze is used over another, the second layer can well be brushed on.

Pottery suppliers are now listing brush-on glazes needing two or three coats. Except for special effects, such as one color reacting with another, it seems a slow and tedious method, although it has the advantage that only a small quantity of glaze is needed. Ordinary glazes can be flicked or laid onto a pot with a brush to produce a rich if somewhat haphazard result. A preliminary thin, dipped coat will ensure that no part is left bare.

Detail of a very painterly design using brush-applied glaze with enamels and other applications. By Karen Firth.

Brushed Slip

A thinly brushed-on slip may appear adequate in the raw or biscuit stages but may disappear entirely under a glaze, particularly an earthenware lead glaze. Use a loaded brush, therefore, and apply generously. Most of the early designs on pots were of slip applied with some sort of brush, but whether the slip remains in its matt state, was burnished or varnished, or was of the gloss type known as "terra sigillata"—the color is probably as solid as when it was made. Slip painting continued after the advent of glaze, though the effect became less powerful. The glaze is often thin and the color strengthened by added pigment. There are some freely brushed medieval pots, though the line is sometimes weak compared with the vigor of the form. The same criticism applies to some modern pots. A brilliantly painted medieval watering pot in the Museum of London and illustrated in Thorp is almost Japanese in its vitality and sensibility of placing. In Fournier (1977), recipes for brushed slip are listed. See also **Engobe**. One of the most effective uses for brushed slip is the **hakame** style, which gives a varied and broken surface as a background for more powerful brushwork in iron or other pigment. **Pate-sur-pate** was a typically painstaking Victorian brushed-slip technique. See also **Slip painting.**

Brushes

Brushes for traditional pottery painting need certain distinct qualities. They must hold enough liquid to feed a long stroke on absorbent material; they should return as near as possible to their original shape when lifted from the pot, but they must not be so stiff as to disturb a dry glaze layer. The bamboo-handled Far Eastern brushes so popular with potters are of very variable quality. At best, hand selected from badger, goat, dog, or deer hair, they are built with firmer hairs in the center and softer ones on the outside—and they are never trimmed. They are softer than the Western sable but are intended for use held vertically, well away from the point, and moved with an elbow rather than a wrist movement. The standard brush type, about 1 inch long and ⅜ inch wide, is called a "fude" in Japan, but there are also a number of other types from Japan and China, many with very soft white hairs. The "hake" is a wide flat brush used for **slip patting** and **hakame**. The "damifude" is large and round and is used to drip color and slip while suspended from a cord. Cardew recommends brushes called Sen Pen Banka (see Cardew), which are more resilient than the norm. For a more striated stroke, as in hakame painting, a rice-stalk brush like a small broom is mentioned by Leach and others. Pounded fiber is also used.

The traditional Stoke-on-Trent brushes were intended for a very different mode of painting: detailed, deliberate, and often guided by transferred or other outlines (see **Pouncing**). They are long and rather floppy. Some have cut ends, either square or at a 45-degree angle, and are called "liners." There are also "mops" for dabbing or laying on grounds; and at the other extreme, narrow "tracers," the commonest of the industrial painting brushes, are used for detail and for lusters, etc. "Majolica pencils" are similar to the range above.

The modern potter will try anything that will transfer color or slip to the pot surface, as have peasant potters throughout the ages. Ken Clark suggests such tools as an old shaving brush or hogs'-hair as an antidote to the ubiquitous **fude**, although, in fact, such experimental types and materials are becoming as common in the East as in the West. Also used in many cultures are frayed plant stems, cloth, and (in South America) chicken feathers and boys' hair.

The general advice for caring for standard brushes is to stroke them to a point after use and to hang hairs down. Harry Stringer recommends applying a little soap to the hairs to keep them in shape when not in use. Even here, there are individual preferences; see end of **Brushwork** article.

Brushwork

To many studio potters of the twentieth century, brushwork on ceramics is firmly linked to Eastern calligraphy: quick, free, apparently spontaneous, but actually the result of a lifetime of practice. It is not, of course, the only type of brushwork. Even in Japan, Tomimoto, for instance, uses the brush in a slower and more precise way to build up structures of pattern, often consisting of repeat motifs. At the other extreme, color is more or less hurled onto some modern pottery.

The brushwork on many early unglazed pots was controlled and intense at the same time: the swirling patterns on the noble Pan Shan jars; the finely balanced geometry of third millennium B.C. Susa, with stylized birds and other motifs more poised, angular, and simplified than even the Greek Geometric; the softer and less disciplined flowers, birds, and sea creatures from Minoan Crete; the list is long. All this work had the advantage that it was painted in opaque slips so that, as long as the delineation was clear in the raw state, the lines and masses remained firm and bold after firing. Drawing, in fact, was paramount, as it was in the last and to many the supreme period of slip painting in fifth-century Greece.

The coming of glaze started a whole new era of pottery color, and although the first Islamic potters—who were, perhaps, the greatest decorators of glazed earthenware—achieved a fairly solid color under their alkaline glazes, the strokes of the brush itself became more apparent and a new quality of color appeared, brighter and with an extended palette. Some of the strokes start and finish with a square end, almost as if made with a wide pen rather than a brush. A similar effect is found on Hispano-Moresque ware. Every type of brushwork and earthenware technique was tried and taken to its limits. On thirteenth-century Minai work, over-glaze enamels combined

Brushwork and sgraffito that "superbly combine flair and decoration" on a Chinese T'zu Chou bottle. Note the irreproachable placing of the main mass of color on the full shoulder and the vivid contrast between light and dark.

A more linear approach to brushwork, the finer strokes being reflected in the sgraffito through the surrounding blocks of color.

Some of the finest pottery decoration developed during the Yi period in Korea, even though the country was poor and subject to waves of invaders. Here the rapid flicks of the brush complement the globular form in a brilliant, instinctive fashion.

Charming and typically impressionistic eighteenth-century Bristol painting on tin glaze. A detail of a plate. The buildings derive in style from Delft but much of the rest has an English flavor.

with the Persian tradition of miniature painting resulting in detailed but freely drawn figurative work.

Enamels have seldom been used with the freedom of other types of pottery; Spanish and modern lusters and Japanese raku are among the exceptions. In underglaze painting, the sixteenth-century Insik designs of flowers painted onto a white slip, while greatly varied and often lively, are stiffer in conception and more formal and purely decorative than were the preceding Islamic designs. Greater verve and vitality resulted from the Islamic/Christian interaction in medieval Spain, and the **Hispano-Moresque** painting of the fourteenth century has been called "the best brushwork in Europe." The highest standards of calligraphic work were less apparent in the spread of tin-glaze techniques to Italy and later to the rest of Europe. To quote Leach, speaking from an Orient-trained standpoint, "By contrast the Italian majolica is generally weak, ornate, and closely allied to third-rate Renaissance [easel] painting." This is an overly-severe stricture on many purely ceramic styles of painting and some extremely attractive portraits and other skillful and direct work with the brush. It must be remembered that realism and illusionism were inherent in the Italian approach to painting.

In the East, the brush was such an integral part of even a lowly-educated person's world that its influence was as all-pervading as typography is in the West today; almost all the brushwork, and it was conjured directly from the brush rather than "painted" in the Western sense, ranged from adequate to superb. In the later period of dire poverty and hardship in Korea—one might even say especially then—the pure brush marks on glaze and the use of hakame as a background to rapid and calligraphic strokes make the pottery of the Yi dynasty one of the most exciting in history. In Korean painting, "everything depends on the brush as an expressive instrument . . . capable of a wide range of rhythms, some swift and fluent, others rugged and broken. In such work no merit, of course, attaches to the rendering of natural forms" (Honey). Probably the earliest Japanese brush painting was the fifteenth century "ironwash" decoration at Shino. The technique was given impetus by the importation of many Korean potters and brushwork rapidly became one of the paramount influences on ceramics and is still important. Leach's work in Japan, combined with his native art training, produced an attitude that is summed up in *A Potter's Book*: "I wanted to work

Simplified drawing with a pointed brush; only six or seven strokes are sufficient to delineate this fish. The crosshatched sgraffito is curiously as suggestive of scales as carefully drawn curved scale shapes would have been. By Charles Vyse.

A more free and lively approach to the fish shape in brilliant brushstrokes by Henry Hammond.

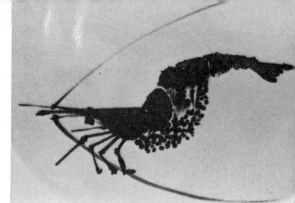

Massive but delicate brushwork in iron on a pale stoneware glaze by Poh Chap Yeap. A splendid combination of long line, mass, and dots.

out a . . . design by repeated painting until I discovered a final simplification of brush strokes and spacing." As a simple example, after watching a robin feeding over several weeks, he found "twenty broad and fine touches of pigment and pale wash . . . to express what I felt in less than two minutes." Two minutes, but with two months' preparation.

To return to the history of pottery painting, on Dutch Delftware, on English tin-glaze, and on the peasant wares of Europe, brushwork often had an attractive simplicity and naiveté though it could be crude and unskilled. Under the influence of the burgeoning fashion for detailed decoration in the eighteenth century, some tin-glaze potters followed suit and produced similarly elaborate designs. Much of the work on tin-glaze was repetition by semiskilled painters assisted by pouncing, though a certain liveliness and variation remained. With the development of the larger factory and the transfer print, brushwork of any individual fluency was largely eliminated in the nineteenth century, apart from a small minority of work by master painters

An example of wide brush application of luster by Alan Caiger-Smith in the manner of the fifteenth-century Spanish-Moorish potters, with overtones of lettering and suggestions of sailing ships. The broad style has been tempered by sgraffito in the center.

A thin line but vigorous bird design by Michael Cardew. Painted in blue-gray on a pale stoneware glaze. This is in a different tradition from the calligraphic brushmarks of the Vyse fish.

Detail of a pot by Staite Murray, a pioneer of the anticalligraphic school, the brush used broadly and without finesse. It still has links with the Leach style in that the brush itself is very evident, that is, it is not used merely as a filler.

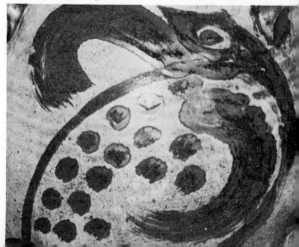

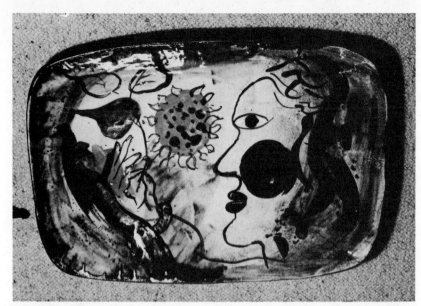

Underglaze painting on earthenware by John Piper. Easel painting adapted to ceramics in a free and individual way.

employed by the factories. There is expert and sometimes voluptuous painting on the earlier porcelains together with "the exact rendering of natural forms," but the splendid organization of space and the joie de vivre of much pre-industrial work has been slowly eroded. Such brushwork as survived into the twentieth century would have made little contribution if it had not been for the stimulus of the rediscovery of Song and T'ang pottery in China and its introduction into Europe by Honey, Leach, and others. This was paralleled by the liberating influence of avant-garde Western easel painting and brief excursions into ceramics by Picasso, Gauguin, and others. This phase has in turn been superseded by more anarchic styles in which brushwork is relegated to a less important role. In raku the brush is often used more like a weapon than a tool, stabbing, splattering, and slashing color onto the pot surface. A similarly vigorous approach is seen in some modern Japanese calligraphy, where floppy brushes a foot wide are used on great sheets of paper with the painter walking over them, reflecting

A lively combination of spattered brushstrokes in color, resist, and enamel on a reduced stoneware dish. By John Maltby.

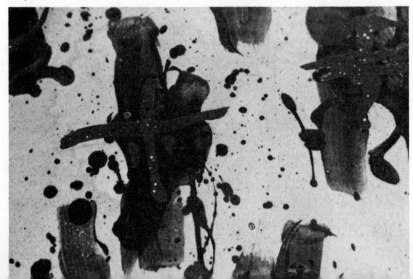

the action-painting of the West. At the same time, pleasant and sometimes gifted if (on the whole) unspectacular brushwork continues the world over on pots and dishes of all kinds, often combined with sgraffito, resist, and other techniques. Alan Caiger-Smith continues a rather lonely but successful trail, keeping the tradition of vigorous luster and tin-glaze alive. As has been said of Leach, apparent casualness combined with subtlety of form and color can inspire his brushwork with a lyrical sensibility combined with strength.

There is no quick route to good brushwork, but a start can be made by familiarizing oneself with the sorts of marks that each brush most naturally makes. Paint freely and you may spoil a number of pieces, but control will come. Many potters confine themselves to a relatively narrow range of designs, which they repeat with variations until it becomes second nature. As Hamada said of his broken reed pattern: "I paint it thousands of times but it is not the same—never the same." Working from detailed drawings from nature is advocated by some teachers, but this approach must be treated with caution. If you start from copying natural objects, put your drawings aside quite soon and develop the pattern in relation to the pot form. It is the nature of the pot itself which is of primary importance.

Do not retouch. Use as fully loaded a brush as is consistent with maintaining a point, and do not habitually drain it on the edge of the pigment vessel. Keep the hand "floating" and free, and move the arm as much as the wrist. Let the brush do as much of the work as possible by varying the pressure upon it. Try all sorts of brushes, including homemade ones; the marks may not have the fluidity of Orient-inspired work but can develop into an individual style along other lines. Some advice on types of brushes and their care is given under **Brushes**. There are always deviations from the norm: my wife is only happy with a brush that is permanently bent almost to a right angle through leaving it, hairs down, in the wax or pigment—but this is eccentric. Thus it is for each to find his or her pet tool—"brushes are like musical instruments; they play in certain ways" (Caiger-Smith).

Bubbles in Glaze _____

Many glazes contain minute bubbles caused by the formation of gases during firing, and some owe their distinctive quality to them, for example, certain celadons. The release of carbon dioxide from whiting and other carbonates is a common source of in-glaze bubbles. The use of calcium silicates, for example, woolastonite, can eliminate bubbles and give a clear, transparent glaze where this is required. Large bubbles can cause pinholes and blistering. Bubble craters are sometimes used as decorative elements. See **Volcanic glazes**.

Burnish Gold _____

Also known as "best gold": a suspension of gold powder in essential oils with a ceramic flux and a mercury salt. The gold is dull after firing and needs burnishing with a hard, smooth stone such as agate. The firing temperature is similar to bright gold (750–760° C.) with ventilation at the early stages. The result has more subtlety and quality than bright gold. Special burnishing sand and burnishing rubber can also be obtained.

The actual tooling and working of the gold surface was carried out on Bristol hard-paste and other wares in the eighteenth and nineteenth centuries. There was also acid etching of gold on plates at Stoke-on-Trent.

A red clay box by Mary Rogers burnished over painted black slip.

Burnishing

Any fine-grained clay, if carefully rubbed over with a smooth tool when leather-hard, will begin to take on a subdued shine. Pebbles, spoon-backs, and other objects are used. If the tool leaves a silky trail, then the clay is ready for burnishing; if the mark is waxy, it is too soft; if it starts to show a lighter color, it is too hard. The surface may be burnished over more than once during drying. After burnishing, the pots should be dried naturally, away from a heat source.

The finish is probably as old as pottery itself and has been used all over the world on low-fired unglazed wares to lessen the seepage of water, to provide a pleasant and cleanable surface, and for its decorative value. Usually the pots are hand-built or molded, but it was a common practice throughout the Roman occupation of Britain and Western Europe to burnish thrown pottery, presumably on the wheel, sometimes with a crosshatched center band left matt. La Tene pottery is burnished all over and inscribed with matt linear patterns of a high order.

The fineness of grain, which is the secret of a high burnish, can be assisted by coating the piece with a suitable clay such as bentonite, or a colloidal (ultrafine) slip can be prepared. Ben Cooper in *Ceramic Review 38* describes mixing clay with a water softener and a small amount of ox-gall or other organic acid (wine lees and urine have been used in the past), a couple of tablespoons for 30–40 pounds of clay. (He has even used iron-bearing sands scooped from rabbit holes!) Enough water is added to make a thinnish slip, which is then stirred every couple of days for a week and left to settle for another fortnight. The alkali helps to break up particles, and the organic acid promotes bacteria growth. The slip will settle into three layers; only the top and finest part is poured or siphoned off for use. This is passed through a 200 sieve, and the result should be almost oily in texture. Alternative surfaces are hematite used alone or in a fine slip. Many clays used for burnishing contain a good deal of iron oxide, such as the Shuei clay used in Japan, where the form of decoration is known as "migaki." In South America a crushed soft shale is sometimes used. A slip recipe suggested by Penelope Burnet is four parts ball clay, one of talc, and four coloring oxide. El'Nigoumi uses Fremington clay (from the west of England) with 10 percent or more of precipitated iron oxide for a fine, shiny, red surface.

The intensely glossy finish given by burnishing on a hand-built pot by Magdelene O'Dundo. Contrasted with a lightly burnished dish by John Ablitt, decorated with colored slips.

Expert burnishing can render a pot virtually water-tight, and because of the low firing temperature (most burnished work is fired between 750–950° C. (1,380–1,740° F.) it can be used over a flame. Coffee pots and the like have been so made and used. El'Nigoumi showed us pots that have been used for some years. Any scratching or incising will, of course, destroy the water-tight skin. Porcelain clays will burnish, although the results are not so striking as with red clays.

The famous Pueblo potter María Martínez burnished her pots to a mirror-like finish, using a smooth stone. Tokomane potters burnish on the wheel using steel tools, and in this connection Hamer recommends reversing the direction of the wheel if the pot has been previously turned. Tools vary widely: stone and steel have been mentioned, but some Africans use a string of hard, round seeds; even the use of shiny leaves, gourds, and leather has been known. Agate stone, used in parts of South America, is said by Litto to leave a crosshatched texture or haphazard markings. The surfaces of some spoon-burnished dishes, on the other hand, are impeccably smooth and clear of any marks from the actural movement of the burnisher. A Japanese master of the technique was Gen Asao, but there are fine burnishers in England and America among studio potters. Asao has an additional technique: he fires the pots to a low biscuit temperature and causes patterns on the surface by touching it when hot with vegetable oil. The result is called "unka" or cloud flower. In a similar way, newspaper burned over a burnished surface at about 800° C. will give a variety of browns and blacks to red slip or clay. See also **Carbonized ware.**

Surfaces need not always be given a complete overall burnish. Decorative areas can be left matt for contrast, as in the Roman example mentioned above. For a very different effect a broken or pitted surface will pick up burnish in small highlights. The burnished surface itself can be scratched or engraved as in the illustrations. See also **Engraving.** Although some burnished ware is fired to 950° C. or higher, clays containing lime may show disfiguring white specks or small areas may scale off. A lower fire to about 800° C./1,470° F. can avoid this, but the clay needs to be a fusible one to achieve the necessary strength.

Today burnishing is used to various ends. Martin Smith combines it with sophisticated forms incorporating metal and epoxy resin. Various nonceramic finishes have been used through the ages to enhance the shine, ranging from the stewed juices of plants or tree bark in Africa to the wax polish of the West. Beeswax, oil, and Danish lard have been suggested, but none represents true burnishing. While burnishing alone is a seductive surface, it is often used as a ground for other techniques as mentioned above. Incising should be done when the pot is almost fully dry. The red clay can, of course, be turned to a lustrous black by clamp or other reduction or carbonizing firings. Certain gold enamels need burnishing to bring up the sheen. See **Burnish gold.**

Burnt Sienna

A calcined ocher giving a reddish-brown pigment. See also **Sienna.**

Cadmium

An easily volatilized metal. The sulphide gives bright yellows, and oranges and reds with selenium. Used mostly for on-glaze low-temperature enamels, it can be released by food acids as a toxic material and so is dangerous on tableware.

Calligraphy

The root of the word is the Greek *kalli,* meaning beautiful. Calligraphy thus indicates

An early stage in the burnishing of a dish by Siddig El'Nigoumi, using the back of an ordinary dessert spoon. Eventually, by leaving the dish under damp newspaper and reburnishing when drier, all traces of the tool will have vanished. See examples under **Carbonized ware** *and in color section.*

beautiful or elegant writing. In the West this would generally mean penmanship. In the Near East some Persian lettering on pottery and much Hispano-Moresque ware has the linear nature of wide pen strokes. In general a calligraphic style is one of free sweeping strokes, whether of a pen or a brush. The "beautiful writing" of the Orient is discussed under **Brushwork**.

The term has been widened from its original meaning of lettering to any decoration in which the nature of the instrument used—be it pen, brush, or sgraffito tool—largely controls the type of pattern made. See also **Lettering**.

A stunning piece of writing on a Chinese Song (Sung) T'zu Chou bottle. The weight, movement, and positioning show the instinctive sensibility of this great epoch of ceramic art. The gist of the inscription might be summed up as "Good wine."

Differing from both Far East and Western "beautiful writing" in its sharper and more angular character, this Islamic bowl nevertheless shows the profoundly decorative qualities of calligraphy.

The somewhat debased script on this fourteenth-century Persian turquoise glazed pot has become a repeat pattern of a single incantation.

The type of flowing brush painting often referred to as "calligraphic," from thirteenth-century northern China.

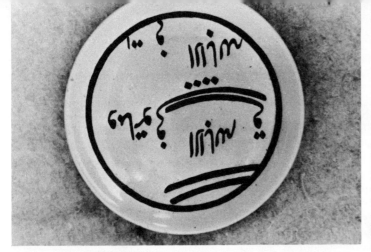

A modern variation on a Near Eastern script, more freely spaced and flowingly brushed on than the earlier example.

Skillful and attractive pen-type lettering by Madelaine Dinkel. The goblet is from the workshop of Alan Caiger-Smith. See also more illustrations of calligraphy under **Lettering.**

Camien Painting

A type of porcelain decoration in varying shades of one color.

Cameo

In the context of ceramics, *cameo* indicates a design in relief as opposed to intaglio, which is incised or engraved. The term is especially applied to self-contained items of ornament, usually carved or molded, laid on a ground of a different color, as in Wedgwood jasper wares and other pieces inspired by Classical Roman gem techniques.

Candle Resist

See illustrations and **Resist techniques**.

Cane Clay

A yellowish firing clay that will sometimes fire to stoneware temperatures. Hamer describes it as a sandy, refined fireclay. It was used by Wedgwood and others in the eighteenth and nineteenth centuries to imitate cane, bamboo, and pastry. Its dry body and crisp finish made it very suitable for such work.

Carbonized Ware, Carbon Smoking

Biscuit ware fired in sawdust, a bonfire, or other primitive, unprotected environment will absorb carbon from the smoke and fuel, sometimes to emerge quite black but often with attractive black, gray, and body-color markings. Porcelain bodies need prefiring to give strength but will develop many shades of gray and black. Pots can be covered with wet leaves or other organic substances toward the end of the firing to produce a black color. Dung is a favorite material in many cultures but is liable to cause complaint in built-up areas!

A resist line made with a sharpened candle, which is then brushed over with pigment. As can be seen, the resist effect is only partial but the broken line could be used to advantage, and it certainly has a different quality from either melted wax or latex resist.

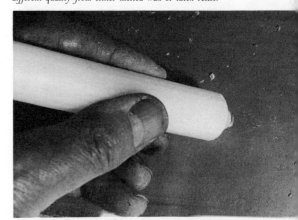

The appreciation of deliberate partial carbonization, apart from some earlier Japanese work, is a modern fashion. The potters of Cyprus, who still fire their reddish clay in wood-stoked beehive kilns, consider variegated pots as failures and could not understand a sophisticated European preference for such when there were so many "perfect" bright terra cotta pots for sale. El'Nigoumi carbonizes his fired, burnished ware over crumpled newspapers on his studio floor (see illustration). This takes only a matter of moments, but the resultant darkening of the color appears to be permanent if polished immediately afterward, and is very controllable. Paper shapes can be laid on ware in a raku firing, held in place by clay pads. These will give controlled carbonized designs as practiced by Karin Hessenberg (see Lane, 1980). Joan Campbell burns away unwanted or too-dark-colored smoke stains with a gas torch.

The deposit of carbon onto glaze during premature reduction in stoneware can cause discoloration (sometimes attractive), which fails to burn out at higher temperatures. This is sometimes known as "sooting."

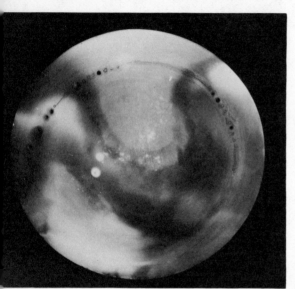

Two sawdust-fired bowls in porcelain body by Sheila Fournier. The porcelain body has been prefired to around 930°C. (Cone 09) to impart the necessary strength to the fabric. The color variations and mottle are due to contact with particles of sawdust and degrees of exposure to smoke. The bowl was lifted partly clear as soon as it appeared in the ashes as the smoldering fuel burned downwards.

A

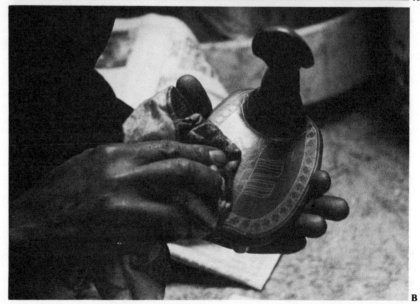

B

C

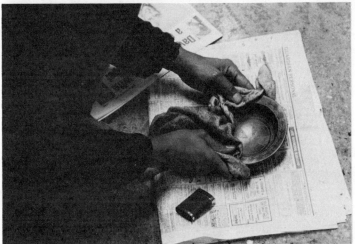

D

E

Five pictures (A–E) showing the very simple system of smoke-staining by Siddig El'Nigoumi. The ceramic is held briefly in the flame of a piece of burning newspaper on the concrete floor of his workshop. The position and shape of the stain are thus delicately controlled. Surface carbon is polished off with a soft piece of cloth. Some newspapers are more effective than others. The bowl is placed upside down on three bricks with burning newspaper wafted beneath it.

Cardium

See **Cockleshell**.

Carved Molds

Many decorated molds are cast from a carved matrix, but some are cut direct, as are the Uchikomo of Japan. Song (Sung) biscuit molds were probably carved direct. Roman

The fine, subtle form and flowing and balanced decoration mark this pottery mold as a Chinese Song (Sung) piece. The cutting is deeper than on many bowls and must have been very carefully designed in order to avoid undercuts, but the impressions would probably have been leveled out somewhat under a thick glaze.

A Roman carved pot showing the slightly ragged marks of the tool.

molds were impressed in the wet clay state (see **Samian ware**), and only the details were cut in. Simple design-carved plate molds were used in the eighteenth century for a form of slipware (see **Molded relief**). Some potters do this type of work today.

Carving

It is difficult to separate carving from incising, impressing, and fluting, but the word suggests a more radical cutting away of the surface, and in this sense it is historically more rare than most other techniques. The potter's instinct has been to add clay decoratively rather than to cut it away. A Maya bowl illustrated in Gerry Williams' *Studio Potter Book* has been cut away to leave whorls and medallions level with the surface, the carved areas filled with cinnebar for emphasis. Chinese Song-dynasty

The dark celadon glaze on these deeply carved Song (Sung) porcelain pieces delineates and gives variety to the patterns. Note also the little creature on the lid.

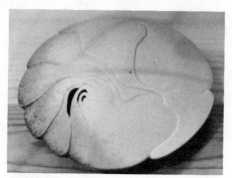

A cut-surfaced "shell" pot by Peter Hayes.

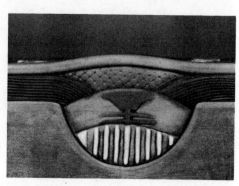

Carving and combing combined to decorate the lid fitting of a special type of casserole by Katherine Denison.

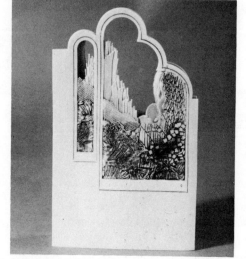

Contrasting styles of surface carving. Rachael Mellors' strange slab image and the intricately detailed and more romantic "Grand Arch" by Gordon Cooke, where the cutting has been rubbed over with oxides.

A crisply cut porcelain pendant by Sheila Fournier. The actual size is only about an inch square.

potters cut the surfaces of bowls and pots, combining vertical surfaces with flatter areas to give a well-defined design, though this is often called, slightly erroneously, "engraving." Sharp knives are reputed to have been used for this work. The relief decoration on twelfth-century Persian jars and bowls is more than merely incised and is either carved or molded. The French studio pottery pioneers DeCoeur and Lenoble carved surfaces in rather rigid abstract patterns. In the late nineteenth century, William Grueby began making carved pots for Tiffany in New York, and the "scarab" vase by Adelaide Robineau, a U.S. pioneer, is said to have taken 1,000 hours to carve. The piercing of the outer skins of double-walled Nottingham stoneware was known as "carving."

Porcelain plate with carved rim. Celadon glaze. By Betty Talbot.

Two examples of surface carving, in this case from slip-cast forms. By Penny Fowler.

Potters, from Han times and before, have been fascinated by the construction of miniature buildings either as models of their environment, as sacred objects or, in this case, as delight in the pattern of a Norman doorway. By Ray Waller.

On the borderline between formal and decorative carving; an attractive cut-rimmed porcelain dish by David Ballantyne.

The very lightly carved face of an envelope form by Val Barry. The roll of glaze, the textures, and the lightly rubbed color are all typically delicate and austere.

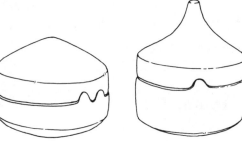

Not precisely carving but showing the decorative effect of the cut lid seating on two charming boxes by Eileen Lewenstein.

Today carving on surfaces and rims of pots is widely practiced. Sometimes slabs or strips are first added to the surface, and the design is then carved from these after the two clays have been allowed to attain a similar consistency by wrapping in polythene for a day or two. A simply shaped cut can develop interesting overall patterns by repetition. Jacqueline Poncelet carves bone china into angular patterns. Many potters cut away the walls of porcelain to enhance and vary the transmission of light in the manner, though not in the style, of Victorian **lithophanes.** The rims of bowls and pots are cut away into conventional foliations or free landscapes and clouds by Ian Pirie, Irene Sims, and others. Some of the "treescapes" and other designs are so fragile as to forbid any function the piece may have otherwise have had. The German Karl Sheid's pots are more muscular, the patterns sometimes suggesting fruit forms. Carving the pot itself into a new shape is somewhat outside the scope of this book, but the effect on glazes of the sharp edges and incidental burrs can be highly decorative. Carving the sides of bowls and pots to produce facets is discussed briefly under **Faceting**.

Surgical renewable-blade scalpels are now favorite tools, especially for porcelain, the cut edges softened with a damp brush. Whatever the tool, the gradual removal of material is generally preferable to fierce cuts, although the free hacking away of a thick stoneware piece is also valid and liberating. At the other extreme some porcelain and bone china is cast very thinly and then carved: here the loss rate might be 50 percent or more.

Celadon

A gray-green to blue glaze on stoneware and porcelain developed in Song (Sung) China and widely (and often badly) imitated today. The color derives from a small percentage—around 2 percent—of iron oxide in reduction. Its popularity in China may have been because of its resemblance to the admired stone jade. The finest kilns were at Lung Ch'uan, where it was of a creamy and unctuous quality and deep duck-egg blue in color. There were also celadon kilns at Yueh, Honan (the northern celadons, a deeper green color), and elsewhere. Fine glazes continued through the Ming period, and the "classic" Song glazes were imitated under the Qing (Ch'ing) emperors with more mechanical perfection but less character. Celadon with body-iron spots is called Pao Pie, or Tobi Seiji in Japan. The origin of the Western term is obscure, its often-quoted derivation being the unlikely one of a particular actress's gown in the French Romantic theater.

The base glaze of celadon is feldspathic, and it is applied fairly thickly. The color should have a translucency that gives it a special quality over carved, fluted, or incised wares, but this very quality means that it can look muddy and dull on the wrong body or when inexpertly reduced. The celadon porcelains of Harry Davis are among the finest made in the West. A very pale version of celadon used by David Leach and others contains only about 0.5 percent of iron oxide and is known as Ying Ch'ing.

Ceramic Literature

A term used by Barber to describe inscriptions or "sprichworter" on early American pottery. See **Inscriptions**.

Ceramic Pencil

See **Crayon** and **Pencil**.

Finely mottled surfaces of grogged clay or "chamotte" distinguish these elegant coiled shapes by Jennifer Lee.

Chamotte

Originally a French word for clay grog, its use has been extended to cover any decorative ware in a coarse, granular body, especially in Scandinavia. Typical pieces are vases, wall decorations, and sculptural ceramics. An equivalent of chamotte as a material in England would be saggar marl.

Chatter

The vibration of a turning tool causing ripples on the surface of clay is normally considered a fault, and every endeavor is made to avoid or eradicate it. Blunt, over-sharp, or slackly held tools, tools made from too thin metal, or clay that is either too soft or too hard for the job can all lead to chattering.

Its presence on some early pots, on some Chinese vessels, and on later Roman Empire pottery appears deliberate, and its effect is controlled and not unpleasant. In Japan an elaboration of the technique is to slip the piece in a contrasting color so that the chatter cuts segments from the slip in the manner of sgraffito. It is called "kasur mon." Sanders illustrates the tools and the method. It sounds even more difficult than is the avoidance of chatter when it is not wanted!

Chevron

A V-shape, sometimes with curved arms, placed in rows. It was a favorite decoration on many early pots. The effect is of a repeated V and inverted V.

Ancient and modern use of the chevron: a detail from a Geometric Period Greek krater with repeated chevrons of varying weight set off the amusing stylized horse; the decoration on the white earthenware slab pot almost resembles stitching. By Janice Heron.

One of the more crowded and formal of the variations on the willow pattern, the most reproduced chinoiserie.

Chinoiserie

Pseudo-Chinese designs, especially of figures and scenes, became popular from the seventeenth century onward, culminating in the ubiquitous willow pattern, which was originated by Thomas Turner of Caughley around 1780 and has continued with variations since then. The original plates are in the British Museum. The term *japonaiserie* also came into vogue in the later nineteenth century and could well be applied to some Eastern-derived styles of brushwork today.

Chrome

A relatively modern ceramic material, the use of which has steadily increased since the early nineteenth century; it is now present in very many prepared colors. Its use as a green pigment was known as early as 1749, but it was not in use in England until some sixty years later.

It is versatile, giving a bright red at low temperatures (around 950° C., cone 08) with lead and silica. At a slightly higher temperature it can impart orange and yellow. Its most common use, however, is to give opaque greens and grays, sometimes rather muddy in quality, or as a stabilizing agent in many prepared colors and stains. It is fundamentally opaque, and large additions do not readily dissolve in a glaze. It will act sometimes as a flux—for example, with the acidic tin oxide to produce chrome tin pink, or as an acid with lead oxide. Its use can produce accidental and rarely pleasant flushes of a hard pink hue in a firing on earthenware or stoneware if tin oxide is present. This is caused by its partial volatility over 1,000°C./1,830° F. Chromate of potash is used in glazes and frits. Blue-greens are possible with chrome and cobalt (0.5–1 percent of each) in a magnesia glaze in reduction at cone 9. See also **Iron chromate** and **Red.**

Chrome-Tin Pink

A rather harsh crimson-pink is derived from chrome with tin oxide and lime. It has a long firing range but tends to be volatile at high temperatures and may stain other tin-containing glazes in the kiln, especially lead glazes. It is normally used on earthenware and is a relatively modern color, dating back only to the late eighteenth century, when it was known as English pink. There is also a chrome-zirconium pink. The color can be used as an underglaze color and as a stain. It may turn purple on a glaze with a high alkali, borax, and low lime content. Nickel-chrome wire can cause chrome-tin pink to develop in an electric kiln.

Chun

A pale blue opalescent glaze. Although a little iron is generally present, the blue color is considered to be due to the scattering of light within the glaze rather than to the addition of pigment oxides. It is named after the Chinese town where it was first made. Examples from Song (Sung) and Ming dynasties often have splashes of red or purple derived from reduced copper. The body clay is of a fairly dark brown-buff color when fired.

This highly decorative and subtle glaze has been variously described as a "glaze in glaze" suspension (Cardew) and subject to "incipient devitrification" (Hamer). The latter may be due to phosphorous (contained in many wood ashes) forming minute nuclei of crystals. Titania and borax have also been quoted as useful additions. (A full discussion may be found in Cardew and Hamer.) The glaze needs liberal application if its essential qualities are to develop.

Cinnebar

The bright red cystalline ore of mercury, very occasionally used as a nonceramic pigment on ancient pots, as mentioned under **Carving**. The material is toxic.

Just how these varied but perfect circles were spun onto this odd-shaped 1100 B.C. Mycenaean jug is anybody's guess, but the precision and skill are typical of the period. The larger circles must have been spun; some of the smaller could have been stamped.

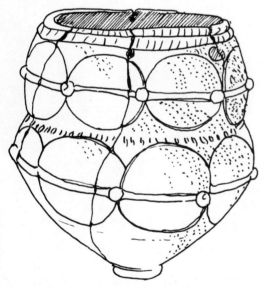

A late Jomon (Neolithic) Japanese pot that treats the circle in a very different way from the rigid Greek Geometric style. The larger incised rings are patterned with rolled cord, and pellets of clay together with the horizontal incisions unite them into a powerful design.
For spiral designs see **Spiral**.

Circle and Spiral

There is a thesis to be written on the character and motivation of peoples as shown by their use of either the spiral or circle in design—they are rarely found together. The spiral seems to be indicative of a "softer," more easygoing culture such as those of the Ancient Egyptians and many primitive tribes. The circle, with its geometric perfection, occurs on pots made by the more disciplined, often warlike, and rigid cultures. The Greek mainland dominated by the Dorians during the first millennia B.C is a prime example.

The spiral suggests growth, endlessness, and a degree of freedom; the circle is finite, defined, and geometrically perfect. Both have been widely used on pottery: the circle with incredible technical precision on the "Geometric" wares mentioned above; the spiral as a simple motif complete in itself, or in imaginative combinations, sometimes eternally circling a pot or combined into maze-like patterns.

The spiral is, of course, inherent in throwing. Inlay, agate, painting, and cutting utilize the spiral on many modern studio pots. As an individual motif it is less common, and the true circle is even more rare. The highly controlled sculptural pot forms of Hans Coper are sometimes decorated with lightly turned circles but without the rigidity of the Greek examples. See illustrations under **Spiral**. See also **Division of a circle**.

Cloisonné Style

This consisted of colors or glazes separated by raised lines either of pigment, trailing, applied clay, or cast relief, and was derived from metalwork of a similar nature. See also **Cuenca** and **Cuerda seca**. The term has also been applied to incised or molded surfaces covered with transparent or semitransparent colored glazes, the varying depths influencing the color.

In both senses the technique has been widespread and is used in various applications today. Because of the possible running of color it is most often used on tiles.

Detail of a large slab form by Shavin Packham showing the use of coarse mesh to give textured variety.

Cloth Patterns

Incidental impressed cloth patterns are occasionally featured on ancient pottery, although the instinct of most cultures has been to obliterate any roughness of surface in the same way that country potters were seldom enamored of throwing rings on pots.

One way (among many) of using loose-weave sacking to give a decorative finish. Beads have been attached to the cloth at intervals. A. The cloth has been wetted and is being beaten onto a leather-hard surface. B. The whole surface is brushed over with a contrasting slip (color or glaze could be used equally well). C. The cloth is removed when the slip has stiffened. D. Detail showing the impression of the cloth and the deeper impressions of the beads.

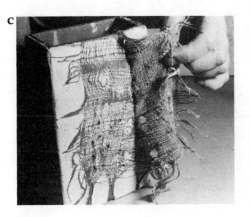

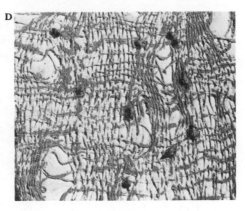

Today, however, when much pottery subjugates utility to fashionable attractiveness, markings from rolling cloths and so on are sometimes left as decorative elements. A number of American and Japanese pots, among others, are textured with coarse cloth or netting over defined areas. The impressions can be further pointed up by brushing with color from a fairly dry brush. Cloth patterns in Japan are called "nuome."

Fabric and weaving designs have also been imitated or used as abstract designs by South American potters and other pottery painters of many places and times. The "brocade" designs from Imari were much imitated in Europe and England. On modern pots the storage jars of Stig Lindberg show fabric-like surfaces, and on a plate illustrated in Beard the cloth weave is broken by seams and what was obviously a hole in the fabric, the latter giving a point of rest. In a bottle by Vivika and Otto Heino, strips of fabric appear to have been beaten into the walls and the pattern accentuated by a thin matt glaze. Ruth Duckworth has impressed porcelain with course cloth textures. See also **Lace**. The cloth used to give the pattern can be either peeled off or burnt away in the firing.

Clouding

An early industrial technique in which pieces of sponge attached to a wooden base were dipped in water, then into a dark-colored glaze, and dabbed onto unfired clay or onto glaze. "The results were crude" (Hughes).

Cobalt

The oxide of cobalt combines with silicates and borates to produce a variety of blue colors. It was known to the Ancient Egyptians and appears on Mesopotamian glazed brick, but it has only been a significant coloring oxide in ceramics since "Mahommedan blue" was imported into China in the fourteenth century, when it swept the field. It had figured on T'ang earthenware and on some Islamic wares before that, but it was the blue-and-white porcelains that gave it ascendancy. It was widely used on Spanish and Italian tin-glaze pottery but only rarely appears on peasant wares. It was not until around 1625 that it started to take Delftware by storm. American potters of the eighteenth century used a blue slip. The Germans have painted it on salt-glaze, to which it is not very well suited. Its consistency of color and ability to record a fine line made it popular in majolica for defining the drawing. Wedgwood used cobalt in a typically subdued form as a body stain for cameos, for example.

The ore has various metallic impurities such as nickel, iron, and manganese. Arsenic and sulphur must also be dissociated before it can be used. Earlier cobalts were rarely as pure as they are today, and some gave more subtle shades of gray-blue, blue-purple, and blue-green. See also **Asbolite** and **Gosu**. A cobalt color for ceramics was developed by Schurer in Saxony in 1545; one quality was known as **zaffre** and a finer preparation **smalt**. The ore was "roasted at a high temperature" after being dissolved in hydrochloric acid to remove "insoluble matter" (Hughes). Some 286,000 pounds came into England in 1754, an indication of the popularity of blue decorated ceramics, although part of the reason for the high level of imports was its use in glass as well. It was known as Bristol blue in consequence of that city's monopoly in the sale of the material. It achieved the very high price of fifteen shillings an ounce. The strident modern pigment is unsympathetic to much studio pottery, and various additions are made to tame it: red clay, iron oxide, nickel, ocher, manganese. A mixture of 30 percent cobalt carbonate, 35 percent manganese dioxide, 25 percent iron oxide, and 10 percent red clay, used as a painting pigment, gives a subdued blue with furry gold/brown areas where thick.

The color is very dependent upon the ingredients of the glaze it is in, on, or under. Alkalis will brighten it and give a feeling of depth, sometimes a purplish hue. With magnesia the tendency is sometimes toward green, while a true viridian green has resulted from its use on a zinc glaze. These and other variations are utilized in the fritting of calcined stains and enamels. Bright colors can be obtained by mixing cobalt with chrome or copper in alkaline glazes on earthenware and stoneware. Because of the intensity of its staining power, very little is needed in a recipe. A thick brushstroke may go black. 0.1–2 percent are the accepted limits in a glaze, but, as with all pigments, experiments with larger additions are sometimes rewarding. In slips the percentages may be higher. See also **Ironing of cobalt**.

Cockleshell

The serrated edge of a cockleshell was used to impress patterns on early Mediterranean ware. The Latin name has given the term "cardium ware," used by archeologists to describe this type of decoration.

Coggle

A *coggle* is given in the *Shorter Oxford Dictionary* as "having rounded protuberances," and in ceramics the term indicates a notched tool used to decorate and to strengthen by compaction the rims of slipware cooking dishes and some pots. The coggle often consisted of a notched roulette wheel, giving the familiar indentations on the edges of eighteenth- and nineteenth-century country pottery pie dishes. Wooden wheels were, apparently, later replaced by iron ones in the nineteenth century. Barber widens the sense of the term to cover a series of patterned roulette wheels used by Pennsylvania German potters, as does Sanders.

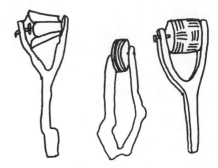

Three Japanese coggles or roulette wheels made from natural forked twigs (from Sanders). The one on the left is probably similar to the type of wheel design that impressed the edges of English baking dishes. See text and following illustrations.

An attempt by the author to make a dish-edging coggle wheel. The indentations proved a little too deep, but the result is reasonable.

Two distinct impressions from one wide cogwheel; from the face and the teeth. Detail of pot by Tony Gant.

Cog Wheels

Small cog wheels from clocks and the like can be used either as rollers or as face-down impressions in the surface of slab pots and the like, though they are increasingly difficult to find in this electronic world.

Coil-Form Decoration

Bowls and other simple shapes can be formed in plaster or biscuit molds by laying and pressing together coils of clay arranged as whorls, parallel lines, circles, etc. This building technique develops its own decoration. It is advisable to smooth over one face,

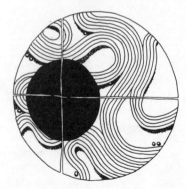

A combination of form and decoration, this interesting use of coils is lively and individual while remaining a simple and basic technique.

A bowl by Gordon Baldwin. Precisely laid coils, broken and stained at one point, have overtones of both construction and destruction.

Flattened coils on a slab base build up this sinuous design by Antoine de Vinck, which he calls "Soul Mirror." The dark oval is in gold luster. Note the small pellet additions here and there which give interest and accent to the flowing lines. (From Lane, 1980.)

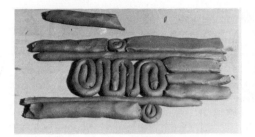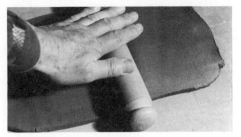

A design built up from coils of clay laid on a flat surface, and with a thin sheet of clay rolled onto them. The coils are flattened and integrated as the reversed slab shows. The technique can be used in making tiles, slab pots, wrap-around cylinders, and other constructions.

normally the inside. The careful thumbing-down of the coils of coiled pots is another application.

A variation of the pressed coil is to lay patterns in a hollow mold and then to press a soft, preformed bowl over them. The coils will flatten somewhat and become inlaid by pressure, giving a distinctive result that resembles some Pre-Columbian American ware. Alternatively thin coils, plain or twisted together, and of contrasting colors may be pressed into the surface of a dish supported by a mold to produce patterns. Antoine de Vinck works in this way. The technique has affinities with **rolled inlay**.

Colcothar

A name for a very finely ground red iron oxide, Fe_2O_3, mentioned by Leach as employed as an overglaze enamel for red colors.

Cold Colors

A term used for unfired pigments. See also **Nonceramic surfaces**. The remains of unfired oxides are found on some early pottery from China, especially on tomb figures, and on some ancient American pots, among others. Cold colors were also used on some English soft-pastes, where the technique was known as "japanning," and painted peasant pots are found.

Today, and in America especially, potters have taken to oil and emulsion colors. In early times the method saved a second firing, helped waterproofing, or made brighter finishes possible. The last reason also operates today, but in the main the use of these materials is iconoclastic. Some pottery suppliers list cold colors, but these are a form of enamel paints rather than ceramic finishes, although they are for use on raw or biscuit clays. They are of some value in elementary schools, especially for modeling, and are often used in conjunction with nylon-fiber or self-hardening clays such as Newclay, but they give no insight into the principles of ceramics and may even mislead. Ordinary water color or poster paint is sometimes used and varnished over.

Colloid

When a finely divided substance is dispersed in another liquid so that it tends to remain in suspension even though it is of a higher specific gravity, it is known as "colloidal." Hamer gives a full account of the colloidal theory is respect to clays and glazes. Copper reds, lusters, and some opalescent glazes owe their appearance to a colloidal condition. The main value of colloids in slips is their use in burnishing and gloss surfaces.

Color-Affecting Minerals

Many glaze ingredients will alter or control the tone or even the hue of pigment oxides. Magnesia and baria will affect copper and cobalt, the one tending to blue, the second to purple. Baria can even turn iron blue. Zinc will deaden some colors. Feldspar, clay, whiting, and flint recipes will usually give "standard" colors from pigment oxides as listed in many books, as will lead/lime/potash earthenware glazes. The results of any variation can only be ascertained by testing. The effects of zinc, baria, dolomite, wood ashes, talc, etc., can be considerable. See also **Chun, Turquoise,** and the headings for pigment oxides.

Colored Bodies

Most clays contain some coloring material, commonly iron oxide, but for agate and similar wares the body may be artificially colored with oxides or prepared body stains. The introduction of china clay and flint in the eighteenth century led to a near-white body and allowed more delicate hues than the buff, brown, blue, and black clays that had predominated previously. Wedgwood developed pale browns, pinks, lilac, blue, and green in his hard-fired Jasper ware from 1775 onward, as did the Meissen factory for porcelain. The addition of pigment oxides will change the characteristics of the body clay according to whether they have a fluxing action or not and, in the case of iron especially, whether the ware is oxidized or reduced. The breakdown of carbonates can lead to bloating.

Colored bodies are used in various ways. See **Agate, Coil-form decoration, Inlay, Marbled ware, Neriage,** etc. Hughto has built up large slab "paintings" from colored clays, with details brushed on in slip.

Color Wash

Color washes have been widely used in ceramics, often as a background to more explicit brushwork. They were used over printed patterns in eighteenth-century industrial wares, as on the Worcester porcelain of the 1760s and are still sometimes used in this way. The transparent water-color nature of most ceramic pigments leads naturally to color washes of weak concentrations over which stronger strokes can be laid. Copper is suitable only for washes or fillings, since it is ill-defined on a glaze. David Leach uses a weak cobalt laid onto a spinning plate or pot as a ground for stronger blue or iron pigments. His father used a mixture of 2:98 of cobalt/ocher for similar pale washes. The hake brush is suitable for this work, as is a mop.

Combing

The factor that differentiates combing from other incising methods is that the tool used has two or more teeth giving parallel lines from a right-angle cut, the lines converging if the comb is moved sideways. In wet-slip combing, three or four fingers held a little apart normally represent the comb, although soft rubber and other materials are sometimes used. Leach, in *A Potter's Book*, mentions slip combs from old tires.

Incised combing has long been used, although only to a limited extent. Some very early Chou-period Chinese cooking pots appear to have been comb decorated, and fine vertical combing appears on Mid-Tumulus Haniwa in fifth-century Japan. Some medieval jugs are combed. The insides of Japanese mortars—"suribachi"—are beautifully scored from the center outward, primarily for the practical purpose of grinding but incidentally as splendid decoration. A steel tool is used at the leather-hard stage of

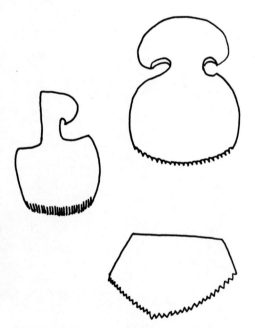

Wooden combs from Japan with a variety of profile and tooth size. "Comb grain" decoration is known as kushime and has been practiced for hundreds of years.

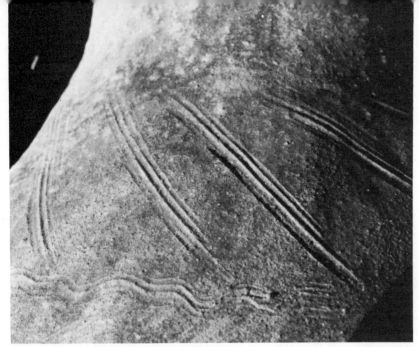

A roughly combed neck portion of a large jug, probably medieval, the shard found during digging near my pottery at Lacock, England.

Combing at its most basic and most effective, the main element of the design cut in one vigorous, sensitive stroke. By Bernard Leach.

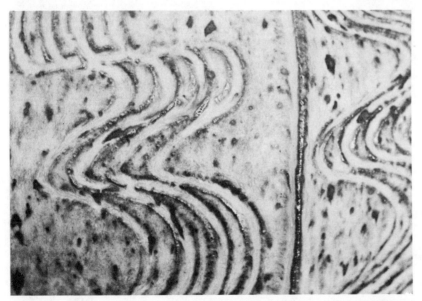

Combing under a stoneware glaze on a faceted pot by David Lloyd-Jones. The edges are emphasized by the pale glaze, which has broken and left a darker line.

In direct contrast to the Lloyd-Jones combing are these fine lines cut through a vitreous slip on earthenware by Michael Casson. The pattern is perhaps a little too delicate for the strength of the modeled knob.

drying. Many potters today use the comb, sometimes as a single motif cut with a swift action, while other potters almost cover the surface, building up crosscurrents of movement into a complex design. John Lawrence, Hans Coper, and others have combed through slips, fired afterward to a vitreous state, in the manner of sgraffito.

The type of tool and the texture and state of the clay will all affect the combed line. Combs can be of wood, metal, rubber, and other materials. A common table fork is

Like the Casson pot, this is also cut through a vitreous coating but in a very different style, amounting to a texture rather than the sharp definition of most combed designs. By Hans Coper.

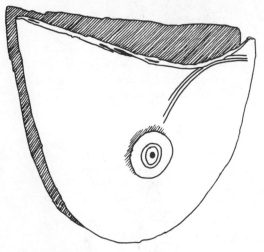

Minimal combing unites this applied circular motif with the rest of the form. A hand-built slab "porcelain object" by Eileen Nisbet.

sometimes used. Flexible prongs are useful for curved surfaces. Wooden and bamboo "kushime" tools are used in Japan. Steel hacksaw blades will give a textured surface rather than typical combing. In general, potters recommend blunt prongs spaced at least ⅛ inch apart. The clay state can vary from soft, wet clay on the wheel to almost dry, and each will give its own characteristic result. The ploughed-up edges of the cuts can be left as a rough texture that will, of course, be much sharper when fired, or smoothed with sandpaper when dry. Grog or sand in the body will obviously give a rougher line and a more broken edge. Various sizes of combs can be used in one design. Leach combined fine combing with brushwork in a satisfactory way. Coarser combing on applied strips of clay can give a molded effect. The combed lines need not be straight

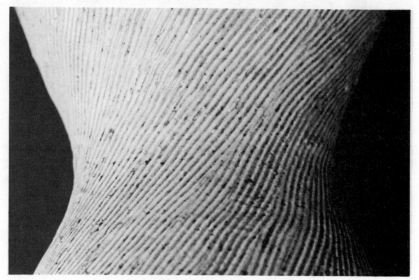

A detail of an all-over textured combing giving spiral movement to the pot. By Sarah Walton.

A dish by Bernard Leach in which the combed areas are almost completely cut away and only the ends of the strokes indicate the tool used.

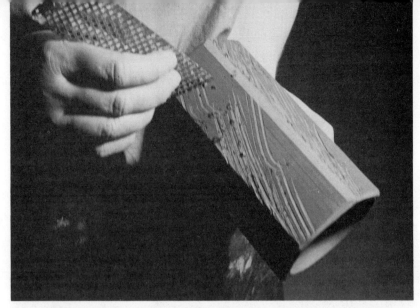

Cutting with free strokes into the leather-hard surface of a pot with a broken Surform plane blade.

and rapid but can be more deliberate, as on the example by Ian Auld. Casson inlays combed lines.

The term *slip combing* can apply to two different techniques. One is allied to sgraffito in that the slip is cut away to show the clay beneath but giving a broader and softer line than the normal scratched line. The work should be done a few minutes after covering, just as the slip is beginnning to lose its first wet shine. The comb, as mentioned above, may simply be the potter's fingers or can be made of wood, rubber, or plastic. A unique tool used by the Fishleys of Fremington consisted of four whale-bone prongs set in a handle, each topped by a baby-bottle nipple! Whatever the material used, the teeth should be blunt or square and be spaced ¼ inch or so apart. A Leach dish shows combing through red slip to a pale body that has taken all the slip away over most of the stroke, simply leaving the broken ends as evidence that a comb was used. This is unusual but is an indication of the variety that is possible. An early name for English slip combing was, incongruously, Welsh ware.

The second type of slip combing is the feathering or marbling of mixed-color wet slips. See **Marbled ware.** Presumably a multifeathered tool was sometimes used, but the term is also applied to marbling done with a single point.

Coperta

The Italian name for a clear glaze layer applied over majolica tin-glaze painting to enhance depth and shine, presumably sprayed on in some way. It was later known as "kwaart" in Holland. See also **Majolica** and **Tin-glaze**.

Copper

Copper was probably the earliest metal to be isolated and worked by man, and the period between the Neolithic and Bronze Ages is often known as the Chalcolithic or Copper Age. Apart from the ever-present iron oxide in clays, it was also the first coloring oxide in ceramics, giving brilliant turquoise in the third millennium B.C. in Egypt. Copper green glaze appears in Roman times, and early Chinese and Islamic

The typical mottled effect of coarse copper fragments in a lead glaze, popular with peasant potters the world over. This example is a charming nineteenth-century money box.

potters used it extensively. Later, in the Far East it was generally relegated to copper reds and enamels. It is less useful at high temperatures. Most peasant cultures used copper extensively, generally with lead glazes, dangerously so as it now appears. Today its function in producing greens has been partly superseded by chrome, especially in industrial colors.

In reduction, copper is only of value in the tricky business of copper reds, but for earthenwares and oxidized or neutral stonewares it is very useful, giving greens and turquoise, a near-blue, browns, buffs, black, and gold. As a stain or painted onto lead glazes the color will be apple-green, moving toward turquoise as the lead is decreased in relation to the alkalis present. On biscuit it will fire black to brown. It will also go black if too thickly painted or used in excess of 3 percent in most glazes. In a glaze the gun-metal black can be attractive, but the surface marks easily. In stoneware it tends to volatilize and in standard glazes is a not very interesting gray-brown, but it can be strongly influenced by the glaze make-up. In a nepheline glaze with rutile it can give an olive-brown; in a high dolomite/barium recipe, turquoise to blue. On biscuit, copper oxide will fire to a rather sooty range of browns and blacks. The metal itself can be beaten into the surface of damp clay to produce spreading black spots on firing, sometimes with a tendency to run.

As a pigment painted onto glazes it cannot be used with any degree of definition. It will spread out from the original line, and its main function is therefore as a filler or a wash. It will also produce a rather watery color in slip, and green slips are often stabilized with chrome. It is difficult to grind the black oxide fine enough to avoid speckle, and the carbonate is often used for painting. Carbonates are, however, toxic. Copper in a lead glaze will increase the danger of lead release into food. Coarse copper or fine filings will give a black and green speckle in glazes, as is often seen on peasant green-glazed pottery. The metal itself can, as mentioned above, be used decoratively on sculptural pieces. See also **Copper/manganese gold** for a reaction of copper on biscuit, and **Copper luster.**

Copperas

A ferrous sulphate that is sometimes calcined to provide low-temperature nasturtium reds (around 600 ° C.) with violet hues in higher firings.

Copper Luster

A metallic ruby-red luster that can be achieved by painting onto a soft glaze with a copper/clay mixture, or by adding 2–8 percent of copper oxide to the glaze. The glaze is normally opacified with tin or titanium; the latter is recommended by some authorities. At Wedgwood's, copper luster was used over a polished red biscuit, which "reflected brilliance back" into the metallic film (Hughes). In-glaze luster is fired to the glaze maturity temperature, normally about 1,000° C./1,830° F., and reduced during cooling, intermittently but fairly heavily. Painted luster is applied to the fired surface, refired to about 780° C./1,420° F. The clay is cleaned away when the piece is cold. In practice all luster work is fairly tricky. More details are under **Copper/manganese gold,** and **Luster.**

Copper/Manganese Gold

Certain mixtures of black copper oxide and manganese dioxide, with a preponderance of the latter, will produce a bronze-gold on biscuit over a wide range of temperatures. An attempt on my part to use copper carbonate produced only black. The biscuit pot can initially be covered all over with manganese, and the copper can then be applied with a brush or sponge where the gold color is required, the rest remaining black. The copper oxide can be itself diluted with manganese, as too thick a coat may turn it ashy black. The effect can be obtained at most temperatures from well-fired earthenware to porcelain. The running of the color is a problem, and the copper should not be applied too near the base of the piece. We have found that temperatures around 1,210° C./ 2,200° F. give reasonable results with a minimum of running. Some potters claim that thick manganese alone will give gold, but I have not found it so. On the first firing the bronze-gold may be crinkled and immature in appearance, but this can be improved with a second firing. The shine can be attached by sulphur gases, which some clays give off during firing. If this happens it can be refired to brightness. The color is preferable

A striking bowl by Lucie Rie in copper-manganese "gold." Although in the text under **Luster** *I describe how copper carbonate failed to give any sign of "gold" at all, Lucie Rie uses the compound to obtain her magnificent examples of this technique—which only goes to show how little its fundamental chemistry is understood.*

to gold metal on most studio ceramics, especially on hand-built and scuptural pieces. The color will sometimes appear on raku but is more difficult to control.

Copper Red

Red glazes from reduced copper pose technical problems. The dictionaries by Hamer and Fournier and expert advice from Rhodes and others cover the subject. When really successful the color is striking and often attractive, particularly when used sparingly with the seductive Chun-type glazes, but many attempts result in brownish or liver hues, which offer little pleasure to the eye. Copper will reduce over a wide range of temperatures, and one of our finest exponents of the technique, Derek Davis, fires at 1,320° C./2,400° F. and higher. The examples by Gerry Williams shown in the film *An American Potter* are incredibly brilliant but curiously out of character with high-fired ceramic. Davis has sandwiched a tin glaze between sang de beouf copper glazes to develop "peach bloom" flashing. Harriet Brisson recommends less than 1 percent of copper in the glaze with a little tin oxide. Fast firing and cooling are essential. It is possible to add copper carbonate in salt-glazing (about 1 part to 60 of salt) to induce copper reds.

Copper Red Painting

Reduced copper red is normally used as an all-over or partial glaze, or as a splash of color. Attempts were made, however, in fifteenth-century China to paint fish and fruit in copper onto white porcelain. The outline was often blurred, but when used with sensitivity on small dishes, stem cups, and the like, it could be very attractive. It is occasionally tried today, especially on raku, but the result is more often the fully reduced metal rather than red.

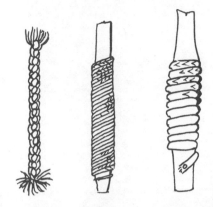

Three types of cord impressing tool, the first consisting of a number of cords braided together; the second and third show cords of various thicknesses wound round a core. These can be rolled onto the clay in its soft-leather state. (Numbers 1 and 2 from Sanders.)

Cord or string impressions combined with circular stamps and incising build up a varied surface. Northern Italy, 900–800 B.C.

Cord Impressions

Rope and string impressions are common on early unglazed pottery, but the actual method used is not always clear. Cords could have been laid onto damp pots and pressed or beaten into the surface, as seems to have been the case with European beakers of the third millennium B.C., which have become known as "corded ware." The impressions are horizontal and fairly close together, encircling the long neck of the vessel. Alternatively, pots may have been beaten with a stick wrapped in a cord, or the wrapped stick can be rolled or pressed onto the surface. An article in *Ceramic Review 62* shows Japanese "nawame," cords that are wrapped around sticks which are then rolled over the surface of damp clay. The cord can be tied in various patterns. An illustration in Sanders shows horizontal sections of a pot rolled with alternate patterns, which have been inlaid by brushing over with slip and scraping down when nearly dry. Thickly woven, plaited, bound, or knotted cords can be used without a central stick; they can then be bent around the contour of a pot as they roll the pattern into the surface. Slabs of cord-impressed clay can be carefully formed into dishes or pots.

Cordon

A strap or raised continuous band around a pot is known as a cordon, especially in books on archeology. Cordons are found on the pots of many cultures and from the earliest times. They serve to emphasize changes of direction and can give vitality and interest to a profile.

They can be formed either when throwing or during the turning of a pot. Karen Karned embodies powerful cordons on her sturdy shapes, and they are featured in the work of Hans Coper and many other potters of today. A strip or roll of clay can also be applied to the leather-hard shape and smoothed into the surface to form a cordon. This technique is generally used for a **frilled cordon**. See also **Applied decora-**

An uncompromising pot from prehistoric Egyptian Nubia. It could well have been made by a potter of the modern "brutal" school.

The cordon on this sturdy mug serves as a springing-off point for the handle.

The rare use of cordons or ribs on the inside of a bowl. By Richard Freeman.

tion. Extremely subtle and delicate surface ridges are shown on a pot by Ryuzo Asami where surface slip has been maneuvered into horizontal strips by the casual stroke of a rib (Sanders, Fig. 74). A ridge or cordon around a beaker or jug is often used as a springing-off point for the handle.

Counterchange

In its strictest sense this is a design in which one half of a pattern is a mirror image of the other but in "negative" colors—for example, one half black on white, the other

Simple paper-resist counterchange by Sybil Houldsworth.

Slip trailing in counterchange style, one half on buff, the other on a black slip ground. The red slip common to both is a uniting factor. By M. Ward.

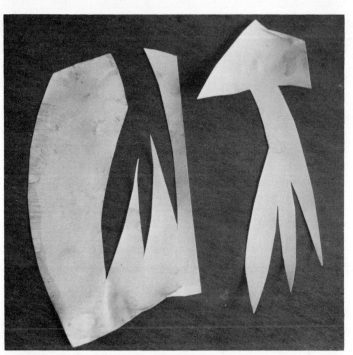

Paper cut to form another variation on counterchange. The use of this design may be seen under **Cut-paper resist**.

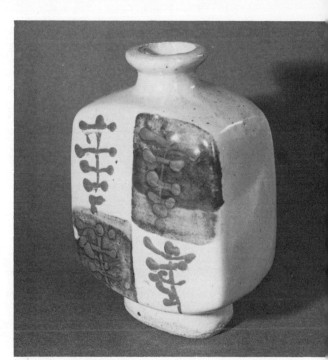

Two variations on the counterchange system by Bernard Leach. Brushwork and resist build up the "tree and mountain" design. That on the press-molded bottle is not strictly true to the style, the iron painting being common to both sections of the design. See also color plate.

white on black. The style is useful as an exercise for students, since it makes clear the fact that the spaces between the elements of a design have as much "shape" as the elements themselves. In a less formal fashion, panels, for instance, can be counterchanged by painting pigment strokes on one and resist brushwork on the other. In an even wider sense the contrasting of the main elements in a composition has been the stock-in-trade of pottery decorators throughout history, giving weight, interest, and variety. Counterchange is especially suited to **sgraffito** where one part of the design can be in contrasting **sgraffiato**. Leach often used counterchange on quartered panels on slab and beaten pots.

Cracked-Ware Surfaces

The attitude toward fire cracks has varied with the period and the culture. In the East today, if a pot or bowl is considered to be a fine piece, a crack or even a breakage repair may be filled and painted over with a gold line that becomes part of the decoration. In the West, on the generality of pieces, fire cracks are considered by the public and by many potters to be quite severe faults. An exception is the work of Daniel and Coombes who worked together in the eighteenth century, and who not only used a fine wire to repair Chinese porcelain but identified themselves on the back in fired-on enamel. On some modern raku, sculptural pieces, and other work, cracks (deliberate or otherwise) may be incorporated into the overall concept. Free-form hand-built pieces may feature a crack or split, sometimes adding pellets of clay or other small elements. A pot by the Japanese potter Arakawa is split from top to bottom, emphasizing its separation from utility. Eileen Lewenstein and others have also worked in this way in England and America.

A distinct form of surface cracking can be induced by laying softer clay or one with

A pot by Eileen Lewenstein that has been deliberately cracked by pressure on the sides. The indentation and shape of the fissure suggest growth and energy.

a greater shrinkage over a firmer base. Continued rolling of clay slabs will also result in a fissured splitting of the surface. See illustrated example under **Texture**.

Crackle, Craquelle

A pattern of fine cracks and fissures will develop in a glaze that has shrunk more than the body in cooling after firing. On a vitrified base, stoneware or porcelain, it can be a deliberate decorative measure, but on most earthenwares it is usually accidental, rarely attractive, always unhygenic, and is known as "crazing." The exception is raku, which is rarely functional and where the blackening of the body gives dramatic emphasis to the crazing.

A coarse crackle can result when the glaze is on the borderline of "fitting" the body; a finer, overall crackle occurs when its coefficient of expansion is at greater variance with the body. The early Chinese crackle, for example, on Kuan ware, probably originated as an accident but was quickly recognized for its decorative qualities. The Chinese call a large pattern "crab's claw" and a finer one "fish roe." It is possible that some pieces have developed crackle years after they were made. A characteristic of some Japanese Awata and Chinese "applegreen" is that an enamel is used over a crackled glaze, giving extra subtleties such as "shining white flakes," known in France as *ailes de mouches*—flies' wings. Crackle was also common on the Shino wares of the sixteenth century. English Elton ware (late nineteenth and early twentieth centuries) used a crackled gold luster over a green ground. Ivy Mitchell, today, paints over crackle in a way that unites the two aspects of decoration. On some British tin-glazed pieces of the 1760s, crackle is simulated in manganese pigment, a style known as "cracked ice."

It is but a step from deliberate crackle to emphasizing the pattern either by staining with pigment oxides, which can then be refired to permanence, or by employing various nonceramic materials: rubbing with inks, soaking in tea, or, to quote Père Entrecolle's notes on Ching-te-chen, "boil[ing] in fat broth—then in a foul sewer for

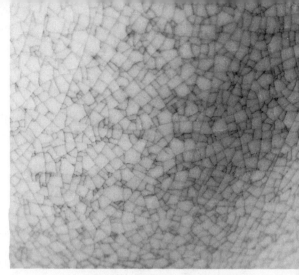

Detail of a "studio" piece from Buller's Electrical Porcelain factory, Stoke-on-Trent, exhibiting a curiously square crackle on a porcelain pot. Long lines can be seen with angular breaks between.

The powerful, stained crackle on this bowl by Mary Rogers is reflected in the rim piercing.

Primary crackle on this Song (Sung) Ting ware bowl has been stained, but the secondary fissures are clear. It is possible that the clear crackle is a later development, but it is also possible that the contrast was deliberately contrived.

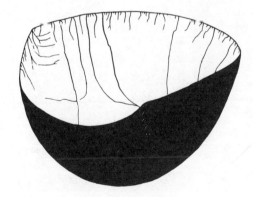

Interesting crackle on a bowl called "Porcelain Raku with Straight Edge," which complements the form. By Susan Sonz.

Crackle defined by spun lines: the rim color painted onto the biscuit with the glaze just barely overlapping; the center lines spun onto the glaze. By Peter Lane.

a month or more," this last rather excessive! Behrens suggests the use of nitrates of pigments to stain crackle. Brian Bevan in *Ceramic Review 73* goes into detail: do not handle pots from the kiln or skin-grease will cause patches when the crackle is stained, but hold the pot in a clean rag while rubbing it over with another rag soaked in a water-based paint. He uses a dark brown stain. If applied to a hot pot, it will take up a deeper color. Washing off in cold water may also set up a secondary crackle, and a couple of hours later an ocher color can be rubbed into the newly crazed areas. To induce crackle just where it is required for a decorative effect, Martin Smith trails a wet cloth across red-hot raku.

Crackle will usually result from an increase in alkalis in a glaze: feldspar, volcanic ash, talc, and alkaline frit have all been mentioned. Hamer's "melt-crackle" is achieved by underfiring a glaze, rubbing the cracks with coloring oxides, and refiring to the full temperature. He also suggests two different layers of glaze, both subject to crazing, to produce "interesting lacework" (see Hamer).

Crater Glazes

See **Volcanic glazes**.

Crawled Glazes

Crawling, like crazing, is normally listed as a glaze fault, but it is increasingly used, often in a semicontrolled way, as a decorative feature on ceramics. This is a modern approach; crawling on celadons and on some other early Chinese pieces was an undesired accident, possibly due to the overgrinding of materials. The Japanese have made a feature of crawling: Hamada's crawled glazes are well known. Ewen Henderson

The typical result of laying a fairly refractory stoneware glaze over black manganese slip. The darker pattern is, of course, from wax resist. By Sheila Fournier.

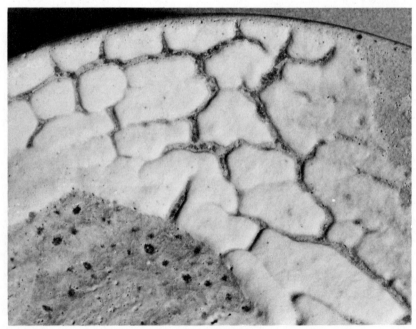

Detail of a John Chalke dish illustrating the somewhat rugged decorative qualities of crawled glaze.

establishes a degree of control in his fine all-over textures. Scratching through a suitable glaze can induce crawling, but recipes can be made up that will bring it about naturally. I manage a fairly close control by judging the precise thickness of a refractory glaze over rough-surfaced pebble forms where most of the crawl-inducing factors mentioned below apply. Lucie Rie managed the effect on earthenware with great panache, but this is unusual because the porosity of the body can allow dirt and moisture to penetrate, and the technique is normally applied to stonewares. The brilliant white-on-black crawled patterns of Robert Sperry are achieved by trailing slip over glaze, a unique approach.

The factors involved in crawling are: a high surface tension in the glaze; an over-viscous glaze; a "loose" ground, such as one containing sand or dust, grog, unfixed color, or rubbed-over dry underglaze color; glaze applied too thickly (a glaze which is normally smooth and well behaved can crawl at the junctions of handles, where it has bridged a gap); and lastly, and perhaps most commonly, a glaze with a high drying shrinkage. Overly rapid drying can also be a factor, caused either by local heat or by a very porous biscuit. High alumina content or the addition of opacifiers, especially zinc oxide, render a glaze more liable to crawl. Such glazes may be essentially under-fired, and the inclusion of more fluxes or a higher fire will produce a smooth surface. The probable extent and size of the fissures can be judged by the rapidity of formation and the degree of cracking as the glaze dries. Excessive thicknesses of glaze are likely to fall off the pot before packing or during firing.

Crayon

Underglaze crayons are now available from several suppliers for temperatures between 1,080 and 1,280° C. (cones 04–9). Use like a nonceramic crayon, blow away excess dust, glaze, and fire. Some potters find them more controllable than a brush but they

Deliberate and controlled crawling of a thick white glaze over what appears to be an agate body so that the spiral of darker clay has become apparent in the different degrees of crawling. By Lucie Rie.

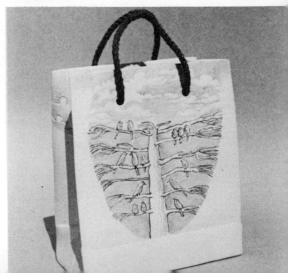

Joan Hepworth uses ceramic crayons exclusively for her individual and amusing designs on unusual forms. She warns, however, that their employment is not as easy as it appears. They need continual sharpening and are soft, brittle, and easily broken. They are sometimes recommended for schools, but they are wasteful and expensive if used by any but the most careful child. See also illustrations under **Pencil**.

will, of course, give a very different effect, generally paler and more allied to drawing than painting. Porcelain by Keith Campbell (Canada) is decorated with crayons (see illustration in Lane, 1980). They are becoming quite widely used, resulting in a new, freely drawn graphic style. See also **Pencil** for details of a homemade crayon.

Crazing

The term is normally applied to an ill-fitting glaze on earthenware, where, except for raku and some nonfunctional ceramics, it is seldom anything but an annoying fault. See **Crackle**.

Creamware

Although not in itself a decorative element, the development of a fine-grain flint/stone/clay body in the eighteenth century made possible a great range of decorative techniques in earthenware, which were previously limited to those possible on a light-colored slip or on a tin-glaze. It also led to the rapid collapse of all other techniques, notably tin-glaze, for the generality of tablewares. In the 1760s, Wedgwood further improved Staffordshire clays by hand-washing them and covering the body with "a brilliant yellow glaze" (Hughes). In 1776, china stone and china clay were added to make a fabric stronger and lighter in weight and color.

Underglaze painting, enamels on a clear glaze, stained bodies, and printing all took on a new significance. Wedgwood treated the material with great respect, favoring "an elegant and sentimental plainness" with the decoration in an Anglicized neoclassical style often confined to a red and black palette. Creamware swept across Europe as "faience Anglais," much of it made by British potters working abroad. Creil, in France, was one such center of production. The pure white "pearl ware" of 1779 was not so successful. Perhaps the principal revolutionary technique was to fire the biscuit to maturity—at around 1,200° C./1,470° F.—and to cover it with a softer, thin, fritted glaze. This reversal of procedure still separates industrial ware from most craft pottery.

Crocus Martis

This is described by Billington as a "natural" iron oxide and by Cardew as ferric iron, but Hamer specifically lists it as an iron salt giving a yellowish color in a lead glaze and "greenish" in boric glazes, using 3–6 percent. It will decompose and release sulphur at 1,200° C. The pure form is soluble in water, but crocus martis of the potter's suppliers' lists is treated to prevent this. It may speckle in stonewares.

Cross Fire

Term applied to the Japanese "hidasuki," straw-marked Bizen pottery. See details under **Fire cord**.

Crystalline Glazes

The devitrification of certain oxide combinations in a glaze will cause the development of crystals that may vary from fine surface crystals, which produce a matt finish or a slight sparkle (see **Aventurine glazes**), to large and spectacular crystalline patterns. The first type is often associated with calcium. Low viscosity is essential, and a detailed explanation of the molecular structure is to be found in Hamer's *Dictionary*. Aventurine glazes were made in the Far East and in the nineteenth century, at Sèvres and

Isolated and unusually formed crystals on 1,280°C. (Cone 9) fired porcelain. Gold/tan on a yellow ground. Electric-fired by Beryl Barton.

Copenhagen. In Cincinnati, Rookwood Pottery introduced the "tiger's eye" crystalline glaze in 1894, and crystalline glazes have been used in twentieth-century industrial and studio potteries.

The crystals are formed principally in the range of 700–900° C. (018–09 cones), and very slow cooling at this stage is necessary. Suitable glazes can be refired to 900° C. to induce crystals, again very slowly through both heating and cooling cycles. Certain rather subdued formations will even appear on stoneware, but a glaze can alter in its character if refired below its maturing temperature. A fluid glaze plus iron oxide in one form or another is usually required. Some crystalline glazes are so fluid that Michael Machtey, in *Ceramic Review 49*, describes methods of minimizing the effects of glaze running and dripping from the base of pots by carefully supporting the inside of the foot and setting the pot over a biscuit bowl to catch the flowing glaze. A great deal of grinding is then necessary. Diane Creber achieves large and magnificent crystals but also has to set her pots on a pedestal from which they are cut away, after firing, with a diamond-tipped glass cutter and then extensively ground. At the other end of the scale, aventurine crystals are so small as to merely give a sparkle. Ash/iron glazes

A comparatively modern stamped Spanish tile decorated with the traditional iron and copper stained glazes, which are held apart by the raised lines of the design.

A molded dish from the Madora factory, Vallauris, in the style of Picasso. The roughly painted-in raised outlines are in the cuenca style. The mold-cutter has forgotten to reverse the numbers at the bottom, as on so many pressed dishes and sprigs.

sometimes develop this effect. Mary White has shown pots with delicate surface enrichment of this kind.

While the results of this technique can be dramatic, their aesthetic value must always be in some doubt. Such restrained effects as are illustrated by Beryl Barton in *Ceramic Review 62* are to be recommended. Crystals can emphasize the full shoulder of a pot or the formally neutral surface of a cylinder.

Cuenca

Cuenca can be translated as "cell type" and is a method of decoration creating separated areas of glaze in the manner of cloisonné enamels. It was practiced in fifteenth-century Seville and has persisted until today. A similar technique was used in Ming China embodying enamels painted onto biscuit. On "fa-hua" pots, threads of slip or incised lines hold the colors apart: at Kochi in the nineteenth century a fine raised line held the glazes in place. But the term is strictly associated with tiles on which a stamped design has given low-relief outlines. Colored earthenware glazes were laid in, presumably with a brush, though they could be trailed or poured, the lines acting as boundary walls preventing the glazes from spreading and mixing (though this sometimes occurs). The technique was taken up with enthusiasm by Victorian tile factories, and a great number of fireplaces are still so decorated. It lent itself especially to industrial production with cheap labor, but with variation and adaption it could still find a place on studio ceramics and to some small degree has done so. In a slightly different way, the slip-trailed lines of Toft-type plates fulfill a similar function, outlining and containing flat areas of slip, as also do the molded raised lines on Samuel Malkin dishes of the eighteenth century. Barumware Art Nouveau vases at the turn of the century have stylized leaves on the side in colored glazes separated by raised outlines (photo in *Ceramics Review 35*). Clay surfaces have also been cut away to leave narrow ribs or walls that are then treated in the cuenca manner.

Cuerda Seca

This technique has affinities with **cuenca**. Although it is known by its Spanish name, translated as "dry cord," it was practiced in the Near East long before its use at Seville and other potteries. It entailed separating colored glazes or enamels by painting lines of a thick mixture, usually of manganese in a fatty medium. Boger (1971) asserts that the dry cord work at Seville was painted over an impressed or incised outline of the design. This could have been stamped or molded into the surface to help semiskilled repetition painters. Quite elaborate figurative compositions were carried out, usually in a broad peasant style. Charleston in *World Ceramics* describes a plate roughly decorated with leaves and an animal in cuerda seca style but as "blue, green, yellow, and brown enamel on a white tin-glaze," probably indicating that colors were painted onto a glaze rather than colored glazes themselves being used.

A variation described by Storr-Britz involves wires welded together and attached (glued?) to tiles. The areas between are filled with colored glazes. The wire melts during the firing and can later be "reduced" with an oxyacetylene flame. The results must have been distinctive to have gone to all this trouble!

Cullet

Pieces of glass. In glass-making, *cullet* describes the glass waste that is returned to the kiln to start the next batch. See **Glass cullet**.

Cupric

The stable oxide of copper, loosely used to indicate copper in a chemical combination.

Cut Brick

See illustrations and **Printing**.

Soft insulating brick or similar material can have designs cut or gouged to provide large-scale stamps. The illustrations show broad and finer patterns of cuts. See also **Printing** *for a system of using similar cut bricks for color application.*

Cut-Paper Resist

The use of paper, adhered to the surface of ware, acting as a resist to slip, glaze, or pigment does not have an extensive historical pedigree. The technique was used in China at least as early as the twelfth century, on some European industrial ware, and occasionally on tin-glaze to form a reserve on a powder ground. It has, however, always been popular with hobby potters and is quite widely used by professionals. Many decorative methods demand a facility and speed that can come only from long experience, but cut-paper designs can be tried out and altered at leisure. They are most suited to comparatively flat surfaces such as tiles, dishes, slab pots, or beaten thrown pots.

For the material, David Winkley suggests thin brown paper, but tissue and other papers are also used. It is helpful if the paper will soften or stretch a little when wet, as this helps it to accommodate some curvature and also to adhere firmly to the surface. It may sometimes be necessary to slit the paper from the edge toward the center in order to persuade it to lie flat. The resisted areas can constitute the design in their own right and can be made less blank by cutouts in the mass of the design, or they can be used as a basis for further detail in brushwork, sgraffito, etc. A brilliant and sensitive use of cut paper is shown in Bernard Leach's "Pilgrim" dishes, where the resist is between dark olive and khaki glazes and where movement and distance are suggested with the utmost simplicity. In another version of the same design the paper is applied to the raw clay and brushed over with a black slip; in a third variation he cuts a figure from the center of a circular piece of paper placed in the middle of the plate, sluices it over with a white slip, and adds details in sgraffito and brushwork. These examples indicate the flexibility of the technique. Thorp suggests washing over biscuit with oxides, dipping into a tin-glaze, and using this as a basis for a cut-paper design, which is then painted over. The initial wash gives color and interest to the resisted areas,

Cut-paper resist of the mid-eighteenth century, with a blue "powder" ground. The resisted areas are used as spaces for painting in whispy strokes. From the Stone Hodges Collection, Bristol.

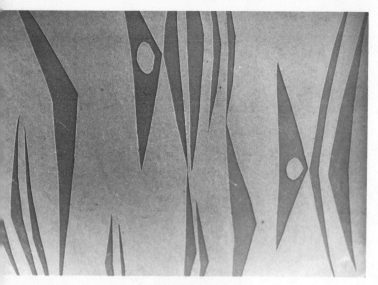

A simple cut-paper element, repeated to form a design.

Powerful yet delicate in detail is this resist horse by Bernard Leach, saved from blankness by the mane and the eye and the odd spot of color.

A

B

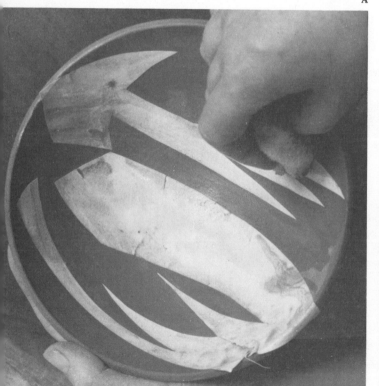

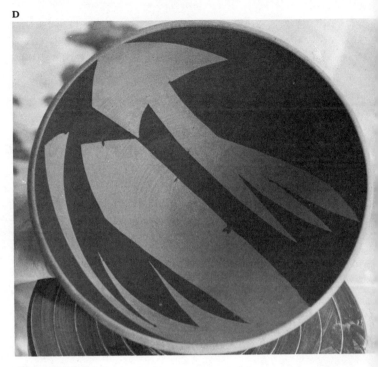

The basic technique of paper resist, the design in simple counterchange using the shape cut from a piece of paper to provide the resist for the other side. A. The paper templates are damped and sponged onto the surface of a leather-hard dish. B. Color is spun over the whole surface. C. The paper is peeled away when the shine has gone from the applied color. D. The completed plate.

As mentioned in the text, slip or glaze could also be used.

On biscuit an emulsified glue (Pritt is a British make) has been recommended, and in this case a thin plastic can be used in place of paper.

The top fish shape in cut paper is blank and uninteresting but when cut in sections at fins, tail, scales, etc., it takes on more decorative qualities. The same system can be developed for any shape, figurative or abstract.

which would otherwise be plain white. He also suggests that the paper can be removed and repositioned for further color. This can give mystery and variety when using any type of paper resist, but on a raw tin-glaze it would be a rather tricky job. In some modern work, simple elements of resist are combined with spraying to produce landscape and other effects. Cut paper inevitably gives a hard, defined edge. This can be softened by tearing the paper instead of using a knife or scissors. See also **Paper resist**.

Cut Sponge

The dense root of a natural sponge or, today, an artificial sponge can be cut with simple patterns to form stamps for repetition work or repeat patterns on a single piece. Pottery suppliers' catalogues used to list a variety of cut sponge stamps. Leach reported that sponge stamps were used in Japan to imitate brushwork, which, even in 1946, had almost vanished from the generality of their ceramics. "Through a shop window it is almost impossible to tell one from the other [but] on closer examination . . . the effect is deplorable." See also **Printing** for a modern use of polyurethane foam.

Dami Fude

See **Brushes**.

Decal

A term used mainly in America for lithographic and other transfers. It comes from the Greek for "off the paper," via the French. An extreme craze for this type of decoration, applied by young ladies to commercial pottery, occurred in the United States in the latter half of the nineteenth century and became known as decalcomania. See also under **Lithography, Slide-off transfer,** and **Transfers**. Some suppliers still list on-glaze transfers, usually of deplorable designs, though their old-fashioned "bad taste" gives them a certain cachet today. A number of firms have started up in recent years that will make ceramic transfers from a potter's own artwork. These are useful for runs of commemorative pieces and for more creative processes and styles. See also **Photoceramic processes** for illustrations of the basic technique.

Making a decal or transfer.

A. The image is first printed in the required ceramic pigment onto a sheet of thermo-flat paper (decal paper) by the method shown under **Silkscreen,** *and lined up by registration with metal rulers taped to the printing bed. This is essential if a number of copies are to be made or if multicolor printing is envisaged.*

B. A screen of 66 or 72 mesh is used to lay on a material known as a covercoat.

C. The screen is laid onto the design and, because the covercoat material is relatively expensive, it is masked off to leave a quarter of an inch or so around the image.

D. and E. The covercoat is applied in the same way as other screen printing but the silk is fixed so that it is stretched about an eighth of an inch above the transfer paper, which is held down by suction on a vacuum bed. The gap is necessary so that the rather sticky covercoat will not adhere the screen to the paper. The photograph shows the screen lifting from the paper behind the squeegee as it passes across it (giving the visual impression of a double image).

F. The image with the covercoat is left to dry. When needed the paper is soaked in water until the gum between the paper and the pigment begins to soften. It can then be slipped from the paper (hence **slide-off paper***) and applied by even pressure, covercoat upwards, to the ceramic. The residue of the gum is used to stick it to the surface. The covercoat fires away. A diagrammatic section through a decal showing the order of materials that make it up.*

A

B

C

D

E

F

COVERCOAT
OIL-BASED ENAMEL
WATER - SOLUBLE GUM
PAPER

Devitrification of Glazes

Glazes, especially on lower-fired earthenware, will slowly disintegrate (devitrify) and develop a patina—iridescent, silvery, or golden. This is apparent on many ninth- to twelfth-century Islamic pieces. As a decorative finish it is hardly a practical proposition for the potter today, although there are probably scientific ways of speeding up the natural process. In the nineteenth century, shiny glazes were immersed in acids to develop a matt surface, and in the United States it was only at the end of the century that the first true matt surfaces were developed (Clark and Hughto).

Dipping

The dipping of a pot into a glaze or slip is not in itself a decorative technique, but it always has its aesthetic dimension. The way in which a piece is held or twisted when removed from the glaze will partly control the distribution of glaze color and effect, as will the speed of dipping. If an area of a biscuit is left exposed, its relationship to the glaze mass is important, even critical. Many country and peasant potters glazed only one- or two-thirds of the other surface, and the contrast between glaze and body is the sole decorative feature. The division may, today, be controlled by a spun wax line and the dipping process then reverts to a more mechanical process.

The deliberate variation of glaze mass (or the area covered by a slip) is a relatively modern feature, although bibs are found on medieval pots, and the Japanese have used asymmetric and double-dipping for centuries. Many stoneware glazes exhibit very different color and other characteristics according to thickness, and this can be utilized. The simple redipping of a knob or other element of form can give interest and focus. A plate can be dipped half-and-half and the overlap controlled in depth and shape by the angle of the dip. The overlap is often adequate decoration in itself. If, instead of an overlap, the inner boundaries of the glaze do not quite meet, the line of revealed

The traditional West Country pale dipped rim, which the glaze just covers. From Lake's Pottery, Cornwall.

The glaze on this dish, dipped first one side and then the other but just not meeting, has not only left a decorative strip of body clay revealed but has also had a highly dramatic effect on the color. By Joanna Constantinidis.

A similar form dip decorated in different ways; side to side, and back and front. As in the Constantinidis dish, there is a bonus in the way the glaze has reacted at the edge of the dip, lighter in this case.

biscuit (which could be precolored) can give a striking effect. Joanna Constantinidis, among others, has used this technique.

Double dipping must be done with care: if the first glaze is allowed to become too dry, pinholing or blistering will take place. The second dip is best made immediately after the shine has gone from the first. See also **Poured glaze**.

Division of a Circle

The method of dividing the circumference of a bowl or plate into two, four, or eight sections is obvious. There is a simple trick for making divisions of three and six. Set callipers to the radius (measure diameter and divide by two), and this length will mark off six divisions around the edge. Five is more difficult, requiring a protractor. The easiest way with a pot is to encircle it with a strip of paper, remove the paper, and divide its length by the appropriate number, marking the divisions in pencil. Then replace the paper and transfer the marks to the pot.

Dotting

Part of the attraction of the large slip dishes of the seventeenth and eighteenth centuries in England lies in the jewel-like dotting or spotting of a contrasting slip along the main trailed lines of the design. This is often overlooked and does not often occur on modern trailing. In the seventeenth century, there was a great vogue for three-dimensional work in all fields: furniture, fabric "stump work," etc., and to a lesser degree in ceramics. A similar fashion, again spearheaded in fabrics, has developed in the 1980s, although three-dimensional ceramic tile-work has been going for much longer. The decoration of pots and bowls, usually in porcelain with tiny dots of color to build up line and mass and often using the halo-like effect of copper, is practiced by Mary Rogers and others with original and delicate effect. See also **Jeweling**. A historical

The dragon on this "St. George" dish of the early eighteenth century has been spotted or dotted to give variety to the infill slips, which are otherwise flat color.

A Portuguese slip dish with the design almost entirely in slip dots.

A vigorous and interesting combination of slip dots and rapidly trailed lines depicting a collared panther, a motif which occurs in heraldry. By Vi Purser.

Glaze-on-glaze decoration of dots and trails by David Lloyd-Jones, building up a repeat pattern on a large dish.

A pointillist technique adopted by Mary Rogers using the spreading and slightly fugitive effects of copper oxide. A combination of inlaid color and surface work.

precedent is the tin-glazed ware of the seventeenth century, where tone and texture were sometimes achieved through the application of a series of dots of paint. The pillars behind portraits of William III and others are so decorated.

Double Dipping

See **Dipping**.

Drilling

See **Pierced decoration**.

Dry Ash-Glaze

Wood ash mixed with china clay will usually give a rather dry-surfaced yellow to orange sintered glaze, which is not suitable for covering pots but can be used decoratively on slab pots and other surfaces, especially of hand-built ceramics. A simple recipe is 65 ash to 35 china clay. Any addition of feldspar or other fluxes seems to destroy the ochrous color, which is its main attraction. It will vary in effect with different thicknesses of application. If too thickly applied a less pleasant paint-like

A refractory ash glaze applied in various thicknesses on a hand-built form by Ian Auld. The texture varies from body-dry through smooth to crawled areas.

mustard color will result. Pour it thinly with overlaps, or sponge it on. It can be used to fill incised patterns or to break up surface color.

Egyptian Paste

This is not strictly a decorative technique, but it is used mainly for the attraction of its unique color and surface. In its original form it was almost certainly the first glazed ceramic surface. The body was principally composed of silica and the deep turquoise glaze derived from a natural copper/alkali ore, natron, found in Egypt. As formulated today the brilliant turquoise shine is not applied as a glaze but derives from materials incorporated in the body that "migrate" to the surface during drying, which should therefore be as slow as possible. The major constituents, flint, feldspar, alkalis (especially soda in various forms), and a pigment (usually copper oxide or carbonate), are bound with just enough ball clay or bentonite to make modeling possible while still retaining the necessary openness to permit migration. The low plasticity of the paste limits the size of pieces. It is especially useful for jewelry, though the Ancient Egyptians managed to construct more substantial work. There is a suggestion that a more traditional type of glaze may have been used on some later Pharaonic pieces.

Cobalt, manganese, and antimony stains have been used as well as copper. The more recently discovered compounds of chromium and uranium have also been used. By the nature of the technique a single firing suffices. Temperatures between cones 012 and 08 have been recommended. Recipes are given in Fournier, *Ceramic Review 39* and *40*, Rhodes' *Clay and Glazes*, and other reference books, and a fairly typical one is given below. Sylvia Hyman (see article in *Ceramic Review 39*) smokes beads raku-fashion to vary the color and to add a copper metal luster to some. She lays the beads on a soft-biscuited bowl or slab to fire and scrubs them when cold. Alicia Felberbaum quotes a recipe—feldspar 34, quartz 34, china clay 5, sodium carbonate 5, sodium bicarbonate 4, copper 3—and notes that copper oxide gives a darker and greener color than does the carbonate. Beads can be hung on nichrome wire to dry, and all pieces should be handled as little as possible, especially when quite dry.

Email Ombrant, Shadow Enamel

A French technique using a deep intaglio design, which when flooded over with a translucent glaze gives a light-and-shade effect. It was also used by the Wedgwood Company in the 1860s. The darkening of the line in incised celadons from Song (Sung) times is a similar effect, and it is used today on all types of pottery. On porcelain it can emphasize the translucent qualities of the body. Melted colored glass on stoneware and earthenware can give a similar effect.

Embossing

Strictly, a boss is a circular motif, but the term is used more loosely. See **Applied decoration** and **Boss**. The rims of some Italian plates and **blue-dash chargers** were pushed up from below into bosses, as were Dutch Delft dishes. But in a general sense "embossed" can simply apply to any relief surface.

Enamel, Over-Glaze Color

The industry, and antiquarians, use the term *enamel* to indicate any soft opaque glaze, generally a tin-glaze, white or colored. In studio ceramics, however, it refers to a low-firing (650–900° C./1,200–1,650° F. range) glassy material, usually strongly col-

A curious little Roman pig model, ca. A.D. 200, with slip trailing and spots of enamel in small "cups" on its back.

*A detail of the teapot illustrated under **Paneled decoration**, showing the combination of colored glazes, glaze resist, and enamel "noughts and crosses." An unusual but very satisfying combination. By John Maltby.*

A Russian Revolution plate (1920) by S.V. Chekonine, painted in an impressionistic Germanic style.

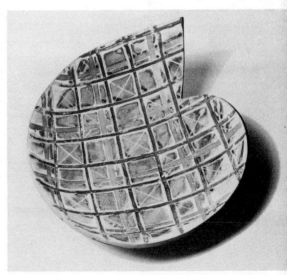

A combination of inlaid clays and enamels on high-fired earthenware by Jaqueline Poncelet.

ored with oxides—a colored frit in fact—and this is the sense in which it is discussed here. Enamel is applied over an already fired glaze and is supplied as a powder approximating to its fired color. Enamels are mixed with an oily medium and ground on a tile or glass slab with a knife or spatula. Turpentine, "fat oil," or plant extract from lavender, cloves, etc., can be used as medium, the object of which is to make it possible

Ruth Dupre combines underglaze painting with enamels, the latter adding brighter and more opaque colors to her lively designs.

to apply the color with a brush and to ensure that it will stay where it is put. One can use plain water, but the color can then be easily disturbed. Brushes are washed in turpentine after use. Colors mixed with fat oil (a concentrated turpentine) cannot be reused if allowed to dry on the slab. The addition of a little olive oil is said to prolong the useful life of mixed colors.

The advantages of enamels are: the brilliance of color which is attainable, including true reds; the fact that the fired color closely resembles the raw one in many cases; and the possibility of having several shots at a design without spoiling a pot. Against this the very facility with which they can be used and the detail possible may lead to fussy work; and they do not always fully integrate with the glaze and may be damaged by scourers and dishwashers. Applying this to transfer work in enamel, I have a completely plain bowl that once boasted a ship in full sail! Enamels have more the appearance of "applied art" than other pottery techniques.

They have been widely used the world over but first appeared on Islamic and Chinese ceramics, quite commonly by the thirteenth century, and from then on used to decorate all types of ceramics, earthenware, stoneware, salt-glaze, porcelain, even straight onto biscuit. The Persian Minai painting used soft colored glazes as enamels in a brilliant fashion. Some of the earliest enamels, late Song (Sung) or Yuan, were reds from iron, greens from copper, and yellow from iron and antimony. They owe part of their origin to the T'ang lead glazes of some 300 years before. Gold as gold leaf was used on Minai (twelfth century). European stonewares were enameled at Kreussen, Germany, from 1622, and a full palette was available by 1660. Meissen used enamels extensively on porcelain from 1715. Because they can be easily attacked by gases from fuel, they were fired in a closed box within a kiln and so became known as "muffle colors." The low firing was known as the "petit feu." They were used to a limited extent on tin-glazed wares, notably in France and Sweden. The later Chinese factories used them, of course, on countless pots and in many different ways. See **Crackle**.

The styles of enamel painting vary widely. In seventeenth-century Japan, for instance, the precise work of Ninsei contrasted with the splashed, bold strokes of Kenzan or, in the twentieth century, Tomimoto and Hamada in similar roles, although they had the greatest respect for each other's work. John Maltby uses small flecks of gold and bright enamel to set off and highlight his very direct poured glazes. The red spots on David Leach's porcelain look like enamel in their bright color but are fired at full temperature. See **Red**.

Most potters buy their enamels ready-made, but some have formulated their own. They are fundamentally composed of a soft frit, an opacifier, generally white tin oxide, a little clay, and a fairly high proportion of coloring oxide. The modern descendants of the Kakiemon family still mix their own enamels, particularly the "kaki" (persimmon red), for which iron oxide is mixed with bark and leaf ash and "porcelain stone," probably a form of china stone. For a base glaze Tomimoto suggests a shiny one with not too much lime. This, he says, helps to prevent the peeling of enamels. He also recommends that the glaze be covered with a thin coat of glue (or saliva) before applying the enamel. These remarks refer mainly to porcelain. A system of dusting powdered enamel onto lacquered glaze parallels the Western industrial **ground-lay** method. Sanders quotes a number of Japanese recipes, a typical example of which is 50 parts powdered lead glaze (soft frit), 5 white lead, and 12 red iron oxide for a red color. The lead, of course, is a very toxic material and not recommended unless used in the form of a low-solubility frit. For gold and silver enamels, see those headings and **Bright gold** and **Burnish gold**.

Enamels should be fired fairly slowly up to 500° C./930° F. with plenty of ventilation to allow organic materials to burn away before fluxing begins. The final temperature will vary with the color, and the advice of the supplier should be followed. Wengers used to recommend firing according to the refractoriness of the glaze: 740°C./1,380° F. for earthenware, 780/1,440 for bone china, 790/1,460 for stoneware, and 800/1,470 for porcelain for the generality of their colors. Most commercial colors are intermixable except for the selenium reds. A thirty-minute soak at top temperature can assist in fixing the colors. For spraying, enamel is usually mixed with 1 percent of starch and enough water to bring it to a thin creamy consistency (Hamilton, 1974). If enamel is applied too thickly, it may peel; where a solid color is required, two thinner coats, with the first coat fired on before applying the second, are preferable. The surfaces to be decorated must be free from grease and can be rubbed over with whiting to ensure a clean surface.

Apart from painting, enamels can be applied by lithography from a gelatinous coated paper, or by silkscreen. The latter will generally lack fine detail, but this can help in broadening one's approach to the material. Photoceramic processes are also used. Enamel will concentrate in hairline cracks in a glaze and show up any crazing or crackle, developing a colored network. This can be utilized as, for example, in **ailes de mouche.** As stated above, cleanliness during the process in essential and this includes the kiln furniture and kiln wall surface: dust or particles floating about during firing will adhere to the surface of the enamel and mar it visually and tactilely.

Encaustic

Meaning, strictly, "burnt in" but applied in ceramics to inlay, especially of tiles. See **Inlay**.

Engine Turning

In this curious industrial technique, a cutting tool is held in a clamp while a pot revolves on a special horizontal lathe in which the pivot or mandrel is moved in a regular way by means of a cam onto and away from the tool. In this way, spaced

An inlaid title of the type called by antiquarians "encaustic": an example made by Mintons, a careful and sensitive replica of a medieval original. See **Inlay** *and* **Tile**.

The remarkable effect of eccentric lathe decoration (engine turning) on a lid, even on the knob. Staffordshire basalt ware, nineteenth century.

patterns or cuts are rapidly formed on the surface of the leather-hard clay. Pots were fired to vitrification and generally remained unglazed. Mathew Boulton made a machine for Wedgwood in 1763, and engine turning was widely used during the later eighteenth century. It had a further short vogue in the third quarter of the nineteenth century. Wavy lines and a form of fluting were common, together with some incredibly intricate and finely cut designs. The alternative term *dicing* may refer to cutting in two directions, giving a chopped-up effect.

Engobe

Orginally a French word for "slip" and now widely used, especially in America. It is useful to keep the word *slip* for more or less natural clays in liquid form with or without added color, and to use *engobe* for the more complex and compounded mixtures that are usually but not always based on raw clay.

Yellow, green, black, and red engobes or stained slips make this Nishapur tenth-century bowl a delight to the eye.

The science and practice of engobes is too involved to be dealt with here: they fulfill a number of functions and merge imperceptibly into glazes at one extreme, firing to a semivitreous state. They can also be designed, by using calcined and low-shrinkage materials, for use on biscuit. Engobes, when fairly heavily loaded with color, can modify and give special effects to the overlaying glaze in both lower- and higher-fired wares. Rhodes and others discuss the principles behind the compounding of engobes for various purposes. Sintered engobes can be made by the addition of borax, colemanite, boron fritt, etc., to clay. A porcelain body base can enhance colors, especially when used for brushwork. See also **Barbotine** and **Slip colors.**

Engraving

The dictionary definition of the term implies cutting into a hard surface, and engraving on pottery should be done on stiff leather-hard clay or on soft biscuit, a crisp, controlled line resulting. Sheila Fournier engraves her almost dry porcelain with a fine pointed knife, the lines in this case being later inlaid. A steel tool can be used on soft porcelain biscuit. This is sometimes done through a color wash laid on prior to the biscuit firing. The fine surface cutting on Ting and other Chinese wares is often referred to as "engraving." See also **Incising.**

For printing onto pottery a design can be engraved on a copper plate or roller, the lines filled with a specially prepared ceramic color, printed onto transfer paper, and hence to the ware.

A Chinese Ting ware dish with delicate engraving made visible by the slight increase in depth of color of the almost white glaze. These pieces were fired on unglazed rims that were copper-bound afterwards.

Extremely delicate but lively engraving under a pale celadon glaze on a porcelain bowl from the Koryu dynasty of Korea.

Skillful and precise engraving by John Ward, emphasizing the form of the pot and its cut rim.

A hand-built bottle engraved with a design suggesting a landscape. By Peter Hayes.

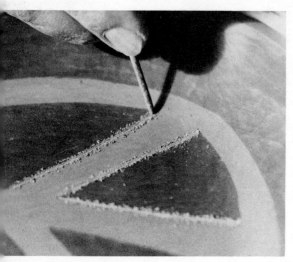

Two pictures of Siddig El'Nigoumi engraving through a slipped, burnished surface to give a lighter line. In the first the design (based on the Campaign for Nuclear Disarmament symbol) has been slip-resisted and the engraving helps to define the boundary: later the darker areas will also be tooled to give further interest. In the second illustration a large dish is almost completed, the background being "pecked" to set off the figures.

Epoxy Resin

A modern material that can be used to strengthen plaster of Paris. A number of proprietary brands are on the market. A curing oven is sometimes necessary, and care must be taken to disperse the toxic fumes that may result from its use. The resin supplier will give advice. Epoxy resin as a solid material has also been used by Martin Smith as an intermediate bedding between his ceramic forms and a metal casing.

Etching

Storr-Britz describes a rather dangerous technique involving covering a porcelain piece with wax, cutting a design through the wax, and then etching the uncovered surface with hydrochloric acid. A somewhat similar system was used in the pottery industry to produce shiny and matt surfaces on gold enamel.

Extruded Clay

Clay pressed or pugged through dies or even simply through a coarse sieve can be used for applied decoration of many kinds. The dod-box is a simple piece of equipment for this purpose. A cake-icing type of extruder can also be utilized to produce soft coils for applying directly to a clay surface, a technique called "sprigging" by Shafer, though this is the wrong term for it. The strands of clay can be beaten flat and then stamped or otherwise decorated. Dies can be used on a pug-mill or dod-box to produce ribbing or other three-dimensional surface decoration. Decorative knobs and handles are also made in this way, by rolling and twisting.

Fabric

See **Cloth patterns** and **Lace**.

A standing form from extruded clay by Peter Wright.

Faceting

This is a borderline technique as far as this book in concerned, but a degree of faceting that retains the basic profile of a pot is obviously more decorative than formal. Normally the facets are cut or beaten from top to bottom of a pot, but there is no need to restrict them to vertical stripes. Short cuts partway down the form can also be tried using a knife or plane. The facets are often used as a basis for further decoration.

A

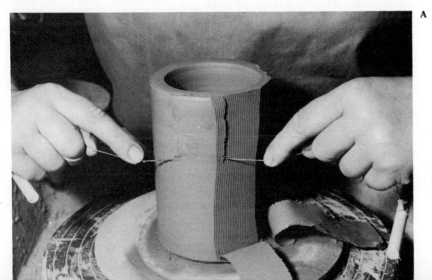

Each of the various methods of achieving facets on a pot imposes its own character. Three are illustrated. A. Cutting with a wire, with the extra dimension of vertical serrations. B. (See page 82.) Planing, giving sharp, well-defined edges and, if a Surform plane is used, striated texture on the facets. C. (See page 82.) Beating: soft edges and a smooth surface.

B

C

Faience

A name given both to the very early **Egyptian paste**, which was most commonly turquoise but also black, reddish, green, and yellow, and also to the tin-glazed earthenwares of France from the sixteenth century onward. It was also applied to similar Dutch wares and as *faience fine* to the cream-color earthenware that flooded in during the later eighteenth century. The word itself is an adaptation of "Faenza," from which city much tin-glazed ware was exported. French tin-glaze was rather more shiny than the Italian, and more colored grounds were used. Archeologists and historians are sometimes guilty of using the term in a very wide and therefore almost meaningless context. French faience was considerably influenced by porcelain styles in its decoration, and the national character was evident in its formality.

False Relief

A term given by archeologists to a type of carved decoration, widely practiced in ancient Europe, in which the cutting away of clay, often in triangles, leaves the original surface in apparent relief. The cutting was also known as "chip carving."

Famille Noir, Rose, Verte

These were Western identifying names given to groupings of eighteenth-century enameled wares under the background color or the color with a leading role in the design. Famille Noir, for instance—rather confusingly a subdivision of Famille Verte—has a dull black manganese covered ground that is covered with transparent green enamel on which other colors are painted. Famille rose was dominated by opaque pinks and carmines derived from gold. Under- and over-glaze colors are used in combination, the one modifying the other in a way that could be studied by the modern potter for use in a different idiom.

Fat Oil

The gummy residue of turpentine used as a medium for enamel colors. Billington (1962) mentions that a small quantity of turpentine left in a cup will evaporate into fat oil but warns that the slightest trace of turps over the side of the cup will cause the oil, by capilliary attraction, to creep into the saucer and onto the table.

Feathering

In this technique a clay form, usually a dish or plate, is covered with liquid slip, and lines of a contrasting color are quickly laid onto it. These lines are normally parallel and quite close together, but radial, spiral, and other variations are possible. While both slips are still liquid a fine, pliable point, such as the center rib of a feather, is drawn across it in alternate directions, generally at right angles to the trailed lines. A highly decorative overall pattern results. The whole operation must be completed quickly, with slip jugs and filled trailers ready at hand. Feathering attempted on too dry a slip or with too coarse or heavy a point has a miserable result.

The use of this type of liquid, flowing style was almost unknown in the ancient world, and the high point of feathered ware was the period from 1650 through the eighteenth and nineteenth centuries in English country-ware potteries, especially in Staffordshire. Feathering was also used to suggest fish scales and birds' feathers, and there were some skillfully feathered bands on beakers and pots.

Because of the need to use very liquid slips, the work is often done on a flat slab of clay that is rather softer than for other slip techniques. After trailing but before feathering, lift and drop the corner of the board on which the slab rests; this will level out the trailed line and give a more integrated effect. The dish is formed when the surface has lost its shine, over a hump mold or, very carefully, in a hollow one. Damp newspaper placed under the slab will help to prevent it from drying out before the slip has stiffened.

Apart from the traditional style there are a number of variations possible: radial feathering from the center of a bowl with the trailed lines made on the wheel, or vice versa; dots of slip between or on the trailed lines; restricting the feathering to bands, areas, or panels. Large blobs and dots—black on red on a white background, for

Detail of a large plate, possibly from Bristol, in which blocks of feathering give variety of tone. Note that the ends of the unfeathered blocks are pulled in opposite directions.

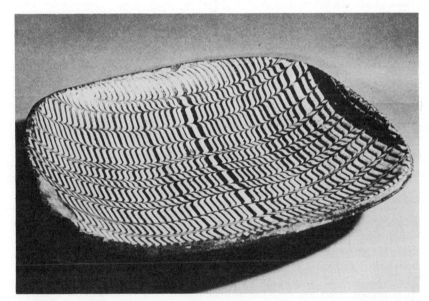

A straightforward trailed and feathered nineteenth-century dish with sufficient variation in spacing and width of line to avoid monotony.

A dish by John Shelley, trailed in circles of black on white slip that have been feathered with skill and precision from rim to center. The middle is strongly and simply treated. Note the little blobs in the center where the feather has been lifted away. The heavier ring was probably trailed after the main feathering was completed.

Generous dots of black slip have been pulled with a feather out to the rim of this pie dish. As with almost all feathering, the work must be done while the base slip is still liquid.

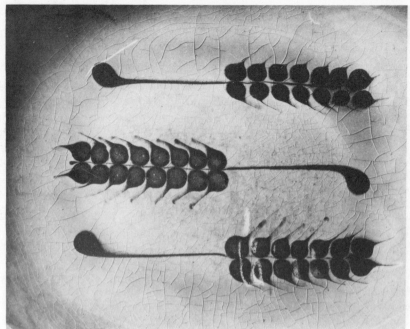

A traditional "wheat-ear" pattern made by laying down dots of slip and feathering outwards.

instance—can be feathered through or outward from the center, but discretion is necessary to hold the design together. Mulitple feathers, mounted on a batten, have been used.

A distinct type of feathering often known as **combing** involves a more random pulling of dots and lines to give a marbled appearance. None of the variations, however, have quite the impact of an expertly feathered straight-line design on a large dish.

Ferric

Meaning "of iron," but usually applied to the red iron oxide Fe_2O_3. See **Iron.**

Finger Combing, Finger Sgraffito

A broad, decorative effect made by sweeping fingers through wet slip to reveal the clay beneath. It is practiced by many potters today and, by Geoffrey Whiting and others, through glaze as well as slip. It is commonly found on large oblong dishes and thrown plates but also on the sides of pots, thrown and hand-built. The displacement of the slip on each side of the stroke is a bonus which gives interest and variety. There is little evidence of early use of the technique, but it is widely used today. Cardew, Peter Dick, Svend Bayer, and many others have made splendid finger-combed ware. It is advisable to let the slip set for a few minutes and then to make the marks rapidly and directly. As mentioned above, the same can be done with glazes on stoneware, especially the dark tenmoku type of glaze, although Ray Finch has also combed paler glazes with lively effect.

Classic, lively finger combing through slip by Susie Cree.

A combination of finger combing, tool combing, and sgraffito by Michael Cardew.

Two approaches to finger combing by Bernard Leach: through slip on the bowl; through glaze on the bottle.

Finger Impressions

As may be expected, these are some of the earliest elements of decoration on pottery, not accidental markings, since it has always been the potter's instinct to obliterate evidence of the forming technique, but deliberate and considered. There are some South American and a few other pots that show the pulling-down of one coil into the other during building, but they are rare. Often the finger was used to notch an applied strip, not only on Neolithic and Bronze Age pottery but also on the more sophisticated Syrian jars of the fourth century A.D. Medieval potters secured the base of a handle with a thumbprint, although the wiping away of clay on each side of a handle terminal does not often occur and is mainly a modern development. Overlapping finger-impressed pellets of clay have been used to imitate rams' fleece, or as a simple decoration since Roman times. Fingernail impressions are also known, but not widely. See also **Finger tipping** and **Frilled cordon**.

Finger Tipping

A term used by archeologists to describe "a method of making small dish-shaped depressions set inside a slight ridge by impressing the wet surface of the vessel with the tip of the finger. A developed form [uses] the broad of the thumb. These indentations occur round the shoulder of a vessel" (Barton). Similar decoration is shown around a flowerpot rim by George Fishley, a country potter of Fremington, England.

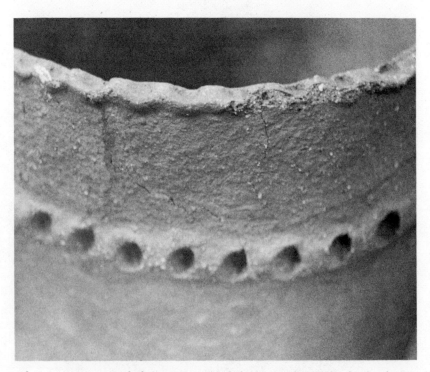

A finger pressed into a ridge of soft clay constitutes the sole decoration on this 1200 B.C. British cooking pot.

Finger Wipe

A single stroke of the finger, as opposed to **Finger combing**.

Fire Change

Attempts to reinstate the traditional Bizen pottery have been made by stacking the unglazed pots in the kiln without shelves or saggars and subjecting them to a pinewood firing of several days, during which the fire is alternatively stoked hard and then allowed to burn low, accompanied by damper control over the atmosphere. The result, not very dependable, is a surface of varying color and gloss from brown to a bluish-black.

Fire Cord, Hidasuki

A Japanese sytem in which straw cords, soaked in salt, are twined around pots before firing. The straw burns away but leaves glossy marks, sometimes in bright red, on an otherwise unglazed surface. Examples are extant from the sixteenth century on. **Seaweed** is also used in the same way, having its own salt to act as a flux.

Flambé

A term applied to copper-red streaks on Chinese porcelain of the eighteenth century. These are less subtle than the flushes on Chun ware. Bernard Moore obtained similar effects at the beginning of the twentieth century. Hamer describes flambé as "iridescent red glaze produced by transmutation of colloidal copper in a relatively transparent glaze." Less than 0.5 percent of copper oxide in the glaze is recommended. Some rather crude modern industrial equivalents are produced by on-glaze methods.

Flashing

A usually accidental effect caused by partial reduction, smoking, local over-firing, or glaze-jumping. It also applies to marks on a glaze surface where a tongue of flame or hot gas has altered its color or character. It can be caused by ash or volatiles settling on a pot during firing. Pine ash picked up by the draft during firing and falling onto the ware can cause shiny and matt black and brown patterns. This was developed by the Japanese potter Kaneshige and is known as "goma decoration." See also **Kiln gloss.** "Salt-glazing is deliberate flashing" (Hamer). Some coloring oxides, especially copper and chrome, can jump by volatilization from one pot to an adjacent one or can even stain an entire kiln-load. Chrome-tin pink or chrome in any conjunction with tin and lime are notorious. More deliberate flashing can be induced by cups of sodium compounds set through the kiln to give flashes of glaze and coloration. This method is used at La Borne, France.

Flashing can thus be decorative and deliberate. Some potters fire individual pots in closed saggars with combustibles that will produce flashing as the main decorative element. Copper and lusters will sometimes develop a spread halo around the painted line, which is a form of local flashing. See also **Fuming** and **Smear glaze.**

Flat Liner

A type of brush used especially in Stoke-on-Trent for banding. See also **Brushes.**

Direct and uncompromising finger wipes through glaze by John Leach.

The simple up-draft wood-fired kilns of Cyprus sometimes gave flashings and markings on pots, which were heaped one on another. Great efforts were made to produce a "perfect" all-over orange color, and our choice of the illustrated kebab pot with its variety of fire-pattern surprised the potters. It is a long way from this approach to the involved, conscious, and expensive fire changes now attempted in Japan and elsewhere.

Flicked-on Color

Slip, glaze, or pigment thrown or flicked onto the surface can complement the form as it flows naturally over the curve of the pot. Very fine flicked color, using a hogs'-hair or similar stiff brush, can provide a texture or background for other decoration. See also **Poured glaze.**

Flint Enamel

An American technique, patented in 1849 by C. Webber, in which a biscuit pot is given a coat of transparent glaze onto which pigment is sprinkled through holes in a small box to produce lighter and darker areas of color.

Flow Blue, Flown Blue

Probably with the philosophy "if you cannot beat it, bear it," the almost inevitable blurring of a cobalt line under earthenware glazes, and some higher-fired ones, came to be considered an added attraction during the early nineteenth century, and the name *flow blue* was coined to describe it.

Flown blue, however, is described by Hughes as being deliberately contrived to spread in a halo-like manner by being fired in saggars with saltpeter, borax, and white lead, as early as 1820 and also by Minton in the 1860s. See also **Scratched decoration.**

Fluting

True fluting consists of a repetition of semicircular cuts like those on classical stone pillars, half a flute in fact. Potters, however, tend to use the word to describe any repeated, fairly regular cut lines, whether of curved, triangular, or any other section. On early Bronze Age English vessels we find a rough kind of rounded fluting, but the

An engine-turned "needle-fluted" basalt ware teapot made by Elijah Mayer of Stoke-on-Trent in the late eighteenth century.

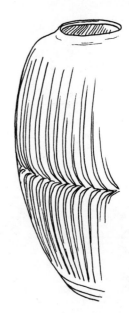

Crisply cut traditional fluting of the "triangular" type using a square-ended tool, by David Leach. Covered with a pale Ying Ch'ing glaze in the Chinese manner. If, in a bowl of this type, the foot is turned after fluting, the lower terminations will be precise and defined.

An interesting variation on traditional fluting made by moving the tool to one side in the middle of the cut. From the Rochester (New York) Folk Art Guild.

acknowledged masters, in the triangular style, were the Song (Sung) potters. Some Korean cutting on bowls is more widely spaced and cut at an angle to the radius, the slope of which is not maintained all around so that an overlap occurs which is lively and spontaneous.

This fundamentally simple technique is capable of varied effects: the confident, relaxed, but precise cutting with bamboo or a hacksaw blade by David Leach; the

Two very different styles of bowl fluting: one done with the broken-off end of a hacksaw blade by David Leach; the other cut with a rounded tool into a large grogged clay hand-built bowl by Sheila Fournier.

Large-scale fluting with a broad tool by Bernard Leach.

Two examples of spaced-out fluting: the first, by Kathleen Pleydell-Bouverie, giving a ridged and furrowed form almost amounting to carving; the second with sharp, spaced cuts alternated with fine combing with a piece of hacksaw. By David Leach.

curved and separated fluting by Yeap Poh Yap; the uneven strokes of Harrison McIntosh; the deep cutting on a mushroom-shaped pot by Karl Scheid; or the even bolder semicircular slashes on a straight-sided jar by Antoine de Vinck. These are comparatively straightforward, though varied in effect and in aesthetic intention, but still more variations are possible, such as fluting with a sharp sideways flick, as shown in the drawing. Alternating sloped cuts, cutting broken by bands, or the wavering diagonal furrows on some Lucie Rie bowls (see Rose) are further ideas. On "shell bowls" from Texas by Eloise Stoker the cuts are deep and break the rim, which is made irregular and deformed in the process.

Fluting on a pot or bowl can be done before it is turned; this sharpens the lower termination. Alternatively a groove is sometimes turned at the upper and lower limits so that a fluted area forms a band of decoration. The pattern will take on a different character according to the hardness of the clay, whether or not it contains grog, and whether the cut is even in pressure all the way down; if this is slackened at the beginning and end, lozenge shapes can be produced. If the cuts are too widely spaced they can look clumsy, but examples show that this is not a general rule. Work is generally done on the leather-hard clay; on softer clay it can be more fluid but also more "fluky," to quote Cardew. Tools vary from sharpened, square-ended bamboo (which may quickly lose its precision) and metal strip, to round-ended turning tools, knives, or specially made tools such as the fluting plane described by Leach in *A Potter's Book*.

Fly Ash

See **Flashing** and **Kiln gloss**.

Frilled Cordon

A twisted narrow clay strap around the shoulder of an early English urn has been described as a frilled cordon. On many examples of peasant and country pottery a band of clay is pressed on with a tool or finger alternately up and down to form a frill. George Fishley, an old Devon potter, and others have used this simple and unaffected element of decoration, but the tradition goes back at least to Roman times, and there are also examples on Song (Sung) stonewares. There is a medieval incense bowl at the Colchester Museum, England, on which a frilled cordon is the main formal/decorative element on both the rim and cup-base.

A delicate frilled cordon pressed with the finger from a thin thrown-on strip of clay on a Chinese lidded jar.

A

B

Two types of frilled cordon are shown; both were used in Song ceramics as well as by peasant potters, the latter preferring the fingered method. A. A strip has been thrown onto a pot and pressed alternately up and down with the finger. B. A carved version of the frilled cordon.

Two powerful bottle forms by Joanna Constantinidis given a lustrous and broken color surface by firing in an enclosed saggar with volatiles.

Frit

Any glassy mixture that has been fused and ground to a fine powder. In the industry all glazes are fritted before use on pottery, but for the studio potter they are normally limited to silicates of lead and high-alkali or borax fluxes. They can be useful at low temperatures for raku, for the development of lead/chrome reds, and for enamels.

The value of fritting is twofold: to render useful materials insoluble which would otherwise dissolve and crystallize in water; and to render soluble or assimilable poisons, such as lead, safer to use by incorporating them into a powdered glass.

Fude

See **Brushes.**

Fuming

The introduction of chlorides, sulphides, or nitrates of metals during cooling at around 750° C./1,350° F. can give variable coatings or colors throughout a kiln or saggar. The kiln room should be very well ventilated because of possible toxic gases. Conrad suggests turning on blowers and burners at the time of introducing the compounds in order to circulate the fumes. This cannot be done in an electric kiln. Alternatively charcoal and sawdust in a tightly sealed saggar can be infused with copper and iron oxides to produce fumed colors and surfaces. Philip Cornelius includes layers of sand between the burnable materials. Copper can give pink, gray, and red blushes; iron and copper may give red to rust if used together with salt in a sealed saggar. See also **Flashing** and **Smear glaze.**

Funk Pottery

A general discussion of the American "funk" style, which had its roots in the West Coast reaction to the "timeless art" concept in the 1950s and perhaps even earlier in the work of the half-crazy potter George Ohr in the 1890s, is outside the scope of this book. There is an excellent summary in Garth Clark's *Century of Ceramics in the United States.* Among the decorative aspects of funk were the reintroduction of bright and lurid colors and glazes used with the maximum shock effect. Technique and materials were of secondary importance to the spirit of iconoclasm, and thus house paint, emulsion, and any finish that came to hand was considered valid. Curiously, the painting and coloring were often treated with greater skill and care than the making of the object. Funk, together with "pop" and other movements in the 1960s and 1970s, was like a blaze of fireworks in its decorative impact (though often applied to crudely sexual and excretal subjects), and like fireworks it was ephemeral and short-lived, although the release from taboos and tradition still maintains its effect. "The work [of Arnison and others] was imitated mindlessly. . . . Because the images of the style were applied without even a modicum of understanding, the funk movement fizzled out" (Clark and Hughto).

Gadroon

A tear-shaped decorative element, often used at the base of a pot, generally embossed and repeated to form a continuous pattern. It sometimes resembles convex fluting and can be vertical or diagonal.

Galleyware, Galliware

There is some doubt as to the precise type of ware covered by this term, but it is generally agreed to have been tin-glazed earthenware, plain or painted, often for medical purposes (ointment jars, pill slabs, and the like), which was imported into England from Italy and Holland in the sixteenth to eighteenth centuries. "Gallipotters" also worked in London, Bristol, and many other centers. Later, with the ascendancy of the Dutch potteries, the term "Delftware" took over.

Gaudy Dutch

A term applied to an early-nineteenth-century style of painted earthenware exported from Staffordshire to the United States, to the Pennsylvania Germans especially—hence the "Dutch." The designs have been described as an "almost frantic" combination of blue, green, yellow, and red on a white body.

Geometric Design

Geometric patterns on ceramics were disparaged by Leach; to quote him, in relation especially to industrial ware: "The accent on geometric design is not one which lends itself readily to the potter; . . . to the deadness of technique . . . is added a further deadness of concept." Against this we can cite the near-geometric patterns on many

Detail of a Greek Late Geometric Period pot from Laconia.

A Geometric Period oenochoe from Cyprus with circles apparently both spun and stamped; or a compass-like instrument may have been used.

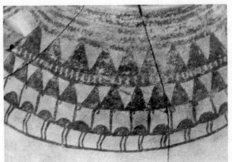

Earlier and livelier semigeometric decoration on a pre-Dynastic (ca. 3500 B.C.) Egyptian pot. Birds, hills, and water are suggested.

A rare squared pattern on a very early glazed bowl. According to Charleston the squares are alternately of white and blue glaze, but they appear to have been in some way cut or sgraffitoed. Possibly from Rome, ca. A.D. 330.

A free version of geometric design on a nineteenth-century hand-built water pot from Algeria. The colors are unfired and varnished over.

All familiar images are grist to the design mill of Siddig El'Nigoumi, in this case a crossword puzzle, which sits very comfortably in this large plate. Burnished and engraved.

Angular resist patterns on faceted pots by John Maltby.

The uncompromising decoration of black and white squares on this ceramic titled "Jerusalem Fruit Bowl" complements the angular construction. By Carol McNicoll.

very fine early pots and the long-lived Geometric Period in Greece, which produced austere but splendid pieces.

Geometry is given in the *Oxford English Dictionary* as "the science that investigates the properties and relations of magnitudes in space," a definition with which no potter would be ashamed to be associated. Originally it constituted the basic science of architecture and produced the finest buildings. But, as Humpty-Dumpty said, "When *I* use a word, it means just what I choose it to mean," and geometry today has become too linked with the ruler and compass and the "deadening of concept." Looking through Garth Clark's *American Potters* for indications of modern design, while there are tendencies to geometry in form, fluidity is the watchword in decoration. This tends to be the historical pattern in the United States: the early tulip-ware and other folk pottery rarely exhibited a straight line, a triangle, or a circle in decoration. The Japanese will sometimes combine a precise semigeometric pattern with free drawing on the same piece in stimulating contrast, as Ian Gregory and some other modern potters do today. A similar arrangement is found in ancient times on the long-spouted lamps from Persia of around 1000 B.C. and in the "geometricized" animals and birds from Susa a millennium previously. Ancient American decoration, while free and immensely inventive, certainly explores "magnitudes in space." The potter El'Nigoumi, working in Britain, has brought geometric pattern to a high state of technical skill and visual pleasure. In a different way Elizabeth Fritsch uses geometric designs, albeit broken and transposed in unexpected ways, on her "optical" bottles and pots, which she calls "a two-and-a-half dimension tactile and optical adventure." Peter Meanley in *Studio Ceramics Today* speaks of geometric perspective imagery in his work. In this book the plate decoration shown under **Optical decoration** (by Tim Jarvis) is a good example of this approach. The techniques most likely to lend themselves to geometric decoration are cut paper, stencils, and stamps. The brush is less adaptable, although Sumerian pots and those of 900 B.C. Greece prove that it can be so used.

Gilding

The application of gold to pottery has been practiced since ancient times, but it was not until the eighteenth century in Europe that gilding was fully integrated by firing onto the glaze, and even then it was liable to scour away. Small squares of gold leaf are found on Persian Minai bowls of the twelfth and thirteenth centuries, and gilding on Chinese Ming wares. One early method was simple—glue the leaf down with gold sizing. Another system mixed gold powder with lacquer. Both wore away easily. In the eighteenth century a ground-together leaf and honey mixture was lightly fired onto the ware. This was rich and fairly durable, and its comparative thickness allowed tooling and chasing. In the later eighteenth century the mixture was gold and mercury, fired somewhat higher, and requiring burnishing. The nineteenth-century liquid gold, used from 1855 (see **Bright gold** and **Burnish gold**), fires to a dependable but rather strident color. Japanese Imari ware used gold decoration, and it was painted on Baroque and Rococo porcelain. Artists in the nineteenth century sometimes lost all restraint and completely covered the piece. A system of resist gilding was used in the nineteenth century. Gold leaf was adhered to the surface with isinglass, over which a transfer pattern in fine lines was laid. The transfer ink was composed of asphalt, oil, and gold size. The uncovered gold could then be washed away with water, leaving the fine transfer-covered lines intact. A thick paste-raised gilding was also used at Stoke-on-Trent.

A number of studio potters today add a touch of gold to freely painted or otherwise decorated stonewares, with acceptable and intriguing effects. John Maltby's dishes are especially successful. Gilding is fired in a muffle kiln like other enamels.

Glass

Glaze is, of course, a form of glass, and a frit is powdered glass. The use of separate pieces or areas of broken window glass or cullet melted onto ceramics is, however, a modern phenomenon. A rare historical example is mentioned by Guilland: a dribbled glaze on a nineteenth-century Virginia jug was made by placing a piece of glass on the rim when it was set in the kiln.

The use today of bottle or window glass as a decorative element is usually on sculptural or nonutility ware. Most commercial glasses contain little alumina and are rich in alkalis, especially soda. Glass is therefore likely to have a high cooling contraction rate and will craze violently, this being further compounded by its thickness, which is usually much greater than that of a glaze. The effect of the crazing can be to give the appearance of shattered ice or a crystalline structure while the actual surface is comparatively unblemished. Several problems arise, however: the contraction can be

A slab table lamp with a double wall and inset melted glass. Note also the applied thrown rings. By Sheila Fournier.

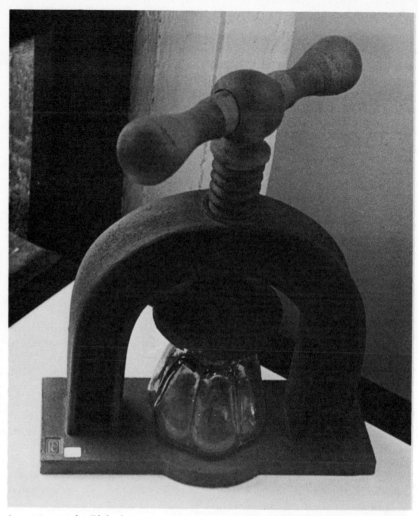

An amusing surrealist "sledge-hammer to crack a walnut" image by Delan Cookson. The jelly is of molded glass, the press of stoneware.

so powerful as to tear the ceramic apart; and local devitrification, especially of colored bottle glass, may cause spots of what look like mold on the surface that, when wiped off, leave a scar. Since the glass is fully liquid at pottery temperatures it will find its own level, and the piece must be set in the kiln to allow for this. It will also flow, and this can be utilized in "frozen" falls from one level to another. Capillary attraction can also cause it to flow upward to some degree. Broken rather than powdered glass gives the most reliable results—there is probably too much air trapped in the powder. If the potter breaks the glass himself, great care must be taken not to cause flying chips. Hammer it between thick wads of newspaper or in a thick sack. Cheap window glass seems less liable to decomposition than colored glass. One way to color the melt is to fire the glass on a generous layer of colored glaze; copper in a glaze will often give a bright turquoise; iron glazes have been less successful in my experience. Low-temperature glass can also be incorporated into raku firings. Enamels are pigments in a frit or powdered glass. Conrad discusses a technique of fusing glass across openings in ceramic pieces but found that the shrinkage caused disaster, and he had to make hundreds of tests. He also describes a classification system for various glasses based on the number of cracks per square inch.

Unfired glass or mirror is sometimes incorporated into ceramics. Delan Cookson used molded glass in some of his enigmatic screw forms, as in his "Jelly Press," where the jelly is of transparent glass.

Glass Cullet

Powdered or broken glass. Conrad mentions an American supplier: Keystone Cullet Co., 426 Willow Crossing Road, Greensburg, PA. See also **Cullet** and **Glass.**

Glass Muller

A flat-ended pestle for grinding and mixing colors, especially enamels, on a glass or ceramic slab. A palette knife is more often used for mixing.

Glaze Decoration

Apart from their individual characters, textures, and colors, one can use glazes as contrasting elements in a decorative system: as a wash, painted like a pigment, super-imposed, and in other ways. See discussions under **Cuenca, Cuerda seca, Flashing, Glaze inlay, Glaze over glaze, Glaze sgraffito, Glaze trailing, Poured glaze, Run glaze, Tin-glaze over slip**, etc.

T'ang potters used semitransparent colored glazes painted or dabbed on in patterns: solid or dotted lines, chevrons, simple flowers, or dappled effects. Sometimes the surface of a piece is incised to assist the separation of colors, but the overall effect is soft-edged and imprecise. Islamic potters poured contrasting swathes of glaze inside bowls. Oribe dishes are frequently divided between two glazes, often a pale amber iron and a copper green with the painting confined to one color glaze. The running of glazes into large drops or folds at the base of a pot is very decorative but difficult to control. Fujioka shows a cut-sided bowl down which the green glaze has flowed "into droplets that gleam darkly like jewels."

A T'ang Period Chinese dish on which the design outline is cut or press-molded into the surface rather than raised from it, as in cuenca. The spaces are filled with colored glazes by brush. This type of decoration persisted throughout the history of ceramics into the industrial era.

On this simple form by John Chalke the quality and overlap of the glaze constitute the decorative scheme. The minute crawls, blobs, and runs of glaze are brilliantly handled.

Something between glaze carving and sgraffito has left the black body as a matt background to this striking design by Maija Grotell (1956).

This tile could equally well be placed under **Glaze over glaze**. Dots of colored glazes are laid on one another with a trailer. During firing they spread and push neighboring blobs aside to give distinctive and never quite repeated patterns. By Alan Wallwork. The work is done on a glazed commercial tile.

An individual approach to glaze decoration. Swags of various color glazes are laid one over another and then cut through to provide detail and a variation of line and mass. By Diana and David Woodcock.

A single glaze can often give a wide variety of colors simply by varying the thickness. Oxidized copper stoneware glaze can produce dark and light grays and a wide range of turquoise to blue hues. Many other glazes will act in a similar way. Dipping, pouring, double-dipping, painting, and splashing can be done to vary the color. The glaze texture will also vary with the thickness.

Glaze Flashing

See **Flashing.**

Glaze Inlay

Glaze may be brushed across the surface of a piece that has been carved, incised, or stamped, filling the depressed lines or areas. The rest of the surface is then wiped clean. Suiko Ito uses this technique on biscuit, scraping and sanding the surface free of glaze except for the cut line. It is also possible to cover the inlaid glaze with a transparent one or one that will allow transmutation of the colored line, but only at a sacrifice of sharpness of definition.

A glaze may also be "inlaid" into another by cutting a pattern through one coat and brush-filling with another. These glazes need to be viscous ones.

Glaze Over Glaze

The science of glaze types and colors and their reactions when overlaid by one another is too wide a subject for this book, but a short discussion of the techniques employed is relevant.

The imposed glaze may be allowed simply to dribble down the sides of a pot, a style used by some of the pioneers of present-day studio pottery: Delaherche, DeCoeur, and Chaplet. Janet Leach and others have shown examples, but the style is considered by some as too simplistic. Pouring, spraying, trailing, and brushing one glaze onto another are commonly practiced. Hamada used a ladle to pour rapid, semicontrolled lines of

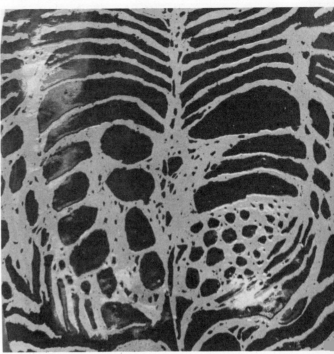

Controlled designs can be achieved in glaze over glaze by a preliminary firing of the underglaze. A contrasting glaze can then be applied either over wax resist or as a solid coating, which is then cut away in the manner of sgraffito or graffiato. The two details of pots by James Tower show different effects; a fine cut line through a damp over-glaze, or a sharper, more defined pattern. The top coat may need a fixative addition.

A strong wax-resist design between a dark- and a light-colored glaze. By John Jeffs.

The effect of a white, slightly crawled ash glaze over a darker and more refractory one. By Denis Moore (1958).

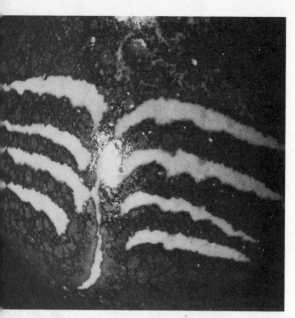

Detail of resist between glazes: a dark cratered iron glaze over a pale smooth one, reduced in a coal and wood-fired kiln. The mottled, broken over-glaze has caused indentations and wavering of the resist line. By Geoffrey Whiting.

white glaze across a darker one, a small hole in the ladle adding a finer line beside the main poured one.

A remarkably decorative glaze-on-glaze method was developed by Alan Wallwork, albeit on the least complicated of ceramic forms, the commercial tile. Drops of glaze, singly or imposed one on another in various colors, were dropped on from a trailer until the surface was more or less covered. During firing, the drops spread out, flattened their profiles against one another, and generally assumed a unique and lively pattern. In an advertisement for these tiles they were described (not by Alan) as "hand fired"—hot hands! David Eeles paints pale and colored glazes onto unfired glazed pots to give a delicate but precise image. Peter Lane recommends latex resist for sprayed glaze: after one coat of glaze, the resist can be peeled away and resprayed. For poured or double-dipping, wax resist is most commonly used. For the subtle merging of one glaze into the other, possibly with the aid of a card template, and for landscape effects, spraying is often the best means. At the other extreme one glaze can be literally thrown onto another—with much less predictable results. Glazes may blister when laid one on another, but if they are "soaked" in the kiln to allow the surface to settle down, this can be a great source of mottled and other effects.

Glaze Sgraffito, Cut Glaze

Cutting through the glaze with a pointed or edged tool has been practiced since the earliest development of stoneware. Earthenware glazes tend to be too fluid, and the body, of course, would be porous. On some of the most stunning of the T'zu Chou bottles a black glaze is cut through to a pale body, often in the block or sgraffiato style, cutting away the background to leave powerful leaf, flower, or figure designs with details scratched in finer lines. A less startling contrast could be achieved by brushing color or slip onto the clay. Sgraffito through the subsequent glaze will give two tones of color.

The character of the cut will depend on the dryness of the glaze and its general character when raw. The work is usually done as soon as the shine has gone from the surface after dipping. It may also be advisable to add a little fixative to the glaze. A round-pointed stick is often used, but potters experiment with other tools, which will influence the line. An easily controlled design can be cut through a raw glaze laid over a fired one. James Tower decorates his dramatic pots in this way, using a dark glaze over a white tin glaze. The process necessitates two glaze firings, and the second glaze should mature at a lower temperature than the undercoat if a crisp finish is required.

Massive and vital Song (Sung) Chinese decoration on a large pot. The glaze is cut away from the background of the design, the blocks of leaf and petal each enlivened with a single cut.

An oxidized stoneware glaze, colored buff with copper, but which darkens with increased thickness to produce this simple but striking decoration. The piece was dipped into the glaze side and side about, and the dark triangle represents the overlap or double dip. By the author.

The colors and textures of varying thicknesses of a single poured glaze are combined with some exposed grogged biscuit on a slab bottle by Sheila Fournier.

Glaze Thickness

Many glazes, especially stoneware, will vary in color and character according to the thickness of application. A copper glaze is mentioned under **Glaze decoration.** Tenmoku can range from red to black, but many glazes are worth testing and exploiting for this decorative "extra." For deliberate and controlled **crawling,** the thickness of application is critical. See also **Dipping.**

Glaze Trailing

Glaze trailed onto biscuit or over another raw glaze will obviously not stay as sharply defined as slip; but a variety of effects are possible, from the style of the bright Ryumonji sake bottles to subtle combinations of blended colors. Some light-on-dark Ushinoto trailing closely resembles slip-trailed patterns. The technique has been used by Cardew. Hamada and others have trailed a black tenmoku glaze over a white or transparent coat, the latter being very effective over **hakame.** With more fluid glazes, such as those used by Ray Finch on fish-decorated dishes, the line will spread. Glazes can also be trailed onto biscuit, perhaps over a color wash. Margarete Schott trails overlapping layers and dribbles of glaze onto spinning bowls; Maggie Berkowitz makes up tile pictures from glazes trailed, poured, cut, and filled. A splendidly original trailed dish by David Lloyd Jones was illustrated in *Ceramic Review 65.* Trailing a diagonal line on a slowly revolving pot can be effective. Hildegard Storr-Britz combines syringe and brush. Janice Tchalenko trails glazes in a close grid pattern to provide an overall, merging color texture. A stark, unglazed, textured-surface plate by Glen Lukens is relieved by three broken, almost free-standing trailed rings of blue glaze on the rim (illustration in Clark and Hughto). The addition of feldspar to a glaze can assist definition by making it more viscous.

*In strong contrast to his usual style (see **Slip painting**) is this striking glaze-trailed pot by David Eeles.*

Glazing

The various methods of applying glazes to pots in their more mechanical aspects are not within the scope of this book and are dealt with in many pottery primers: Tony Birks' *The Potter's Companion* is fairly detailed, but there are many others including my *Illustrated Dictionary of Practical Pottery*. The decorative dimension is discussed at the various headings mentioned under **Glaze decoration.**

Gloss Ware

A number of cultures, prior to the general introduction of glaze, and especially in Greek and Roman times, made use of a very fine-grain, high-iron slip that took on a gloss in the firing. According to Cooper (1972), alkalis "such as wood ash" (probably for the soluble soda and potash they contain) were added to red clay slip to act as a deflocculant. Only the finest particles in the top third or so of the slip would be used, poured or siphoned off. Further additions of organic acids—urine, wine lees, etc.— were made to balance the alkalis and give a final smooth slip, which was then used as a pigment for painting, dipping, or pouring. See **Burnishing** for details of a modern potter's system. Red and black colors, combined on one surface, are considered to have been achieved by reduction and partial reoxidization of different thicknesses of slip

A gloss-surfaced pot, the gray ground enlivened with bright red, green, and white slips. By Fiona Salazar.

painting. The control must have been very skillful! The Romans tended to use a redder clay than the Greeks but with a similar gloss finish, normally of a single color that varied from purple-black to bright coral. It is surprising how few pots show any variation or admixture of colors. Catherine Johns asserts that a highly oxidizing fire is essential for the gloss on Samian-type ware. See also **Black- and red-figure painting.**

Gold

Gold can be fired onto ceramics at enamel temperature. For details of the various types see **Bright gold, Burnish gold,** and **Gilding;** the last includes a brief history of the use of gold on ceramics. Leach mentions the admixture of gold dust with the red enamel to soften the crudity of the color, and in a similar way gold has been painted over red enamel. Gold and tin oxide give **purple of Cassius.** Pinks and reds can also be derived from gold, sometimes accidentally if the gold is over-fired. Gold enamel is obtainable in the form of a felt-tipped pen for line drawing (listed by Celtic Ceramic Crafts in Great Britain). Gold and silver can be applied with a metal lettering pen for script or fine lines. Liquid gold must be thinned, if necessary, with a precious metal essence and not with turpentine. Gold enamel is sometimes called gold luster. See also **Copper/manganese gold.**

A splendid high-temperature bronze-gold on porcelain, with banding and sgraffito, by Lucie Rie. See also **Copper/manganese gold** for details of this technique.

Gold Eraser

Special gold erasers for removing unwanted smudges of fired gold luster are available from specialist suppliers.

Gold Size

A thin mixture of standard carpenter's glue and water heated in a double saucepan.

Goma Decoration

Goma means "sesame seed" in Japanese and is applied to two phenomena. "Iron-spot goma" refers to fragments of iron compound breaking through the body or glaze and giving brown or black spots on the surface. See also **Bleed-through.** It is also applied to the variegated shiny and matt, black and brown patterns caused by pine ash picked up in the draft during firing and falling on the ware. Kaneshige is an exponent.

Goose Quill

Once an essential item for slip-trailers, set in various types of reservoir. Multiple spouts were common. The quill would probably still be preferable to its modern glass or plastic equivalent, giving a finer line and a greater range of apertures.

Gosu

The name given to "natural" cobalt in Japan, an ore called "asbolite" in the West. It is "found in pebble form in creek beds particularly in China" (Sanders). It is ground with a boiled green tea solution. Examples by Tomimoto have a subtle grayish, eggshell quality. Gosu may turn black in oxidation and gray-blue in reduction. It is now rare. Leach used a cobalt/ocher mixture as an alternative. See **Blue** and **Cobalt.**

A red, black, and white stamped and incised bowl from the Hallstadt culture of southern Germany some 1,000 years B.C. The black areas are of graphite and the red of hematite.

Graphite

A natural crystalline form of carbon found in Mexico and other places. Its main use is as a refractory under reduction atmospheres, when it has the remarkable melting temperature of 3,500° C./6,300° F. Its decorative use has been as a surface coating in primitive and necessarily reducing clamp and bonfire kilns. It will take a high shine and is intensely black. The black areas of the designs on South German Hallstadt wares are reputed to have been graphite.

Green

Copper, the first metal to be worked by man, was the source of the earliest color in glaze. Green and turquoise were the most common colors during the first 2,000 years of alkaline and lead glazes. Much nearer our times, cobalt/antimony and cobalt/iron mixtures were occasionally used on tin-glaze for green pigment. Millions of pieces of nineteenth-century industrial pottery were copper green glazed (now known to be a hazard in lead glazes leading to increased solubility), and there are references to "the eternal matt green" in America at the turn of the century. From the late eighteenth century, however, chrome came increasingly into use.

Copper and chromium are still the main sources of green stains and pigments, and they are discussed under those headings. Reduced iron in recipe percentages of about 2 percent give the familiar celadon blue/greens. A bright green can result from cobalt in a zinc glaze. Nickel gives drab green-grays, but it is unstable at stoneware temperatures and can cause scum. Vanadium is used to modify copper and chrome greens, and mixtures of the latter two oxides will also produce various tints. Mixtures of cobalt and iron and cobalt with antimoniate of lead give greens, sometimes of a broken color. Prepared stains are made by cobalt/uranium, praseodymium phosphate, and zirconium/vanadium combinations.

Grogged Surface

Grogs and stones set in the surface of bowls have been used for practical purposes, such as the grinding of foods. Decorative "clay grit" was dusted onto the surface in bands of Nottingham eighteenth-century salt-glazed beakers. It was used to imitate fur on "bear jugs" and other models when it was known as "breadcrumb" decoration.

Grogged or tempered clay bodies have been common since the beginning of pottery manufacture, but its deliberate use to impart tactile qualities is probably a modern preoccupation. Grogged and textured clay is known as **chamotte** in Europe and especially in Scandinavia. Red grog can be beaten into leather-hard clay for varied texture and color. See also **Texture.**

An excessively rough-textured Japanese tea bowl, provenience unknown. The white glaze has barely covered the stonier areas.

Ground-Lay

This technique has been widely used in industry, but because it demands skill and time it is being superseded by more mechanical methods. It gives an even coverage of enamel color over a fairly large surface such as the well or, more often, the wide rim of a plate. The special ground-laying oil is brushed on as evenly and thinly as possible in a dust-free atmosphere. When it has dried to a sticky state it is further evened out by patting with a piece of silk wrapped around cotton wool. The powdered color is then applied with cotton wool, but the material itself must never touch the oil directly, always retaining a layer of powder between. The surface is dry enough to touch in 24–40 hours according to the atmosphere. Designs can then be cut through the enamel in the manner of **sgraffito.** Resist with a watery syrup is also possible: this will take the color like the oil but can be washed off when the oil is dry. The preparation of the "oil" is rather complicated and a proprietary brand is advisable.

The technique is probably too slow and laborious to appeal to many potters today, but experiments could be made with spraying the oil, which would bypass the most tedious part.

Haematite

See **Hematite.**

Hakame

A rapidly brushed-on striated slip, normally on stoneware, which may have been invented and was certainly widely practiced by Korean potters on Pun Ch'ong wares. The early Yi period is considered the finest; Honey calls it "the pattern of a gesture." It traveled with captive Koreans to Japan. Says Leach, "the unconscious beauty of Korean work has always been deeply felt by Japanese connoisseurs but Japanese potters have rarely if ever been able to equal it." It is largely to Japanese efforts, however, that we owe the popularity of the style. "Hakame" can be translated as "brush grain." It was often used as a ground for iron brushwork, but there were also two other types: an all-over near-white coverage that could be cut away to the gray body in broad areas, which was called hori (carved) hakame; and a second style, possibly the forerunner of the more usual brushed slip, known as kohiki or powdered hakame from its appearance, which covered even the foot of pots on a gray-brown body. In mijihakame only the upper part of a pot was covered. The kohiki is scratched through and has "a distinctive primitive appearance" (Boger, 1971) and is sometimes painted. The original concern of the Korean potter was likely to have been not a conscious aesthetic effort but to effect a rapid and workmanlike covering of the surface; as it is summed up by Yanagi, they made their bowls "without noticing."

The overall effect will vary with the brush used and the user. The soft hake brush will give one effect and a more broom-like tool, "made of the ends of rice straw" (Leach), coarser striations—what the Japanese call "the rough touch." Application can be free-hand in straight or curved strokes (see illustration in Fournier, 1977) or while the pot is spinning on the wheel. It can be considered as sufficient decoration in itself

Korean hakame painting of the most fresh and vigorous type. It appears to result from a single stroke with a wide, hake-style brush. It is covered with a meager transparent glaze, all suggesting haste and poverty but also an enviable vitality.

A Japanese nineteenth-century tea bowl from Karatsu Pottery, the brushed slip being the sole decoration. Unusually, the lines are applied in a wavy pattern on the outside, giving an illusion of facets.

Hakame slip and painting in the traditional Yi Korean style by Shoji Hamada. The slip is more evenly spread than on much Korean work.

Bowl decoration in hakame, giving a sense of continuous movement. By Peter Smith. Coal-fired high-temperature earthenware.

In the absence of the Leach rice-straw brush, an ordinary cheap house-painting brush can be used. It can also be cut as in the illustration to give a more striated line, as seen on the spinning cylinder below.

or be used as a lively background to further brush painting, glaze trailing, and the like. A hakame wash, for instance, can form part of a more considered handscape design.

Traditionally the hakame slip is of a lighter color than the body. Leach mentions Pike's siliceous ball clay, possibly with china clay and feldspar additions. However, many clays will be found suitable, the character of the style suggesting as "natural" a material as possible. Variations include **slip patting** or the dabbing of slip to build up plant and other forms, though here we are entering the field of **slip painting.** Much excellent traditional work is still being done by Bill Marshall and others, although the technique is not as popular as it was a few years ago.

Hake

A wide, soft brush, used to repair Japanese paper screens with starch, which was adapted as a slip brush in ceramics. It is used especially for **Slip patting.**

Halved Design

This is a curious organization of pattern where the piece, generally an open dish or plate, is glazed or decorated roughly half-and-half in a very contrasting fashion, one section sometimes having a relationship to the other but, in the case of some Oriental dishes, having apparently little in common except skill and elaboration. Kutani dishes of the seventeenth century, for instance, are painted in a part fabric–part flower design. Some forms of counterchange halve the pattern, but these are closely related in line and mass. Rhodes (1960) shows a bowl by Warren Mackenzie, which appears to have been glazed all over in an oatmeal glaze, one half redipped in a rust color that is cut through in a linear design to show the oatmeal beneath. This is a very acceptable form of halved design.

A typical Japanese halved design in green and white glazes with brushwork. Much Oribe work is in this style, though it is sometimes divided into three sections.

Handles

Much work has been done on handles through the centuries in excess of that demanded by their practical use: ribbing, notching, twisting, modeling, the occasional applied figures, elaborate thumbstops, and junction wipes. The curve and flow of many Greek handles was emphasized by painted or modeled decoration, especially at their

A strongly modeled "stop" on an Etruscan jug, ca. 750 B.C.

Handles on a Song (Sung) Chinese cup that are modeled with dragons beyond the practical requirements; they become, with their extended tails, almost purely decorative.

An elegant handle combining utility and ornament. By Bill Brown.

While the handle itself, on this large storage jar by Michael Casson, is of practical use, the wipes at the end are largely decorative.

lower junctions, in order to unify the whole concept. Country potters nearer our own times have added handles to pots in numbers far exceeding practical requirements, and the innocent joke has been imitated by modern potters on teapots and other pieces. The "handles" on Ron Nagle's cups are conceived purely as formal variations or decorations with no useful aspect. In general, however, handles lie in the realm of form and outside the scope of this book (see Fournier, 1981).

Hardening-on Fire

An intermediate firing is necessary when using underglaze colors on biscuit. Prepared pigments are often made to fix at about 800° C./1.470° F., but neat oxides need the higher temperature of 1,060/1,930, and these are best used on raw clay. See also **Underglaze colors.** The hardening-on fire is more common in industrial work where the underglaze is applied by transfer or other mechanical means. It may be necessary for studio potters using similar methods of decoration.

Hare's Fur Glaze

The name given to mottled or streaked dark-brown glazes of the tenmoku family and especially those on Chinese Ch'ien Yao ceramics. They can be of a soft, smoky nature or with fine, lighter flecks. Rhodes considers them to be slip glazes similar in composition to the Albany slip of the United States, and Hamer also mentions this possibility. The streaks are probably caused by local fluxing and subsequent running of the color. The later hare's fur examples had yellow streaks. Spots of a similar color can appear on iron/ash glazes in oxidation. A blue-gray type Hamer suggests to be the decomposition of magnesium sulphate in the melted glaze, but the precise composition is not known. A similar effect occurs in high-iron glazes in reduction.

Harlequin Set

A title given to mid-nineteenth-century tea services with cups and saucers of different colors, the obvious reference being to the multicolored Harlequin costume. The term and style had a further vogue in the 1920s and 1930s. Potters seldom avail themselves of the practicality of this type of tableware, though the problems of matching are sometimes considerable.

Hausmalerei

Although these seventeenth-century specialist pottery decorators of Germany, who worked outside the factory system (the word means "home painting"), had degenerated into hack painters by the end of the eighteenth century, in their heyday they were a unique group of fine independent craftsmen who also often signed their work, presaging to some degree the modern individual potter. Some of the finest and the poorest German enamel painting was by the hausmalerei.

Hematite

The earthy type of this natural iron ore was used by early potters for their slips and colors. In Bronze Age England and the Hallstadt Iron Age it was crushed and used as a powder pigment on the surface of pottery, but this technique does not seem to have continued, although it was occasionally used as a stain in slip. It is a very pure iron oxide, its name deriving from "blood," which refers to its color. Red ochers are impure hematites and are useful in burnishing and in crystalline glazes.

Henri Deux Ware

See **Inlay.**

A Minton copy of the curious inlaid French pottery known as "Henri Deux."

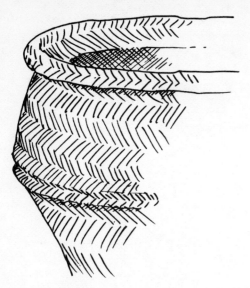

Herringbone

A design motif of great antiquity appearing, for instance, on Aegean Cycladic pottery of 3000 B.C., but also a staple element in pottery decoration.

Hidasuki

See **Fire cord.**

High-Temperature Colors

Underglaze colors that will stand the full heat of stoneware or porcelain firings are the oxides of cobalt, iron, and manganese, the first being the most stable of all, with copper, chromium, and antimony to a lesser degree. At one time the term was used for tin-glaze colors, as opposed to enamels. Vanadium as ammonium metavanadate will survive fairly high temperatures. The behavior of oxides depends in some degree on the kiln atmosphere; copper, for instance, will still give reduced red at 1,340° C./2,450° F. Another term, used in books on the history of pottery, is *grand feu* color.

Hispano-Moresque

The amalgam of Islamic and European influences on the painted and luster wares of Spain in the fourteenth to seventeenth centuries has become known as Hispano-Moresque, although the Moors were only the last recipients of a long line of tradition in ceramic decoration. This magnificent ware is discussed under **Brushwork, Luster,** and **Tin-glaze.**

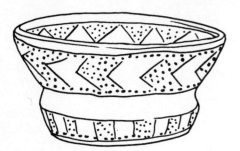

The herringbone pattern occurs widely on early pottery. The two drawings show adaptations: an all-over incising of alternate sloping lines on an English "Yorkshire" type Bronze Age vessel; and as a separating line between two textures on an ancient bowl.

A luster dish from Valencia which still shows strong Arab influences. The museum caption reads "Fair ladies in profile on a lanteen rigged ship."

While the lettering on this fine Hispano-Moresque plate is Gothic, it still retains an Arab-type flourish through the stem of the H.

Cobalt and luster combined on a Spanish plate of the fifteenth century. Western influences, especially of heraldry, are strong.

Honey Glaze

The richness of the old slipwares was due in part to the impurities in the galena and other glaze materials that helped to blend and unite the colors. The nearest we can get to the honey-colored glaze is to add small quantities of iron oxide, preferably as red clay. A tiny amount of copper and manganese may also help.

Illite

A widely distributed micaceous clay. Its name derives from its isolation from other clay minerals by scientists in Illinois as recently as the late 1930s. No precise formula can, however, be given for it. Kaolinite is thought to have been altered to illite by the action of ancient seas. "London clay [may be] 90 percent illite" (Cardew). The micaceous element is reputed to be useful in burnishing and gloss ware and may have been featured on Roman Samian ware.

Ilmenite

A hard beach sand of ferrous titanate, similar to rutile but coarse in grain and richer in iron. It can be used to give a speckled, "peppery" (Rhodes) appearance to bodies, glazes, and colors. Up to 1 percent or so will assist the development of crystals in a glaze. It has also been used for brush painting on glazes, giving a yellowish color.

Impasto

At Doulton of Lambeth in the late 1870s, a thick underglaze color was painted onto

This remarkable object is a roll in cuneiform text of an Assyrian king's campaigns, ca. 700 B.C. The amount of precise and detailed stamping is mind boggling, since it must all have been done on fairly soft clay and there is no trace of any variation of impression or smudging.

a raw stoneware body, giving a slight relief under the glaze. The same effect could be achieved with heavily pigmented slips (engobes). A thick, deep blue, raised pigment was also used on early Florentine majolica.

Impressed Decoration

The plastic nature of clay has ensured that impressed decoration of one sort or another has been practiced since the inception of ceramics, and there is a natural integration between pot and impressed designs that has appealed to the twentieth-century potter. The edge of a cockleshell was used to impress patterns on pots by Western Mediterranean potters of 5,500 years ago, but most decorations tend to be geometric or abstract and depend on the repetition of a simple motif. Bones, stones, plants, fabric, cord, and many other found objects have been brought into use, as well as fingers and thumbs and the more considered cut stamps, toothed, and other tools, over the eight millennia of pottery history. There is also the long period when history was written on pottery: the Babylonian, cuneiform, and other scripts pressed into clay. The great aesthetic pleasure that many of these tablets offer can give clues to the successful use

Obviously made by a single stamp, these unusual little dogs have been impressed into a scored tile, the scoring possibly for breaking into four sections after firing. Medieval, from Pipewell Abbey, Northants, England.

An unusual piece by Lucie Rie with small circular impressions on the shoulder.

Two examples of patterns built up by the repetition of impressions from a single simple tool: the first a large jar by Michael Casson; the second shows the angled cut of a bamboo sgraffito tool in action.

of tool impressions today. A "survey tablet" on a circular block of clay illustrated in Cooper (1972) is an object of considerable abstract beauty, while many of these stamps are models of subtle placing. In a more representative style, two impressed fish appear on a first-century Han dish, and there are countless other fine examples.

Medieval tiles were decorated with overall impressions from wooden blocks: plain, inlaid, or slipped and glazed. Such large impressions, however, are unusual, and most designs are built up from simpler and smaller elements. While found objects can be used—broken wood ends, plants, or man-made objects such as a cogwheel, a ball of string, or a bottle top— these may have too positive an identity to harmonize with the ceramic piece. As a contrast, an intriguing incongruity, or a visual pun or joke they can have value. A fairly neutral impression, on the other hand, such as the end of a ruler or a triangular stamp, can be built up into significant patterns that can also complement and heighten the formal values of the pot. For beginners especially, limitation to one or two motifs is more likely to release invention and have satisfactory results than a number of conflicting or naturalistic impressions. Similarly, a single, well-placed impression can have a considerable effect.

For larger and more consciously designed stamps, chalk, wood, or plaster can be cut or cast. Stamps can also be cast from one another to form positive and negative images that can be effectively combined into one design. A form of simple roulette can be made by carving the sides of a stick of chalk, rolling it across a slab of clay or around the neck or shoulder of a pot. Plaster and chalk will quite quickly disintegrate, but the former can be strengthened with glue or epoxy resin. A useful impressing tool, either for its original purpose or used purely decoratively by repetition, inversion, and so on, is printer's type—particularly large wooden letters and symbols. Many charming flagons and other pieces of the seventeenth and eighteenth centuries are type-stamped and sometimes inlaid. Indian textile blocks can be used, although the designs are often too figurative for creative use. See **Stamping.**

The state of the clay will dictate the character of the impressions: too dry will obviously give a weak or partial image, too wet will give a cushioned effect with the clay riding up around the tool, which may also stick. On the soft side of leather-hard is the general rule. If possible, on a pot, support the wall from the inside. Impressions

Robert Kibler's "Microcircuitry Tea for Me," slab-constructed earthenware with underglazes and a computer-generated surface pattern. Photo courtesy Phil Starrett.

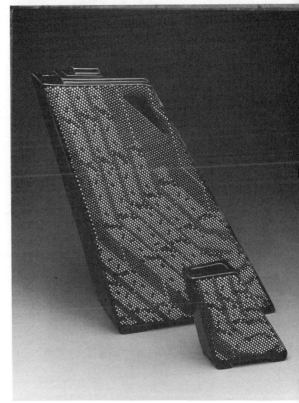

113

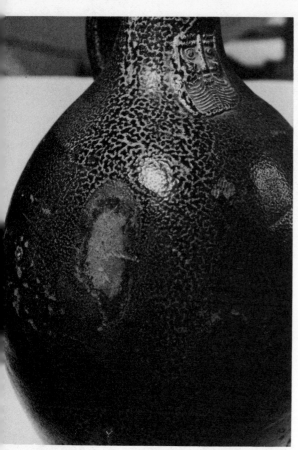

The traditional firing of salt-glaze, the pots heaped up one on another, resulted in scars and uneven salting, which are truly incidental to the technique and comprise a large part of its attraction in modern eyes.

can also be made onto a pad on the surface of the piece. See also **Applied decoration, Seal,** and **Stamp.** Nonrigid materials such as fabric need completely plastic clay to leave a significant mark. For more physically active techniques, see **Beaten patterns.**

Tiles are a special case. If impressed to any extent they will distort. This can be minimized by using a frame, but it will often be necessary to plane or fettle the edges. Alternatively a relief pattern in plaster, wood, or biscuit can be set at the bottom of a tile frame and the clay pressed onto it. It is sometimes a help, or maybe an added decorative item, to cover the stamp with slip. The walls of slab pots can usefully be stamped or impressed before assembly.

A dusting with oxide or a wipe over the impressed surface with a color-loaded sponge or a large flat brush can emphasize the design, leaving the impressions in the body color. The reverse—inlaying the line—can utilize pigment, slip, or glaze. See **Inlay.** Small combustible items such as rice grains can be impressed into or right through the surface, but the kiln will then need to be ventilated. See also **Printing, Rice-grain pattern,** and **Roulette.**

Incising

The term *incidental* is defined by *Webster* as "being likely to ensue as a chance or minor consequence" and, less complimentarily in the *Little Oxford Dictionary,* as merely "casual, non-essential." Unplanned happenings, however, are often integral to modern studio pottery—and the bane of the industry. We make allowance for them or even partly plan them, but they fuel the impatience that makes one open a kiln too soon, even after a lifetime of such events. Leach's famous paragraph in *A Potter's Book* distinguishes the incidental from the accidental in the ceramic process. The second may be due to bad luck or carelessness, but the former—as manifested in fire-flash, bleed-through, degrees of reduction, glaze variation in different parts of the kiln, the running of color, even the crawling of glaze in some instances—can be considered as peculiar to the process of firing natural materials and is often happy evidence of it: "They are incidental to nature rather than accidental to men."

Before this century, in most Western cultures, these incidentals were generally put down to primitive and undeveloped techniques, and it is true that "development" in the scientific sense can all but eliminate them. Today their acceptance is due in some degree to contact with Japan, but they are sometimes taken to absurd lengths. Such mishaps as shattering and cracking are added to acceptable decorative/formal effects. Shock rather than pleasure is often the aim, arising from the fear of complacency in an affluent society. As ever, the best work, usually that of the originators, surmounts the apparent chaos with brilliance and aplomb. Incidentals have come a long way in forty years.

Incising

Incising implies cutting with a sharp tool, usually a metal one. Engraving is a form of incising. The term is often used rather more loosely in ceramics to indicate any cut line or design including scratching, which is characterized by a broken-edged line.

The ninth- to thirteenth-century Chinese and Koreans were masters of the fluent but crisp and controlled line, "flowing, sensitive, varied, and eloquent" (Honey). Centuries before them there is evidence of brilliantly sharp and vital cutting on some Roman Empire pots, a definite chisel edge being used on fine-grain clay without hesitation or double cutting, an object lesson in its type. A vast body of early pottery is incised, this being one of the few decorative possibilities before glaze, and incising

The sides of flasks were fertile ground for incised and other decoration in the seventeenth to nineteenth centuries. Sharp and clean lines, combined with thin salt and other glazes, ensured that the cut remained significant even when shallow and fine.

Very close hatching within the elements of this design by the Nigerian potter Ladi Kwali has given an illusion of a darker color and of being in relief from the smooth pot surface.

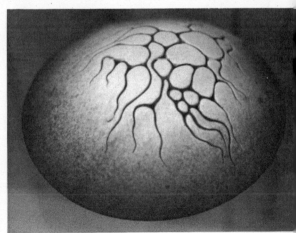

Bernard Leach cutting the first strokes on one of his "Willow" designs. A cut line must be firm but unhesitating if it is to be alive.

A deeply cut and color-filled curved form by Maggie Barnes.

The rough body gives considerable strength to this carved and incised form by Ian Godfrey. Like a Persian rug the design at first looks regular but is, in fact, anything but.

is often better and cleaner without glaze. A red-gloss cup in the Ashmolean Museum, Oxford, is cut with triangular curved strokes in the manner of engraved glass. The incising and cutting away of porcelain to enhance its translucency has long been practiced, a famous example being the eighteenth-century Te Hua Fukien blanc de chine, cut on very thin material with a fine point, the design being visible only by strong transmitted light. Fluting may be considered a form of incising, especially the triangular cut as used by David Leach, but it is often nearer to carving. Generally an incised pattern is a line pattern, though it may vary in character from the blunt and vigorous to the fine and nervous, and be graduated in breadth and depth. It is possible to cut soft biscuit with a sharp, hard tool, useful on delicate pieces and occasionally practiced today.

Many potters use incising either as the main or as a peripheral aid in decoration. Hans Coper's pots have cut lines that gently emphasize forms or give movement to them. Work by Michael Casson shows the free sweep of sharply cut lines, which are given mystery and sensitivity by the overlay of slip and dry ash glaze. On Ladi Kwali's fine jars are blocks of pattern so closely crosshatched as to give a feeling of being in relief.

As has been suggested, the work should be done with a sharp, hard tool: metal, bamboo, or, as Leach mentions, pine with the bark removed. Clay needs to be fairly stiff if a clean cut is required. Such is the variety, skill, and simple perverseness of potters, however, that all rules are often broken to good and original effect. See also **Combing.**

Indentation

An impressed mark normally leaves the identity of the tool or object, but indentation can also distort the formal character of a pot and so becomes more of a shaping than a decorative process. A number of modern pots, by Eileen Lewenstein and others, are

A sure and lively stroke of a tool has resulted in a mark somewhere between impressing and indenting, altering the profile of the pot and forming lobes. By John Huggins.

deeply and effectively indented. A stoneware bottle by John Tuska illustrated in Rhodes (1960) has been deeply indented into vertical furrows down which a very thick glaze has run. Less radical finger and other impressions have figured in pottery through the ages, but they are much less common than many other techniques. See **Finger tipping.**

In-Glaze

This may refer to either colors that are painted onto a raw opaque glaze (majolica) or those that are transmitted through an opaque tin or titanium glaze from below, the latter also known as transmutation colors. They are distinct from **underglaze** and **over-glaze** (enamel) colors.

Inlay

The most striking and expert historical inlay work was by the fourteenth-century Koreans under the Koryu Dynasty. It featured finely cut and often quite realistic flowers, trees, and animals together with stamped repeated motifs, all in a sober black and white on a grayish body under a pale celadon glaze. The method has persisted or has been revived in Korea today. In an article on a modern Koryu-type pottery south of Seoul, Jill Kato shows how the design—still a reflection of the early style—is cut free-hand with a fine hooked tool, and only the bands are inked in. Cuts are rapid, direct, and skillful. Several coats of white slip are laid on with a wide brush and, when dry, are scraped down to the inlay with a triangular-headed metal tool, which, though it looks unhandy, leaves the surface quite unscarred. Some of the historical ware was stamped with rather monotonous little starry flowers, and this technique was copied in Japan, where it became known as **mishima.**

Apart from the Korean work, inlay is not common in the ancient world. Slip was brushed into incised or stamped lines to pick them out more clearly, and there are some Roman inlaid lettered pieces. Small brightly colored tiles were inlaid with small shapes in Pharaonic Egypt. Inlay work was practiced in Sri Lanka (Ceylon). The major development of inlay, however, was in medieval floor tiles. In an explosion of activity, acres of flooring in abbeys and churches, and occasionally in manor houses, were

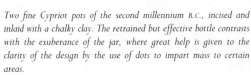

Form and decoration are one in this indented cylinder by Eileen Lewenstein. The shadows and the darker (or lighter) central hole make light itself the main factor.

Two fine Cypriot pots of the second millennium B.C., incised and inlaid with a chalky clay. The retrained but effective bottle contrasts with the exuberance of the jar, where great help is given to the clarity of the design by the use of dots to impart mass to certain areas.

117

On this Korean bowl much of the design, including the little studs in the circle in the base, is in relief. Slip has been washed over them and roughly scraped away, leaving a white background rather than the more usual inlaid white pattern.

At first glance this appears to be typical Korean Koryu Period inlay; the flower outside is in traditional mishima style but the swirling interior pattern is in reverse, achieved by cutting away and inlaying the background rather than the elements of the design itself.

Detail of a typical English Sussex lidded jar, the design cut and stamped into dark clay and filled with a white slip. Lettering and date stamped with printer's type.

covered with these long-wearing inlaid (encaustic) tiles. Reputedly they were stamped with wooden dies and the impression filled with soft clay or slip, although hard evidence of the stamps, which must have numbered tens of thousands, is scanty. There is also a theory that slip was applied to the stamps and "printed" into the tile. It is difficult for a potter to imagine this happening effectively, especially at the speed that must have been necessary. The designs are quite intricate, often with considerable areas of buff clay inlaid into a red body. Individual, self-contained designs are complemented by superbly worked-out schemes extending over a large number of tiles. Shields, heraldic devices, hunting scenes, ecclesiastics, facing birds in Persian style, kings and queens, beasts, and plant forms were all grist to their mill. But in all cases there is a feeling of great unity in a floor of these tiles. It was a peak of decorative effort in ceramics in Great Britain and Western Europe and is one that continues to give great pleasure and instruction. The Victorians must have destroyed many thousands of medieval tiles, but they also developed industrial methods of copying them fairly faithfully to repair certain floors which remained, notably at Westminster Abbey. They also tried a rather slow system of first dust-pressing the "inlaid" areas of the design face

Two modern tiles cut and inlaid in the medieval fashion. The lively pig was drawn by a schoolboy, the abstract pattern by Sheila Fournier. See **Tile Decoration** for examples of medieval inlay.

Lines and masses are built up on this form by Maggie Barnes by a series of pinholes, filled with a darker pigment.

A variation on inlay. A cylinder has been planed into facets that are alternately plain and combed, the combed line filled with a black engobe and covered with a white stoneware glaze, which has been scraped from the plain faces. By Sybil Houldsworth.

A form of "neriage inlay" into porcelain by Gerry Wornell. While the effect is intriguing, the floating areas of pattern appear somewhat dissociated.

down in a metal mold and then dust-pressing the background clay onto them. It was a curious reversal of inlay with uncertain results.

During the sixteenth century a fragile ware was intricately inlaid at St. Porchair in France: a white body with brown, black, and ocher ornament in French Renaissance style. It is often called Henry II (or Deux) ware, a curious on-off development. Delicate plant-form inlay was used by the U.S. pioneer potter Mary McLaughlin. Today, as well as the slip inlays described above, oxides, high-pigment engobes, and glazes are also used.

A very simple form of inlay is to lay a strip or other shape of one clay onto a slab of contrasting plastic clay and to roll it into the surface with a rolling pin. Somewhat amorphous shapes can result, but delineation will improve with practice in the relative consistencies of the clays. Kuino Uchido impresses strips of contrasting clay into the walls of half-thrown pots, giving spirals and rings of inlaid color in the finished piece— halfway to agate ware. And as with agate ware, scraping or turning the surface will sharpen the pattern. In *Ceramic Review*, Hylton Nel shows thin, flat pieces of colored clay rolled onto slabs, which are then mold-formed into bowls. The thinness of the inlays accounts for the comparative crispness of the result. Val Barry obtains a mysterious and satisfying variety of shape, texture, and color by rolled inlay, the clay stained with unground oxides.

For the more usual slip or soft clay work, the base clay is used at the leather-hard stage, the walls of the cut-away areas being upright so that the design is not distorted when scraped clean. A soft plastic clay can be used over stabbed, impressed, combed, or stamped depressions, though many potters prefer slip. As well as the more considered type of drawing, the surface can be textured by repeated pecking or stabbing with a tool. A splendid example of this is the Sudanese hyena model illustrated in

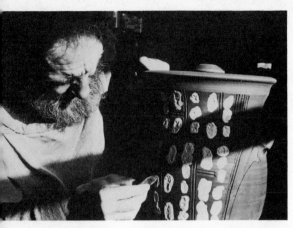

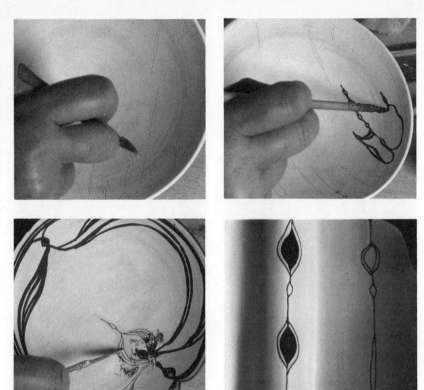

Five pictures showing two styles of inlay technique. Mick Casson is applying soft clay to a broad inlaid pattern; when stiff, the surplus will be scraped away to reveal the motif. The porcelain bowl shows, in contrast, fine-line inlay, cut with a pointed knife, filled with a high-pigment engobe, and scraped clean with a curved scalpel. The detail of an upright curved form by Sheila Fournier shows the latter type with actual apertures through the wall to give variety.

Hamilton (1974), where the dark clay is covered with stabbed dots set in a subtle pattern of lines and filled with white. A dramatic variation is seen on Mayan pots, where a burnished surface is cut away and filled with a white inlay. A very individual approach is that of Nick Homoky (the line cut with a pocket knife, according to Lane, 1980), whose inlaid porcelain is sharp, very consciously placed, and austere in style, if often amusing in content.

The only major technical problem lies in the different shrinkages of the body and the inevitably wetter inlay. With the narrower lines this is not serious, but larger areas may shrink away. Some have tried flint and grog additions, but the latter must be very fine if striations are not to appear during scraping off. In Japan, by the hari-tsuke process, plastic clay is applied to a roughened and slipped surface and the inlay rubbed and pressed outward when leather-hard. This applies, of course, to the large areas of inlay. Old English tiles with their high-shrinkage red clay bodies and white (pipeclay?) inset slip represented an ideal combination of materials. The deflocculation of soft clay has also been tried. When slip is used, it is necessary to top up two or three times to leave the final leather-hard inlay slightly proud of the surface. A brush or trailer can be used. If the slip spills out of the cut it does not matter, since at a suitable stage of dryness the surface is scraped over with a ruler or flat tool to reveal the edges of the pattern and leave all sharp and clean.

Not all potters, however, desire clear definition: Michael Casson, for instance, inlays a red-firing stoneware with a soft white clay and then covers the whole surface with a slip of the same color. This is scraped away sufficiently to reveal the inlaid line, but the slip left in the roughness of the body gives a speckled appearance, which softens the impact. He uses porcelain body with 20 percent ball clay for the slip. In a similar way, oxides or slips can be rubbed or inset into freely cut or combed patterns and left judiciously smudgy. In the sharp and crisp style Eileen Nisbet inlays her sophisticated porcelains at the leather-hard stage with slip loaded with commercial stains and oxides. Homoky adds 10 percent of bentonite to his slip and blobs it on with a brush until it is proud of the surface.

Oxides alone or with a little clay are widely used to inlay fine lines on porcelain, normally into the raw clay, although Jenny Lind cuts into low-fired biscuit and uses an ordinary eraser to clean the lines. Sheila Fournier uses a pointed knife to cut into almost dry porcelain clay. Small impressed dots may be filled with pigment which can then spread into an overall mottled surface under the glaze, as in the work of Mary Rogers. The incisions can equally well be filled with glaze. Suito Iko (Sanders) inlays colored glazes into carved porcelain and covers the whole with a transparent glaze, giving delicate pastel hues. One glaze can also be "inlaid" into another. See **Glaze inlay.** In this connection Clive and Margaret Simmonds use a technique of firing wax-resisted glaze onto tiles and later filling the empty spaces with other glazes by brush or trailer. **Cuerda seca** could be considered an inlay of this type. See also **Agate** and **Scratched decoration.**

Inscriptions

Since written language began, there have been words and phrases impressed, scratched, or painted onto ceramics. Leaving aside the official "libraries" of clay tablets in Egypt, Mesopotamia, and elsewhere in the ancient world, descriptive names were sometimes scratched or painted on Greek red- and black-figure ware. The earliest surviving example of Greek characters appear on a jug of *ca.* 750 B.C. The lettering on Near Eastern pots was generally of a religious character, and poems appear on Chinese pots as early as Song (Sung) times. But the heyday of the extended inscription was the seventeenth- and nineteenth-century country and peasant pottery, sometimes pious, often earthy. The inscriptions are sometimes of more interest than the pots themselves: of the American nineteenth-century Pennsylvania German ware, Barber rather un-kindly says that "without these inscriptions the ware would possess . . . little interest either for the ceramist or the historian." This is not always true. The basic elements of life are reflected in the sayings plus a good deal of homely philosophizing. "A pipe of tobacco does a man as much good / as though he spent his money on the girls," or "Luck and unluck / are every morning our breakfast." With direct reference to his trade—"Luck, glass, and earth how soon they are broken / out of earth with under-standing the potter makes everything," and hopefully, "All beautiful maidens hath God created / they are for the potter but not for the priest." On a resigned domestic note, from a woman this time: "I cook what I can / if my son will not eat my husband will." There are some admirable sentiments: "I like fine things / even though they are not mine / and cannot be mine / I still enjoy them," and a more disillusioned idealist of 1805: "I have ridden over hill and dale / and have found disloyalty everywhere." These are all translations from the German and are culled from the charming book mentioned above, Barber's *Tulip Ware.*

In England the inscription is not so common. A rare series is known as the "Merryman" series and is painted across six plates: "What is man / let him do what he can / to entertain his guests / but if his wife do frown / all merriment goes down." The original spelling is somewhat more erratic. "Money wanted" slip trailed onto another American dish probably indicated "no barter," which was a common practice.

Tin-glazed wares are usually limited to the names of their contents, herbal or medical, but a few rhymes and other sentences occur, amorous, religious, or indicative of the patron. Attractive type-impressed flasks and other pieces were made in

This enigmatic statement, perpetuated on ceramic, is typical of similar inscriptions through the eighteenth and nineteenth centuries, although this particular plate is from the Gouda Zenith factory and was made circa 1980. The edge decoration is transfer, but the lettering is painted on a tin glaze.

A nicely lettered reminder of mortality on an English tin-glaze plate.

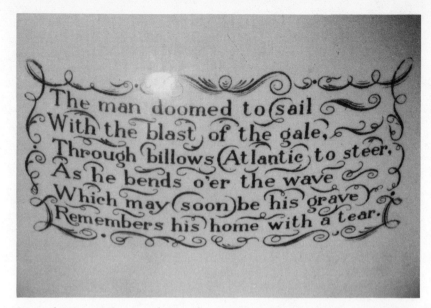

The sort of rhyme, applied as a transfer, that often appeared on nineteenth-century bowls, usually with a sailing ship in color inside.

eighteenth-century England. A salt-glazed tea caddy from Bradford, Yorkshire, is inscribed "Jesus is Preshious to a believin heart." A great many industrial pieces had inscriptions: doggerel about the sea and sailors was popular and also, of course, the "Trifle from Lowestoft" kind. Some early Bernard Leach beakers and plates are lettered in slip or sgraffito (but not very well). Inscriptions, except on specially made commemorative pieces, public or private, are comparatively rare on modern studio pottery.

Skilled lettering in slip is uncommon today, but the length of this proverb on a plate by Godfrey Arnison shows great confidence. The division of words by four well-placed dots is interesting.

(Too specific, perhaps?) As mentioned, Leach and Cardew decorated bowls and dishes with sayings and even poems, but it was not until the early 1980s that an increasing number of inscribed pieces began to appear, especially in slipware. Broken or unfinished scraps of sentences sometimes feature on sculptural pieces as a clue rather than a statement.

Intaglio

An engraved or incised design as distinct from cameo, which is in relief.

Iridescence

A prismatic, opalescent intermingling of colors on the surface of a glaze or enamel, resembling that on soap bubbles, gasoline, etc. It is often an effect of long burial in damp conditions, causing surface devitrification through the dissolution of the alkalis by carbonic acid. It is common on Islamic pottery and on Roman and other ancient glass. The effect sometimes occurs on high-concentration manganese glazes and on lusters. Raku pieces will show occasional iridescence. It is the principal quality of tin-and-bismuth lusters.

Iridium

A rare metal of the platinum group, the oxide of which has been used to produce black in ceramics. "Fine, stable blacks and greys" (Billington).

Iron

Iron oxide has always been the commonest stain in pottery, being present in most clays and in many other materials. In a fairly pure form it is found widely as such easily crushable rocks as hematite. Its role in glazes is complicated, as evidenced by Hamer's twelve columns in *The Potter's Dictionary,* but in general it produces yellow-buff, orange-reds, orange-browns, browns, and blacks, with greens, blues, and grays in reduction. High-iron stoneware glazes or brushstrokes can produce near-reds by saturation. In ash glazes, in oxidation, the same recipe can give red or an almost mirror-black depending on the wood and the style of its burning, that is, its carbon content.

In earthenware, iron gives variable results when used as a pigment, and a single brushstroke can vary from yellow through to black. There are a number of types of oxide, red, black, and ocher. Some authorities recommend the black oxide, which has some fluxing properties in or on soft glazes. Magnetic iron (spangles) is a coarse form and will develop speckles during firing. The bright red crystals of the raw ferric oxide (a disappointment to beginners when fired) can be maintained at enamel temperatures, or, as mentioned above, to some degree in stoneware. The mineral known as "bole" can retain its redness at earthenware temperatures when applied thickly, as the sixteenth-century Isnik potters proved. Even on porcelain, David Leach uses a red clay with nepheline to trail bright red-orange dots onto the glaze. The alkalis in the nepheline probably have a role here, as they do in maintaining brighter colors from iron at lower temperatures. Very small additions of titania can brighten iron yellows and oranges. The quite bright iron reds on Bristol and other Delftware of the early eighteenth century can be picked out by touch, not having blended completely with the glaze. Lime in a body or glaze will bleach iron, as is seen when a pink-orange biscuit becomes a buff-gray stoneware. Zinc in a glaze will kill the typical iron color.

A somewhat excessive bleed-through of body impurities, with some brushwork. By Helen Pincombe.

Iron Chromate

Used as a stain in bodies and glazes (0.5 to 2.0 percent), iron chromate gives grays in most glazes, browns if zinc is included in the recipe. It aids crystallization in glazes, and is used as a modifier of colors and as an opacifier. Iron chromate can "bleed" with various colors when used as an underglaze pigment. Its coarser qualities are used to create spotting in glazes.

Iron Spot

Natural (or deliberately added) iron pyrites in a clay body will cause iron spot on the glaze. The small nodules are drawn by reduction to the surface where the iron concentration forms darker and sometimes slightly crystalline specks and spots on the surface. Crushed granite and other materials are added to clay in Japan and the resultant iron spot is called "goma" (sesame seed). Crushed granite from the Quyle kilns at Murphys, California, will give a similar effect in bodies (Sanders).

Specks and splashes of brown can also be incorporated into glazes, although it is difficult to keep them in suspension. Iron spangles in its coarser form has been recommended. A Kyoto pottery burns leaves in an iron drum, the ash taking up small specks of scale. Fine spots can also derive from 10 percent or so of coarsely ground, hard-dried red clay in the glaze mixture. See also **Bleed-through.**

Iron Wash

A term used by Fujioko to describe "simple unsophisticated" designs, sometimes consisting of a single wide brushstroke in iron oxide under a feldspathic glaze on Shino ware (sixteenth and seventeenth centuries). It varied greatly in color and bleed-through and was practiced on roughly shaped tea bowls and the like. An iron-bearing clay called "oni-ita" formed the pigment. It is reputedly the first type of brushwork on Japanese ceramics.

Ironing of Cobalt

Reddish or black patches may form on cobalt painting, especially on stoneware. It is due to the crystallization of cobalt silicate (Dodd). Though normally considered a fault caused by too heavy an application, certain mixtures can also give a furry-edged golden brown, which is attractive. The author uses a mixture of 2 cobalt, 4 manganese, 3 purple iron oxide, and 1 red clay, which gives this effect on a fairly fluid tin-opacified stoneware glaze in oxidation at 1,260° C./2,300° F.

Iron Spangles

See **Magnetic iron.**

Italian Maiolica

As a class of pottery that relies so heavily on surface decoration for its distinctive qualities, a short account may be of interest. Its chief characteristic is its glowing color. This results from clever handling and juxtaposition of the palette, which was restricted to blue from cobalt; yellow through orange to brown from an ochrous iron; green from copper; antimony yellow; and manganese purple brown—all enhanced by the white tin-glaze background. Although today maiolica (or majolica) is associated mainly with pigment color, it had its origins in the lusters, sometimes with blue, which came over from Spain. In fact a great deal of luster ware, albeit in a very different style, was made in Italy.

The great period spanned some 150 years, from the first quarter of the fifteenth century to the third quarter of the sixteenth. Within this time, 1480–1535 is considered "classic," although to the studio potter earlier and later styles are often more sympathetic. Many of the factories of town-based groups of potters had only some thirty to forty years of production before they began to decline. Nevertheless, probably millions of pieces were made. A bold, naive, and "imperfect" beginning was made in Florence and Orvieto, at first in copper and manganese and at Florence in a thick impasto blue. Simple motifs—oak leaves, fleur de lys, dogs, and occasional faces—were painted. Probably the greatest center, Faenza, was early in production, making drug pots and plaques of great distinction. Deruta and Gubbio became famous for their luster, which was also added to work from Urbino and Castel Durante, which had many workshops and specialized in "istriato" (historical or mythological scenes). The earlier rather spare designs tended to develop into all-over painting in the style of the current easel pictures. Siena and Urbino were very active from early in the sixteenth century. An overall bluish cast is evident in some later work. Francesco de Medici founded Cataggiolo in 1506. Rome made maiolica and Venice started late in the period. There was some resurgence at Montelupo, at Castelli, and in Sicily in the seventeenth and eighteenth centuries, but the initial drive had been dissipated, and although tin-glaze is still made, much of it has been derivative and generally without distinction.

Savonarola tried to destroy "profane" and pagan pictures at the end of the fifteenth century, but maiolica customers continued to prefer decorative scenes and figures to religious subjects, though there were also many of the latter. Actual portraits are rare, but some pieces show pleasant women and handsome men. Drug pots, of course, were for general use as well as for decoration—the pharmacies must have been a splendid sight. Large dishes were probably fruit and table pieces, and the smaller "tondini" had a deep central well for sweetmeats, etc. Holes in the feet of dishes and plates show that they were hung. Wall tiles, plaques, and pavements were made for churches.

In a museum, maiolica is overwhelming and often unsympathetic to modern eyes, but an individual piece can show the skill and often the charm and strength of a great decorative period in ceramic history.

A portion of an octopus motif in black on red; an early form of dotting or jeweling on a Mycenaean cup or kylix. The dots may have been applied with a sort of trailer or with a loaded brush.

Jasper Ware

This was a fine, hard stoneware embodying sulphate of barium in the recipe together with coloring oxides. See also **Colored bodies.** It was developed by Wedgwood and was later replaced by a white body covered with colored slip called jasper dip.

Jeweling

A term sometimes applied to the white spots of slip on a trailed line of red or black slip, which was the general practice in the heyday of trailing in England on Toft ware and other dishes and pots. See **Slip trailing.**

In a more realistic sense, not only have small shapes of gold foil been covered with a thick enamel and fired to the surface of ceramics in (probably distant) imitation of rubies and other jewels, but in 1872 real jewels were imbedded in the clay before firing (Hughes). In a similar way the term *jeweling* has been used for drops of colored enamel on a gold or silver ground at St. Cloud and, in the 1780s, at Sèvres.

Enamel can be applied with a toothpick or other pointed tool to achieve this effect. The tiny blue spots on some of John Maltby's otherwise broadly decorated dishes could be so described, and the result is highly attractive.

Tiny spots of pale slip on a black line enliven many a slip dish, of which this is an example from around the turn of the eighteenth century. Staffordshire. The spaces within the black trailed lines are filled with red slip in the Toft style.

The color and texture of this pot by Janet Leach are evocative of the fire through which it has passed.

A charming knob modeled beyond the strict requirements of use, and a fitting crown to a strong, simple form. By Michael Casson in tin-glazed earthenware.

Kairaku-en Ware

A Japanese system of colored glazes separated by ridged outlines in the **cuenca** manner. Made by Eiraku in the early nineteenth century (Boger and Boger).

Kaki

The Japanese word for persimmon, referring to a broken, rusty-brown glaze color resulting from an iron crystal layer on the surface. See Fournier, Hamer (under Rust), Leach (1940), and many other authorities for details of principles and recipes. Rhodes includes kaki under slip-glazes. See also **Black** and **Tenmoku.**

Kiln Gloss

An often inadvertent thin glaze coating or patch caused mainly by ash falling onto the shoulders of vessels during a firing. See also **Flashing.** It could have been the clue that led to the first high-fired glazes in the Far East. Other factors may cause a gloss on the clay surface, such as the iron and flux content of some red clays that will "self-glaze" at high temperatures. Salt-glaze may be considered as kiln gloss in the widest sense. See also **Fuming** and **Smear glaze.**

Knibis Technique

An impressing technique described by Storr-Britz whereby a sharp-edged wooden tool is rocked on a clay surface to produce rhythmic square and wavy ornaments and bands. See also **Rocker tool.**

Knob

The lid knob has often transcended its practical purpose to become a highly decorative element but is a borderline case as far as this book is concerned and is more fully dealt with in Fournier (1977 and 1981).

Kwaart

The Dutch name for the thin coating of transparent glaze over majolica painting, which enhanced its gloss and color. See **Majolica** and **Tin-glaze.** It is called *coperta* in Italy. Today the second glaze could be sprayed on. It was used in England during 1720–1730, and the effect was a good imitation of Oriental porcelain.

Lace

Around 1770, models were made at Meissen clothed in lace that had been soaked in porcelain slip, the lace burning away, leaving a fine tracery of porcelain. Variations could give texture and decoration to modern ceramics in a less figurative and specific style. Lace has been used to impress the background, as in "Singer in a Boob Tube" by Gillian Still (illustration in Lane, 1980).

Lajvardina, Lajvard Ware

An early Islamic technique in which black, red, white, and sometimes gold enamels were painted onto a blue or turquoise glaze. It was a development from Minai.

Variations on this type of work on black and other stoneware glazes are practiced by potters today, often using red and blue enamels.

Lamination

Characteristic dishes can be made from slabs sliced straight through a layered pile of different colored clays, but laminating is usually a precursor to further blending by throwing, cutting, rolling, etc. Small segments of parallel layers can be built up into complicated designs, such as those produced by Dorothy Feibleman and others. Mary White rolls very thin slabs of stained porcelain clays to build ragged-edged laminated forms touched with gold luster. For Ewen Henderson, laminated and agate techniques produce "forms organically related to decoration." See also **Agate ware, Marbled ware,** and **Neriage.**

Landscape

Rolling hills, trees, and clouds have been appearing on pots, bowls, and dishes by artist potters since the mid-1970s: cut, sprayed, and modeled. This may have been a reaction

It is difficult to know under which heading to put this interesting surface decoration, which is a combination of coils and blocks of slightly different porcelain clays pressed together and forced against a flat surface to amalgamate them. See also **Coil decoration**. *It is called "Temporal Font" and is one of a series by R. Lynn Studham.*

A

B

C

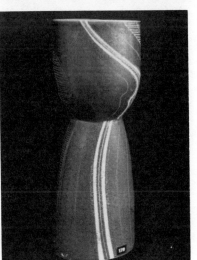

D

Well-defined laminated or agate decoration on a coiled stoneware form by Jennifer Lee.

Four pictures illustrating the approach to landscape design by the Cassons. A. The type of countryside that inspires the work. B. Mick Casson's incised, combed, and inlaid evocation of hill and cloud. C. and D. Stages in the stylization of ploughed field and sky by Sheila Casson.

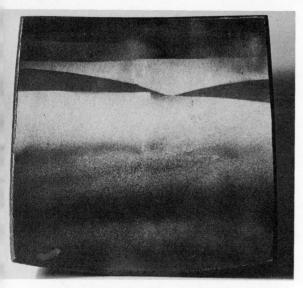

A dish that will conjure different land or seascapes according to which way up it is held. Oxides sprayed onto a porcelain-slip-coated stoneware body. By Sheila Fournier.

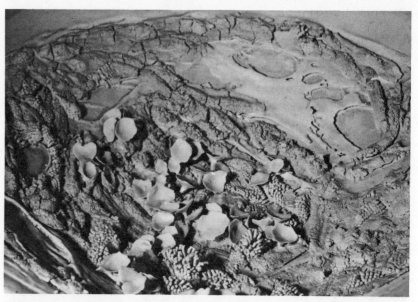

Three-dimensional "landscape" dishes. The first by Peter Simpson; fungi, outer space, and volcanic eruption are suggested in the careful planning of this crowded scene. The Ian Godfrey detail more overtly encapsulates wide expanse, desert, and pyramid, using the controlled crawling of a refractory glaze.

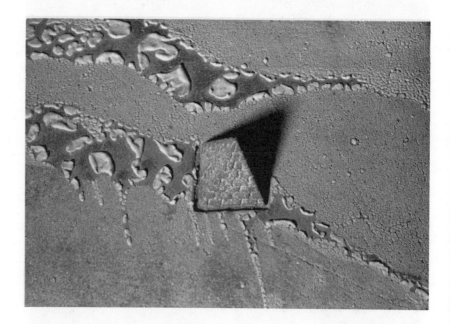

to the abstraction of the 1950s, although landscape itself is rapidly creating its own abstract patterns. Two of the earliest and most successful were Michael Casson and his wife, Sheila. In an article in *Ceramic Review 73*, they discuss the assimilation of the essence of the country around them, the ploughed fields, the underlying structure of land, which betokens its shape and history. Sheila's are "about surface and pattern while Mick's are about the elements—the constant winds that blow are reflected in his designs." Their work deals with abstractions, designs with overtones of natural form.

This is a different approach from depiction of landscape on most historical pots. In Egypt 5,500 years ago, attempts were made at suggesting the Egyptian scene, water and reeds, but the important element was always a creature or a boat. Greek scenes are totally figure-oriented; in the Far East the Chinese painters' preoccupation with gorges and misty mountains is not reflected in the pottery, although the Hill Jars of Han times may be considered an exception. It was not until the fourteenth and fifteenth centuries that stylized but comparatively realistic landscapes began to appear, generally as backgrounds to figures or animals, later becoming common all over the world. Some of the most charming are painted on Delft tin-glazed tiles and dishes. They were only rarely integrated with the ceramic form, however, and they became increasingly naturalistic and "applied," culminating in the photographically detailed nonsense of the nineteenth century.

A number of designs by Leach and Hamada suggest landscape, although they are more often "items in space." Leach is the more explicit with hills and trees and suggestions of wind and cloud, with more realistic drawing such as that of a Cornish tin mine on a tile. Stylized landscapes have appeared in the work of several potters in stoneware and porcelain—David Lloyd Jones' dish centers are especially successful. More explicit scenes are carved into the rims and walls of pots, but great variety and ingenuity of design and method are increasingly employed. See also **Carving, Inlay, Mocha, Pierced decoration, Spraying,** and **Template.**

Lappets _____

See **Scales.**

Laqabi _____

Although literally meaning "painted," this style of piece from twelfth-century Kashan in Persia had the body clay carved back to leave raised lines, the spaces between being filled with color: "an almost jewel-like effect" (Cooper). It is basically similar to **cuenca,** though not in method or effect.

Latex Resist _____

A form of resist that can be painted on and that sets to a thin coat of rubber. This can be peeled away after the resisted coating has been applied, leaving a clear, sharply

Lappets or scales representing a pineapple, a favorite subject in the eighteenth century. Here the applied decoration has become the form itself. St. Cloud "blanc-de-Chine" ca. 1730. See also **Scales**.

Two examples (by David Frith and John Maltby) of how latex resist can be used to obtain a blank area that can be further decorated with glaze, color, slip, or sgraffito after the film of rubber has been peeled away.

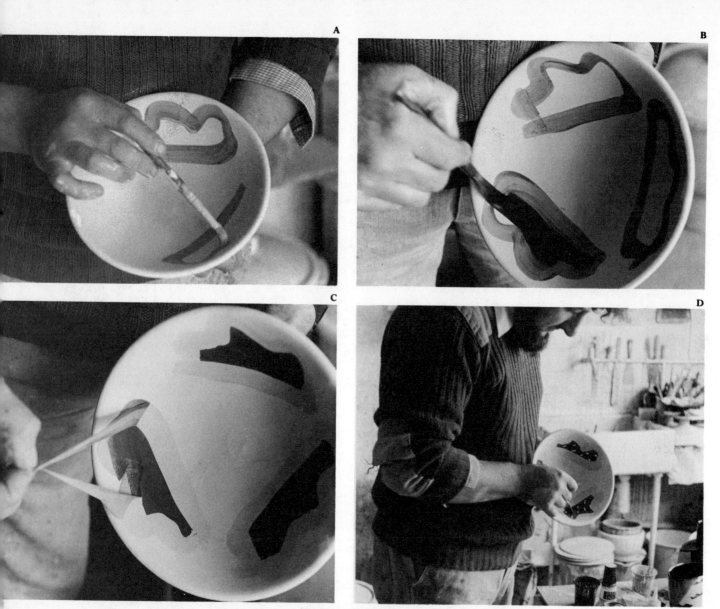

A   B

C   D

John Maltby using latex resist. A dish has been lightly covered with a thin wash of glaze. This enables the latex to be peeled away more easily when required. A. B. A design is painted with latex and color applied. C. Peeling the latex away. D. Cutting a pattern through the color. Additional decoration may then be applied, and the whole then covered with a clear glaze. Maltby uses a dilute latex with four parts of water to make brushwork more flowing, and he also lightly stains the mixture with an organic dye to make the strokes more visible. He cleans brushes with Polyclens. A recommendation from another source is to keep the brushes in a solution of household ammonia and water.

defined space. It is useful for sprayed color or glaze, which tends to leave a mist of droplets on wax. Latex permits the overlapping of color by peeling away and repainting between color applications. It may take glaze with it if peeled from a raw coating. It is very transparent but may be stained with a vegetable dye such as Coldron. If it is not peeled off before firing, the fumes are more noxious than those from burning wax. See further notes on latex and on brush cleaning at illustration captions.

For this evocative design by Bill Brown, the outlines of the main darker areas were painted onto a plaster slab and the outline and background (white) thickly painted in latex. This could be peeled from the plaster, dampened, and laid onto the porcelain plate to form a stencil, resisting sprayed colored slips. Details were later cut through to the porcelain body in the manner of sgraffito.

Leaf Resist, Leaf Impression

The use of plant leaves as a resist material has appeared only occasionally on pottery. There are examples on Chi-chou ware (China, thirteenth century): here a pair of leaves, one cut away in a circle suggesting fruit, is set in a bowl, resisting tenmoku glaze. The leaves are strangely realistic, with pale veins and markings. In the early nineteenth

A slip-resisted spray of leaves on a pot by Fishley Holland (1950), a country potter of Devon, England. The veins may have been cut in or may be the actual impressions of the underside of the leaf.

Detail of fern resist on a raku dish by Marcus Finch. With cut-through glaze.

A double-resist design, the leaf being pressed down onto the buff clay and the background waxed. The leaf was then removed and the central area sluiced over with black slip. Veins and holes were later marked out in sgraffito. The variation of tone arises from the fading of the slip under the glaze (see **Slip painting**) *during the firing, in this case a honey-colored earthenware lead glaze. By George Martin.*

century, Pennsylvania potters used leaf resist with slip, sometimes two slips, first white, then red. A sgraffito motto often appears: "This dish is made of earth / when it breaks the potter laughs." The Fishleys of Devon in the twentieth century have used leaf resist, again combined with sgraffito.

Handled with restraint, as in the beautiful Chi-chou example, the technique can achieve some subtlety. At worst it can be mechanical and, because the leaf is in simple silhouette, rather blank and dull. A worm-eaten leaf can give more interesting interior markings, or a leaf can be cut along its rib lines. Alternatively, a prior coating of slip or pigment can provide a basis for marking in details. It is sometimes difficult to stick a leaf down onto the clay, and only certain types are suitable.

Fleshy leaves can be pressed into soft clay to leave an outline with the ribs as shallow indentations. A strange system called "natural process" was used by J. Low of Chelsea, Massachusetts. A leaf (one would imagine a fairly fleshy one) was forced into the clay surface with a screw press. The leaf was then removed or burnt out and the impression used as a mold to form a relief image by casting.

Lettering

Lettering has been scratched, carved, stamped, trailed, and painted onto pottery, but, perhaps because literacy was not the lot of many early potters, it is not common. The great exception is the multitude of stamped "tablets" of the Babylonians and others for whom a slab of clay was equivalent to a sheet of paper. The Greeks sometimes named the hero on black- and red-figure pottery, but even these are often sketchy. The first surviving Greek letters were found, however, on a *ca.* 750 B.C. Corinthian jug. Some Roman pots are cut with letters that are filled with a whitish pigment. Discounting the close relationship between Chinese painting and script, actual characters appear on a fine T'zu-chou bottle in bold sgraffito, but this is a fairly rare example. A long

A Hebrew magic incantation from sixth-century Nippur.

incantation appears on a Hebrew plate of the sixth century. Islamic lettering is probably the script most commonly found on ceramics, a recognition of its intrinsic decorative qualities. Spread around a bowl or the shoulder of a pot, or cunningly placed in space, even the Chinese brushwork pales a little beside the vigor and variety of its forms. The Cufic lettering around Samarkand ware of the late ninth century may have been the work of a single master potter and his pupils. Lesser, illiterate Near Eastern potters copied phrases without understanding, but the lettering retained some of its decorative value. The Islamic feeling for bold script influenced the Christianized Hispano-Moresque luster potters, who painted some vigorous Gothic lettering. Some historians, in fact, suggest that the luster was applied with a square-ended quill in the manner of ink. This seems technically doubtful (Caiger-Smith shows a similar type of line made with a flat brush), but the style of the best painting has the same flow of thick and thin lines as

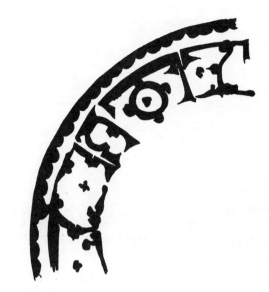

Detail of a ninth-century Nishapur (Persian) plate painted black on a white ground and showing the highly decorative character of one form of the Cufic script. Other interpretations of the letters are more rounded and flowing. These are parallels in the variety of form of our Western Roman script. See also **Calligraphy**.

Typically illusionist decoration on a Faenza early sixteenth-century spouted bottle with ornamental lettering in deep cobalt blue. The rest of the design is reversed on a dark blue ground.

Two country pottery styles of lettering in slip: the Soil Hill, Yorkshire, example is skillfully applied with a fairly liquid slip; that from Devon with thick slip with blobbed terminals. Note the lively dotted filling in the first example. See also **Inscriptions** *for a modern example.*

A charming child's plate from the late Victorian period. The transfer design largely ignores the form of the plate, although the diagonal inscriptions in the corners take some account of the central well.

The brilliantly skillful lettering of Mary White, the word "Ovid" effectively punctuating the circle of the rim.

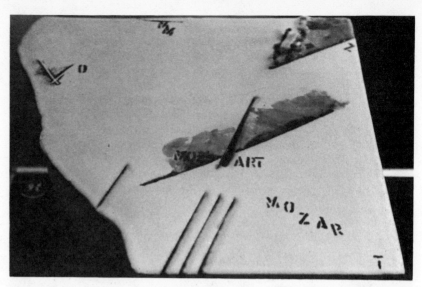

Two examples of the cryptic approach to lettering on much modern ceramics: the first on the lid of a box form by Gordon Baldwin, "ART and MOZART" giving a punning effect; and an amusing trompe l'oeil piece using sketches and lettering by Jan Oosterman.

has modern calligraphy. From quite another school comes a Lombardic pot (*ca.* fourteenth century) with what looks like printer's type stamped haphazardly over its surface, foreshadowing some modern approaches which treat letters as purely decorative items as distinct from literate symbols.

Majolica and, later, faience and Delft were frequently lettered, most often with the name of the contents—drugs and simples—or with the title of a portrait. This is always adequate and attractive without often being striking. Somewhat cruder but still lively are the slip-trailed or scratched names, dates, and short mottos (see **Inscrip-**

tions for some entertaining examples) which appear on seventeenth- to nineteenth-century peasant and country wares from Eastern Europe to America. Some London Metropolitan slipware is described by Boger (1971) as "distinguished by pious inscriptions and poor lettering." Today Cardew and many others have produced the typical red and honey-colored slipware with names and other lettering inscribed. Script has, however, been generally considered alien to the free-textured work of the last thirty years, though scraps and fragments of writing and newspaper collages appear on some Pop and other modern pottery styles. Among the few who use lettering, the brilliant and skillful work of Mary White stands out.

Lift-off Slip

A technique described by Shafer by which wet slip is absorbed into cut stamps of wood, plaster, biscuit, or fine-grain artificial sponge (the last can be cut with a hot metal point). The work is done with a dry stamp on wet slip, the design being made by lightly pressing the stamp onto the slip, thereby partially absorbing it. The result is a slightly fuzzy but distinct image of the stamp.

Lithography

A method of reproducing images by printing from a stone surface, drawn with either a greasy crayon or ink. In chromolithography a number of stones are used, one for each color, and special registration equipment is needed. The principle is the mutual repulsion of oil and water. A roller bearing greasy color is passed over a stone on which a design has been drawn in an oily medium and on which the blank areas have been dampened with water. A print is then taken by pressing paper down onto the stone. Metal plates are replacing stone ones today, and the process has been adapted to photography. See **Photoceramic processes.**

A commercial plate (Susie Cooper Ltd.) on which the lithographed design is sandwiched between two layers of glaze.

Paul Astbury "incorporates litho images with pre-fired reduction glazes. The lithos are underfired to give the correct quality at 750° C. This gives a broken, dry texture." These appear to be photolithos. The "correct quality," of course, refers to his particular and personal use of the medium. Lithography in general is of limited and specialized value to the potter. Ceramic **transfers** can be made by printing in lithographic oil, dusting with pottery color, and applying to ware coated with a tacky varnish. The paper is soaked away with water. Known as **decals** in the United States, they are now generally replaced with slide-off transfers.

Lithophane

The light transmitted through a translucent body is controlled by the thickness of the material. By varying the depth of carving into the wall of a pot, bowl, or tile, designs can be made to appear in shades of gray when the article is held up to the light. The lithophane, a porcelain tile or bowl, had a design cast intaglio to reveal all-too-realistic scenes and images and portraits—illuminated engravings, in fact. They were technically brilliant but usually aesthetically unimportant. The idea originated at Meissen in 1825 and had a long vogue in England and Europe.

Today, potters use the same technique in a more abstract and integrated way, or so we like to think. Victor Margrie and others cut the walls of their pots to thinner sections or even pierce them. Alan Whittaker casts and sandblasts patterns to a wafer thinness over whole areas of tall bowls. Some of the most remarkable pieces with the same general effect are those of Rudolf Staffel, where clay is lapped and folded to build up his aptly named "Light Gatherers." The technique can also be very effective for light shades, and in the nineteenth century these were actually made for gas lights.

Lizardskin Glaze

See **Snakeskin glaze.**

Luster

The deposition of metallic films onto glazes using the precious metals gold, silver, and platinum, as well as tin, bismuth, and copper, is fairly easy to comprehend in theory but difficult to carry out successfully.

The first luster dishes appeared in Mesopotamia in the ninth century and quickly assumed a variety of colors. Some of the earliest pieces treated the lusters as colors, and polychrome dishes were made, a feat which is still very difficult. The technique spread across the Islamic world and was especially successful under the Fatimid dynasty in the tenth to twelfth centuries. Green, brown, and yellow hues, tawny red, even a deep olive, and eventually a pure red-gold (from copper, not gold)—the last reaching its peak at the limit of the Arab Empire, in eastern Spain—were all produced with the typical metallic, lustrous surface. Lusters were generally on a cream-colored ground (tin-glaze) and occasionally on blue glazes. For some reason, lusters were abandoned in their probable birthplace of Persia in the fourteenth century and reintroduced only in the late seventeenth century. In Egypt and other centers the production was continued. Iridescence appears on many lusters, and some may have been developed with this quality in mind. From a treatise by Nasir-i-Khuaran *ca.* 1050 (quoted in Cooper, 1972) is the passage: "They make colors . . . like those of the stuff called bugalimun [a type of shot silk]. The colors change according to the way in which the vessel is held."

From the Islamic/Christian melange that was fourteenth-century Iberia arose what Leach has called "the best brushwork in Europe," the Hispano-Moresque ware with its fruitful combination of Arab, heraldic, and Gothic styles producing one of the pinnacles

Victorian lithophanes were often in the form of tiles, but this lampshade (probably made for gaslight) shows the effect of light shining through a translucent body of varying thicknesses. Great skill and effort have gone into this curious object, which dates from the beginning of the twentieth century.

of the potter's achievement. With the complete rout of the Moors in the fifteenth and sixteenth centuries the work slackened, lost some of its vigor and quality, and took on a more garish, coppery luster with less variety. By then it had spread to Italy, where some centers took to luster with enthusiasm. At Gubbio (*ca.* 1498–1540) a bright luster ware was made by Georgio Andresli, sometimes signing as Maestro Georgio. Deruta produced a ruby luster and a yellow color combined with blue and ocher painting: "Some of the world's most beautiful majolica [and] luster." Although surviving pieces from this period appear expert and assured, there are sixteenth-century documents that suggest that a firing may produce only about 10 percent of real successes. Iridescence is a feature of some Italian work. Later European lusters never reached the same high levels as the Spanish or Italian. They were used sparingly on Meissen porcelain. They did not appear on English ware until the nineteenth century, when, as well as a yellow-gold and not very durable ruby colors, luster over purple of Cassius gave a shot-silk effect. "Burgos luster" is quoted in Dodd as a red luster used on porcelain made by diluting a gold luster with bismuth and tin, both of which promote iridescence. "Cantharides" was a yellow luster from silver, so called because it had the surface appearance of beetles' wings. Mixed tints of gold/tin purple lusters were called "Moonlight" by the Wedgwood factory. Oil sprayed through a tube, the end of which was covered with muslin, gave a mottled effect, a technique similar to that used today by Geoffrey Swindell. Manganese was used with platinum for a "polished steel" surface. Luster was sometimes dusted onto a tacky oil medium transferred from copper plates. Similar effects could be gotten today using lino cuts. The deposited metals of gold and silver (the latter color usually from platinum) were, of course, widely used, covering entire pots in the nineteenth century. Bismuth was used on some Beleek and Worcester ware to give a mother-of-pearl effect, and similar pieces came from Paris. In the later nineteenth century a group of potters headed by William De Morgan tried to revive the Persian styles and materials with some success and produced attractive pottery and a large number of tiles. The painting was expert but, inevitably, of its own time. Leach is less kind: "The attempted revival of lustre painting under the Pre-Raphaelite influence led, as one might expect, to nothing fresh or vital . . . in decoration." The Far East appears to have ignored the technique, probably because it is associated with soft earthenware. Mary Perry, working in Detroit in the nineteenth century, produced "cloudy, rich, in-glaze lusters" (Clark and Hughto). Pilkinton produced a highly controlled luster from 1880 onward, and Wedgwood issued a "Fairyland" series in the 1950s.

From Rayy, Persia, ca. 1200. Finely drawn camels in luster.

Today there is a limited but quite intense interest, and some potters have devoted a large part of their effort to it. A specialist is Caiger-Smith, and his book *Tin-Glaze Pottery* is an exciting story of discovery and struggle by potters over the last ten centuries. He treats his own work in a fairly traditional way. In other hands the technique is broadened and byways are explored. Sutton Taylor has evolved some startling effects with brilliant multicolored lusters and various resist methods. Raku has given a new slant, while copper and manganese can be used on stonewares at high temperatures without resorting to reducing atmospheres (see 5 below).

Lusters may be incorporated to become an aspect of the glaze itself, or they can be applied to the surface of an already fired glaze and developed at a lower temperature. There appear to be as many ways of compounding lusters as there are potters doing it. Frank Hamer helps to sort out the main types in the *Potter's Dictionary*. The first three are on-glaze or painting pigments. The fourth deals briefly with in-glaze effects; and 5 is painted onto the raw biscuit.

1) The precious metals are dissolved in acid and made up with a medium for painting. The medium burns out in firing, reducing the chloride back to a film of metal (see **Bright gold, Burnish gold,** and **Silver**).

A large luster and blue plate from Valencia ca. 1430 with strong influences of Near Eastern design combined with Gothic lettering. At once grand and amusing in concept.

Innocent, rather haphazard luster painting on nineteenth-century bone china.

2) Copper oxide, painted onto the raw glaze, can be fired in reduction to the melting point of the glaze and then given a second, lower temperature reduction. See also **Copper luster.**

3) Copper may be mixed with clay that has previously been calcined to at least 200° C./390° F. above the luster temperature. Ocher is often quoted as a suitable material. The luster is produced in reduction during cooling, and the coating of clay is washed off when cold. An added silver nitrate will help if a more golden color is required. This system is called by Hamer "transmutation luster." Bismuth nitrate dissolved in resin and oil will fire to a mother-of-pearl surface (disparaged as "slimy" by some commentators). The usual firing temperature is around 700° C./1,290° F.

4) Tin or copper in-glaze lusters. The iridescent tin effect has become familiar on raku reductions. 2–8 percent of copper in a glaze may be used to give a reduced layer of luster on the surface of the glaze. Reduction is during cooling and must be in fairly intense bursts. The glaze is normally a soft one, maturing at below 1,000° C./1,830° F.

5) A subdued bronze color can be obtained from copper at almost any pottery temperature up to 1,270° C./2,300° F. in oxidation. It is used in combination with manganese (some assert that manganese alone will do it) and is painted onto the biscuit. See **Copper/manganese gold.**

This theoretical background, however, masks a multitude of problems. For example, in 5 the reaction at 1,200° C./2,190° F. is often wrinkled and somewhat immature in appearance; at some 50° higher it is smooth—but it runs like water. After a number of fairly calamitous kilns, a double firing at about 1,215° C./2,220° F. proved the best solution. Another unexpected effect arose out of the difficulty of laying the "luster" on. A pot was sprayed using copper carbonate because the black oxide clogged the jet. Result—unrelieved black! Simply replacing the oxide with the carbonate totally inhibited the effect. According to the caption on one of Val Barry's porcelain bowls in Lane (1980), a crinkled gold can result from the use of a heavy application of manganese alone. Lucie Rie uses the same bronze-gold on her bowls strikingly combined with blue and black, or even pink.

Commercially prepared lusters are generally of type 1 and, while fairly reliable, they lack subtlety. They are available in many colors including black, which may be covered with a mother-of-pearl luster for special effects. Caiger-Smith use types 2 and 3 and has spent years in experiment, building up his experience, as he says, from nowhere. His success rate from four kilns a year was 15–80 percent. In an exhaustive series of experiments Clive Fiddis, in articles in *Ceramic Review 61* and *62* called "The Lure of Luster," quotes a very wide range of recipes. Discussing type 2 he suggests that lead in the glaze inhibits luster and that a high-alkali recipe is preferable. The pigment, applied to the raw glaze, is subjected to fifteen minutes or so of reduction during cooling at around 725° C./1,000° F. Too heavy a reduction will blacken, and partial reduction can give a turquoise center and lustered edges to a brushstroke. A tendency to the "bleeding" of copper red from the edges is common, and a number of Caiger-Smith's pieces show this effect. The pigment can vary from 100 percent copper to 10 percent copper/90 percent bismuth. He suggests using the carbonate of copper. High-bismuth mixtures give a pale gold. He found no totally successful method for the oxide and clay type.

Other advice for special or particular applications include: shiny glazes accept lusters better than matt ones; salts for use in luster include silver sulphide, silver carbonate, and cupric sulphate, a suitable base for which is 85 percent alkaline frit, 10 percent china clay, and 5 percent whiting; Alan Barrett-Danes in Lane (1980) lists a number of variations on silver and copper mixtures for subtly different colors. A silver luster can be derived from silver compounds but is liable to tarnish so platinum is usually used. Silver will generally give a yellowish finish, and fine silver lusters are found on

The powerful but integrated effect of an amber luster on a grayish glaze by Alan Caiger-Smith.

early Islamic ware. Piepenburg lists two parts silver nitrate to one of tin oxide for a gold color in raku. For a "copper penny" color the following is suggested: eight ocher, two black copper oxide, and one cobalt oxide. Raku lusters may be impermanent.

Conrad divides luster types into "hard" or "Persian" and "Arabian," the latter composed of metal salts, ocher, and a binder, the former fired to glaze temperature and reduced during cooling through 950–550° C. Salts of copper, chrome, silver, uranium, and manganese may be used for hard luster, which is more durable and becomes an integral part of the glaze, which is normally a glossy one and which may mature at cone 02 or higher. The thickness of application is important: too thick may flake, too thin may disappear. As with all luster work, surfaces must be kept absolutely clean. A wipe over a glazed surface with whiting can help. Brushes should be washed in benzol. Tim Mather, in *Ceramic Review 33,* discusses a mother-of-pearl luster on salt-glaze obtained by adding a few teaspoonfuls of stannous chloride into the kiln chamber as the glow fades on cooling. A very interesting variation (which has historical roots) is that by Geoffrey Swindell, who sprays his brushed-on lusters with detergent or paraffin (kerosene) to break the surface tension and cause a honeycomb-like texture. Further applications can blend this into a mysterious and decorative surface. Subtle and noble lustrous surfaces are obtained by Joanna Constantinidis, who fires in a sealed saggar containing mustard seed, salt, and other materials for "flashed" effects. The pots are previously sprayed with copper or iron oxides. A crackled glaze can be wiped over gold luster and cleaned off with thinners. The crackle will generally fire to a pinkish line. Oldrich Asenbryl prints blocks of luster by silkscreen onto a translucent glaze. Robin Welch enhances the richness of gold by painting it over a glaze saturated with black copper.

The modern users of lusters are thus exploring many byways, which are by no means exhausted. An occasional meditation on the sublime work of the fourteenth-century Spanish potters will, however, help to retain a perspective.

Magnetic Iron, Magnetite

A heavy black ore which will respond to a magnet. By reason of its great hardness the ground black magnetic oxide (Fe_3O_4) is coarse in grain compared with other iron oxides and can therefore produce speckle in glazes, bodies, and colors, more particularly in reduction. An alternative name used by some suppliers is iron spangles. A synthetic version is **blacksmith's scale.** Leach refers to Hamada's use of a magnetic iron pigment from a crushed local rock. Brushstrokes will dry to a brown sandy texture, which is fluxed by the glaze to produce a broken color of more interest than the purified oxide.

Majolica, Maiolica

When the technique of painted and lustered tin-glaze spread from Spain to Italy it became known as maiolica (pronounced *majolica* is identical), reputedly derived from the stop-over island of Majorca. More recently, historians have suggested a source of the name in Spain itself. With a similar transference of source-name maiolica from Faenza became "faience" in France, and tin-glaze from Holland "Delftware" in England. Early English tin-glaze ware of around 1570, however, was known as English majolica. See also **Malling ware.** American Delftware was made as early as 1685, great quantities of which are said to have been shipped to Barbados and Jamaica, though none appears to have survived. See also **Italian maiolica** and **Tin-glaze** for further general discussion.

Malling Ware

The earliest English tin-glazed ware, mid-sixteenth century. Globular jugs or beakers were mottled, splashed, or flecked with manganese, a pigment giving an almost turquoise blue, blue with orange flecks, and other colors. It was a strange beginning for English majolica, possibly in imitation of the popular "tiger ware," a Rhenish salt-glaze.

Manganese

The dioxide of manganese can be used at all firing temperatures as a stain or pigment, but it is more frequently found on lower-fired wares. It alters during heating, but there is some confusion as to its precise action in a glaze. It can act as an active flux at temperatures above 1,080° C. (Orton cone 3) but glazes have been used that contain up to 25 percent of manganese and that do not run or bubble at 1,260° C. (Orton cone 9). The bubbling or blistering of earthenware glazes around 1,080° C. can be due to an alteration of the manganese oxide. Firings should, therefore, be below or fairly well above this figure. Brian Newman adds manganese to his clay "to give sparkle."

Manganese normally produces a warm brown, purple-browns, or near black. It is essentially an oxidizing color. As well as staining bodies, slips, and glazes, it can be used without a glaze to give a rather ashy dark gray or black. Some potters assert that a coppery bronze is possible with manganese alone used thickly on high-fired unglazed bodies, but in my experience an addition of copper oxide is necessary to achieve this. The make-up of the body may be critical. See **Copper/manganese gold.**

Marbled Ware

The imitation of marble or agate by means of colored bodies is dealt with under **Agate ware.** This article is limited to the marbling of colors on the surface of a dish or pot by means of slips or glazes. The practice has been widespread for many centuries, and peasant communities in Europe and further east have produced marbled pieces in profusion since the seventeenth century. Earlier, Song (Sung) Chinese pots occasionally used marbled slip as part of their decoration. Nearer our own time, Dwight of Fulham Pottery, London, decorated stoneware beakers with marbled bands in white, brown, and gray. Seventeenth- and eighteenth-century Staffordshire produced many marbled pieces. Nineteenth-century industrial wares were sometimes marbled, for example, Caillote, a marbled ground from Sèvres. The traditional Sussex Pig money-box was dipped in marbled slip. The term *Welsh ware* was used for eighteenth-century English combed slipware, which also included "cloudy slip," which was presumably marbling.

The running and intermixing of glaze colors was the principal technique of T'ang potters; it is less common on Islamic pottery and was ignored during the long ascendancy of majolica. Whieldon and others used intermixed glazes on modeling, and Wedgwood developed a form of glaze marbling, which Hughes calls "slip glaze," in 1770. Opaque white glaze was marbled with oxides in Sweden (Marieburg). A type using mixed tones of manganese on Staffordshire work was called "tortoiseshell," a term also applied to other mixed-color slip or glaze decoration.

There are two basic slip-marbling techniques. First, slips can be poured, trailed, or spooned in dots or larger areas onto the clay or onto a wet slip-covered surface, normally the latter, and the typical veining achieved by stirring the liquid slips around with a feather or comb (hence the alternative name "combing" for this type of decoration), or by sharply twisting the dish or plate. Any surplus can be run off the edge. It is fatally easy to overdo the twisting, giving an indecisive and muddy pattern. The colors tend to become less defined after the glaze firing due to thin overlays showing the color beneath. A variation on bowls is to trail from the inside edge onto a wet slip coating, allow the blobs to run down to the center, and then give a sharp tilt or twist. "One must use one's judgement as to whether the effect obtained has aesthetic merit or merely exhibits dexterity" (Leach). Second, marbling can be produced in slip itself by spooning or trailing different colors into a bowl of slip and giving them a minimum of veining with a stick or brush. This is similar to the way inks are used for paper marbling. The piece is then dipped into the slips and gently extracted. The advantage is that pots and models can be decorated. The disadvantages are obvious:

A rare example of marbling on a Sung T'zu Chou bottle, not blending very happily with the precise brushwork above it. Perhaps fishes would have been a more apt motif!

An English bowl ca. 1800, marbled and banded outside. It is difficult to see how it was done; possibly dipped into marbled slip, as in the next illustration, with the rim and foot cleaned up afterwards.

Slip-marbling the back of a piggy-bank money box by dipping into a dark slip into which blobs of a lighter color have been introduced with a spoon.

141

A sharply delineated geometric dish by Marian Gaunce, which she calls "marquetry."

Blocks of various clays assembled to form a strong pattern. By Ewen Henderson. It represents the antithesis of the filigree work of Feibleman and others and indicates the great range possible with "marquetry" and other neriage techniques.

slips rapidly become intermixed and are more or less valueless afterwards. The system is most economical if a number of pieces are on hand to dip in a single session.

A splendid marbled plate by Anita Satenau Scott, showing just how attractive and strong the technique can be, appeared in *Ceramic Review 63*. Multicolored marbled techniques are known collectively in Japan as "nerikomi." See **Neriage.**

Mark

Potters' marks or stamps are rare on historical pottery. A few Greek and Roman pots bear the names of potter or decorator, and the bolder "Toft" and other names on seventeenth-century slipware may have been potters' signatures. Marks on Chinese wares such as the t'ang (hall) marks (not to be confused with the T'ang dynasty) and others are of uncertain significance. Individual potters rarely marked their work, a tradition continued in Japan by Hamada—to the eternal confusion of collectors. Japanese marks in general are, however, "numerous and misleading" (Boger), and signatures are no more to be taken at their face value than are Chinese reign marks. Authentic marks are confused by differences in family and "art" names and by son-pupil continuations of a name. There are also patron and place names. Western factories, of course, stamped their wares, often including numbers and codes indicating clay body type, decorator, and other information. These **backstamps** may be accompanied by or incorporated into charming engraved fanciful scenes. See also **Seal** and **Stamping.**

Marquetry

A term sometimes applied to the **agate wares** of the **neriage** type. See discussions under these headings.

Masking Tape

This can be a useful resist material, usually for enamel color on a fired glaze, but it could also be used on biscuit. It gives a crisp and sharply defined line, typically in straight stripes. Martin Smith utilizes masking tape dramatically on raku and polished earthenware. See also **Terra sigillata.**

Masking tape used as a resist material on a ceramic construction.

The typical clean-cut lines of a masking tape design on an equally geometric form by Martin Smith. The starkness of the effect is offset by the staining and crazing from reduction raku firing.

The decoration on these "Ceramic Sculptures" by Roy Lichtenstein were at first applied as decals but later sprayed on through perforated masking tape, opening up a new way of using this resist material.

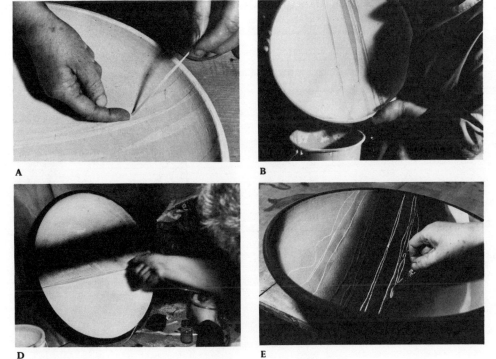

Sheila Fournier decorating a large landscape dish using masking tape. A. Tape, cut to shape, is adhered to a biscuit bowl, which is then glazed. B. It will be seen that the glaze has flowed from the tape, which has a nonabsorbent surface. C. The tape is removed, leaving a biscuit line. D. Spraying with various pigments. E. Sgraffito lines suggesting landscape are cut through the color (but not the glaze).

The completed plate. The resisted areas have taken up the sprayed color to produce a dark tone while paler colors result on the glazed areas. This is simply one use for masking tape. There are many others.

Meander

A running design of repeated spirals, squares, or other shapes, consisting of a continuous line weaving in and out.

Melted Glass

See **Glass.**

Merryman Plates

See **Inscriptions.**

Mesh Pattern, Lace

See also **Beaten patterns, Cloth patterns, Impressed decoration,** and **Lace.**
An open-weave mesh or net can be laid onto a clay surface and very soft clay smeared over it. A raised negative pattern will result when the material is peeled away. Alternatively, net, gauze, or lace soaked in slip and applied or draped as required has been used in the industry. The cloth fires away, leaving a fragile pottery (often porcelain) substitute. The method can be used in less explicit ways to form textures on pottery, but one can anticipate aesthetic and practical problems.

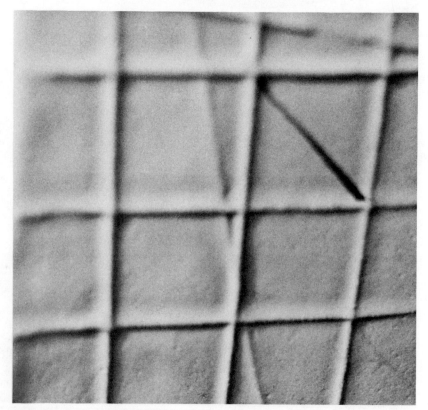

Detail of a ceramic piece by Gordon Baldwin. The surface appears to be cast from a mesh-impressed surface.

Metals, Metallic Finish

For details of metallic finishes on pottery see also **Copper/manganese gold, Gold, Luster, Silver.** Metals themselves can also play a part in surface decoration. Iron filings of various grades can be beaten in, and so can small copper turnings, which will go black and spread out in a stoneware fire. Under some glazes they will show a

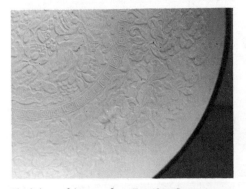

The dark rim of this magnificent Ting (Song Dynasty) ware dish is of fine sheet copper that has been beaten onto the unglazed surface necessitated by the practice of firing the porcelain upside down.

Copper fragments (the larger ashy-black areas) and iron filings were beaten into a grogged clay to build up a surface. The white shape is poured refractory glaze. From a stoneware "pebble" form by the author.

Wire and metal set into a strange dish-like form by Almuth Hargreaves.

A

B

C
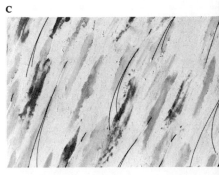

D

E

F

Variations on the use of fired-in Kanthal wire by Irene Vonck. A. The potter inserting wire into the leather-hard clay. B. Simple spikes of wire protruding vertically from an "envelope" form. C. Doubled-over wire. D. Wires that have been coated in black slip. E. Feathers slotted over the wires, combined with painted feather-forms on the surface. F. Wire used to hold "shells" of clay on the surface.

Steel insets in a hand-built form by Gordon Baldwin. These have a more integrated appearance than many attempts at combining clay and metal. See also **Silver**.

green halo. Other metals can be used—even nails are suggested by Riegger—but results must be tested by experiment. Brass filings are interesting as they will dissociate in an oxidizing fire into zinc (a flux) and copper, giving a speckled effect, again occasionally with a green halo. In *Ceramic Review 19* we read of aluminum being used by F. Borza of Hungary, burnt into porcelain to produce a dark lacy effect. A silvery metallic surface is mentioned by Leach, using 25 percent of glaze mixed with magnetic iron for brushwork on raw glaze and fired in reduction. A remarkable suggestion in Storr-Britz is to lay thin plates of copper under a glaze firing at around 1,050° C. (cone 04). The practical difficulties must be considerable!

The use of unfired metal strips and other shapes to inlay ceramics is becoming more widely practiced. In historical times silver and other metals have been used as mounts on German and Chinese pieces but rarely actually inlaid, since the work was not done by the potter. Today silver, steel, aluminum, and other metals are used in various ways. Gordon Baldwin and Martin Smith use strips of metal, Smith sometimes setting ceramic forms into a metallic outer skin. Debbie Pointon goes further and inlays intricate metal forms into soft-fired, smoked porcelain bodies. A tracing is taken of the carved-out design, and this is reproduced in silver, carefully filed to fit, and glued in.

Mica

This is a group rather than an individual mineral and is associated with clays and spars. It is separated from china clay by levigation. Its massive form is more or less transparent and will cleave like slate. It is naturally present in some early pottery; in Neolithic unglazed cooking pots from China, for instance, it glistens in the body, and it forms a lustrous sheen on vessels of the Roman period, possibly in imitation of metal. It can be used on the surface of earthenware; above 1,050° C. (cone 06) it will begin to decompose. According to Hughes, however, Nottingham salt-glaze made by Morley

Fragments of mica are sometimes found in ancient pots. The one illustrated is, in fact, a copy (by Sheila Fournier) of a prehistoric Chinese vessel, the glistening specks of mica having been beaten into the surface.

was rendered smooth-surfaced by coating it with a mica- and iron-bearing clay from East Morr, Derbyshire, giving it glistening specks. Raku and sawdust pots can make use of mica. Mica fragments can be scraped from some composition roofing tiles. Ground mica (a difficult process) is used to produce mullite in clays. See Fournier (1977) for chemical details.

Minai

This was one of the earliest Persian styles (*ca.* A.D. 1200) to use enamels on tin-glaze. The body was usually a thin and brittle "frit-paste," possibly in imitation of porcelain. Hobson does not mention the term *minai* but calls the pieces "Rhages enamels" from the main center of production. The colors were composed of pigment oxides in finely powdered glass. Strong hues were obtained, and gold leaf was often added. Many designs were of horsemen or figures, resembling the famous miniatures of the time. The best minai is on a nearly white ground; later colored grounds, pierced walls, and other modifications heralded the decline of the technique. As a style it repays study by the modern potter for its brilliance of color, for the placing of disparate elements in a

design, and for its special spirit, "aristocratic, romantic, elusive, in which the treasures of the rugged world were gathered into the small compass of an enchanted space" (Caiger-Smith).

Mirror Black

A fine black porcelain glaze of the K'ang Hsi period, also called Wu Chin or "black gold." It was reportedly derived from a "cobaltiferous ore" mixed with "iron of coffee brown" (Boger, 1957). The surface has brown and bluish reflections. A shiny black, 1,260° C. (cone 8) glaze has been obtained using iron alone in a laurel ash recipe. Manganese can also be used alone in shiny black earthenware glazes. In stoneware glazes up to 22 percent can be used, but test with care.

Mishima

Also called "zogan": a Japanese term for a style of decoration involving stamped and inlaid starry flowers, circles, and semicircles, originally used on Koryu- and Yi-period Korean stonewares and porcelains. The general class of wares is known as "pun ch'ong." It was much imitated in Japan, where the name "mishima" was applied,

This technically advanced Minai dish (Persia, thirteenth century) combines underglaze colors, enamels, and gold leaf. The gold leaf has remained remarkably bright and intact and the whole still shines with its original brilliance.

A delicately inlaid bottle from the sophisticated Koryu Dynasty of Korea. Black and white clays have been inlaid, and the starry flowers are very typical. A celadon glaze over.

Black and red burnished slips with a pattern cut through to a lighter body. Fired at about 800°C. By Siddig El'Nigoumi.

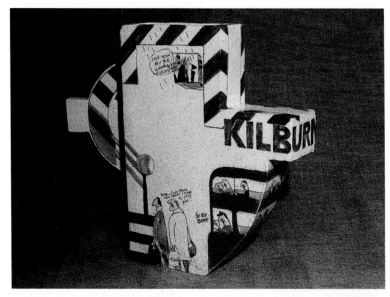

Two examples of the use of ceramic crayon or pencil with underglaze colors by Ruth Franklin and Alison Britten.

An industrial crystalline glaze from Doultons of Staffordshire in the early twentieth century. The glaze contained zinc and is reputed to have been fired to 1,450°C.

Free and lively use of red enamel on a raku pot by Wally Keeler.

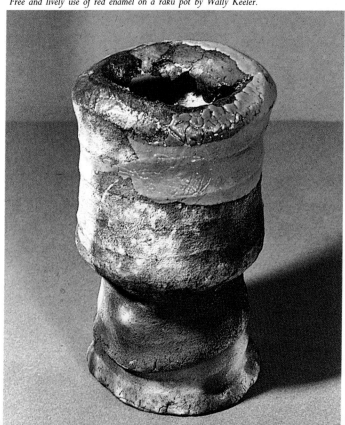

A single glaze poured on in swags of varying thickness gives a terra cotta color, the body burning a very thin layer black and white to turquoise blue, on a hand-built bowl by Sheila Fournier.

A modern use of gold enamel on a constructed piece by Tony Hepburn.

A delicate flush of color on an unglazed surface: a happy incidental flashing characteristic of wood firing. By Anita Roddis.

A delicate and evocative landscape by David Lloyd Jones, using sprayed color and stencils.

A luster pot by Alan Caiger-Smith showing the right-hand half as it came from the kiln and the left after cleaning and polishing.

Magnificent multicolored lusters by Sutton Taylor.

A mocha "landscape" by Rupert Andrews (see **Landscape***).*

Silkscreen printing by Glenys Barton achieving a brilliant flat color with enamel.

A late-seventeenth-century English majolica plate with a liberal use of sponging to represent foliage.

Underglaze painting by Alison Britten with chrome colors in brushed-on strokes of green and brown contrasted with finer lines.

An easel painter's approach to ceramic decoration in lively brushwork that differs in style from the calligraphic approach of many purely pottery decorators. One of a set based on Virginia Woolf's novel Orlando. *By Vannessa Bell and Duncan Grant.*

Detail of a coarser Korean inlaid bowl but with the same stars, although the trefoil motifs are unusual. Some of the work may have been stamped, but the wavy line is likely to be freehand.

A bowl inlaid in the Korean style but with unmistakable Japanese overtones in its form and handling. By Shoji Hamada when working at St. Ives, Cornwall, in the early 1920s.

possibly from Mishima Almanacks, which had radial characters. There was also a mesh or hatched pattern known as "koyomi-de."

Some mishima has a carefully cleaned surface giving sharp outlines to the stars; other examples are "swimming in a ground streaked and clouded in white or grey" (Honey). The latter sometimes incorporated sgraffito on the lower part of the pot. Some of the earlier Silla funerary bowls were decorated with a single stamped motif (yoraku), which is roughly inlaid, the ridges around the stamp turning brown in the firing. According to Tomimoto the profusion of mishima in Korea in the Koryu period (in the tenth to thirteenth centuries) was due to the Emperor's ban on blue and white porcelain for anyone not of noble rank. There is a variant on the slip-inlay where the pattern is filled with a gray glaze. See also **Inlay.**

Mocha

If a coloring oxide is mixed with certain weak acids and a drop is applied to wet slip, it will travel by local deflocculation to form "dendritic" (tree or mosslike) patterns that fill with pigment and become permanent. The name has probably arisen from a resemblance to "mocha stone," an Arabian quartz.

Its use was common in Europe and North America around 1800 but declined through the nineteenth century; its commercial use came to a virtual end about 1910, although it was still used by T. G. Greenwood at Church Gresley, Derbyshire, up to

Nineteenth-century English mocha decorated beaker, trimmed and banded top and bottom, as was usual for the day.

the 1930s. It was also known as seaweed, fern, or moss pottery. One of the earliest dated pieces is 1799. Industrial mocha creamware was usually decorated in a wide band with colored boundary lines above and below. The usual color was iron or manganese brown, but blue, green, and black occur. The ground color also varied: brown, green, cream, or a terra-cotta orange.

Today a few potters experiment with the technique, including Rupert Andrews, who expands on his methods in the article "Mocha Magic" in *Ceramic Review 69*. He achieves mysterious "landscapes with trees" and utilizes the happy accident that a bluish color appears where the slip has been disturbed by the "mocha tea" to suggest water and lakes. Robin Hopper (illustration in Cooper, 1972) flows irregular bands of white slip onto his basalt bottles and induces mocha diffusions in a purely decorative way. The mechanical ease with which the patterns can be made to grow is, of course, a danger in itself, and Leach's strictures quoted under **Marbled ware** apply.

The deflocculating agent or "tea" is most commonly brewed from tobacco. Andrews suggests ½ ounce (15 grams) black rolling tobacco in a pint of water to which is added a teaspoonful of red iron oxide. Harry Horlock Stringer offers one cigarette mashed in boiling water. The pigment must be finely ground and, together with the tea, passed through a 120- or (better still) 200 mesh sieve before each use. Many other materials have been used over the two centuries of mocha: hops, tansy, urine, turpentine—an odiferous mixture! Citric acid from orange or lemon is reputed to assist the spread of the pattern, while Storr-Britz recommends apple cider vinegar. For color, as well as oxides, "dry printer's ink" has been used and underglaze black is also recommended. Whatever the mixture, it is applied with a large brush or syringe as soon as the base slip has been poured or dipped. The pattern travels partly by gravity, and experiment, as to the most useful angle for the piece, is necessary. Rupert Andrews applies a rapid stroke around the base of a pot (held upside-down) and then a second stroke—"It is during these final strokes that the magic of mocha occurs—complete landscapes suddenly appear."

Modeling on Surfaces

See **Applied decoration, Barbotine, Boss, Carved molds, Cordon, Embossing, Frilled cordon, Molded relief, Poppyhead pots, Rope decoration, Rusticated slip, Seal, Sprigging, Strip decoration,** and **Studs.**

Moko Pottery

A form of splashed-on mottled slip using a flexible brush made from the long hairs of a donkey's tail (Hughes).

Molded Relief

Surface decoration obtained from molds carved intaglio is probably as old as molds themselves, but the first great phase of molded pattern developed in the Roman period from 200 B.C. onward, probably in imitation of silverwork. The red-gloss ware known as Arretine is finely and skillfully cut, the details unobscured by glaze. Figures, swags, and decorated bands encircle the outer surfaces of cups, bowls, and pots. The biscuit molds have been found. An interesting aspect of Roman molded ware is that the decoration is on the lower section of the piece, contrary to the normal position on the shoulder. This arose from the exigencies of the technique. The relief would be damaged or destroyed unless taken from a slightly flaring shape. The top portion of the piece would have been thrown onto the molded section and was therefore plain, apart from

A Roman mold for Samian ware with the decoration almost certainly impressed. See **Poinçon**.

horizontal ribbing. Islamic and other potters overcame the problem by throwing the lower half and luting on a cast shoulder. Finds at Samarra on the Tigris, a caliph's palace that was built about 838 A.D., show quite delicately molded pottery covered with yellow or green glazes or painted with lusters. Tenth- and eleventh-century Persian bowl molds have been found and the later Seljuk pieces from the thirteenth and fourteenth centuries were molded in relief on faceted shapes. The most famous of Chinese molded wares were the ivory-white Ting plates of the Sung Dynasty. Hill jars and other pieces had been molded with reliefs in the Han period and probably earlier. Glazes softened and rounded the edges of relief decoration, although the Ancient Egyptian frit pastes (see also **Egyptian paste**) maintained a certain crispness. German salt-glaze stonewares also made much use of cast relief, the thin, hard glaze maintaining detail. Similarly the white salt-glazed tableware of the mid-eighteenth century was a perfect material for molded relief decoration, marvelously sharp and defined in the fine-grain material. Delicate jelly molds were produced, jelly (Jello) then being a much more upper-class delicacy. Wedgwood creamware and similar sophisticated clay bodies were equally suitable for sharp modeling. Octagonal Pennsylvania molded dishes are found. Cast relief appeared on millions of Victorian jugs of every type, from the charming to the truly horrific.

As with other types of molded pottery the primary purpose has been to produce shapes that cannot be thrown and to reproduce pieces in quantity. In this way the considerable labor of cutting the original design can be redeemed. Neither of these considerations is very relevant to the studio potter. The sparingly cut eighteenth-century Staffordshire plate molds, which gave a raised outline subsequently to be filled with slips, have been imitated by a few potters. The technique was a debasement of slip-trailing but has its own curious charm. An individual style, which is not truly cast relief but exhibits a three-dimensional patterned surface, is that of Mary Keppax, who

Two examples of the molded relief plates that replaced much slip trailing in the eighteenth century. On the clock the spaces are only sparsely filled, while on the sun-face the boundary lines are all but obliterated. Note the continuation in relief of the "jeweling" from the old slip-trailed plates, which can just be seen at the edge of the face.

A plaster cast from a rubber mat used to create a relief pattern on a clay cast. See **Translucency** *for its specific use.*

places clay trimmings onto the face of the mold before pressing the form. These appear to be immersed in the surface of her spheres and other shapes. Shafer describes using clay coils in a similar way, placing them in the mold before pressing. Cut press-molds are rarely used in Japanese artist pottery.

The appearance of molded relief is always somewhat mechanical, but variation and development will certainly occur to studio potters who use any form of molding in their work. Jewelry, harking back to Ancient Egypt, is an obvious field.

Mop

A large, floppy brush, usually without a point, used for laying on washes or large dabs of color or slip.

Mother-of-Pearl Luster

A luster, containing bismuth, developed by Bottger at Meissen. Tin oxide can also give a similar effect. See **Luster.**

Muffle Colors

A term applied to enamels fired in a muffle kiln. With the exception of lusters, these colors need firing in a protected space so that they will not be contaminated by a reducing or smoky atmosphere.

Muller

See **Glass muller.**

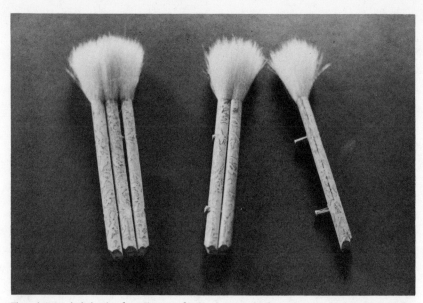

These charming little brushes from China are fitted with pegs and holes so that they can be combined into a single, wide head.

Multiple Brush

A number of brushes, set like a comb, were probably used to produce multiple wavy lines on Mazapan ware by the Toltecs of Mexico (*ca.* tenth century). A Chinese double brush, the short handles pegged into one another, is used as one wide brush, the width of the stroke variable according to the number used. A number of intriguing designs could be envisaged using various types of multiple brushes.

Mussel Gold

An old form of ceramic gold. Sugar or salt were rubbed with gold leaf, the paste traditionally stored in mussel shells.

Naples Yellow

A yellow pigment, a compound of antimony and lead oxide. See **Antimony.**

Negative Painting

A term sometimes used to indicate a resist technique, especially the decoration on some ancient American pottery.

Neriage, Neritage

A specialized form of agate ware, using layers of colored clays. The general style is known as "Nerikomi" in Japan. The pattern is usually finer and the overall design under greater control than in the general run of agate ware. It probably originated in Song China, was used on Shino ware, and became popular in Japan. The vogue for porcelain among studio potters in the West has led to neriage being widely practiced

An early example of Chinese neriage, probably Song (Sung) period. It appears to have been made from a slab that has been cut from a large circular block—mass-produced neriage?

in the late 1970s and the 1980s. The jewelry and bowls of Dorothy Feibelman and the "petaloid" pieces by Harry Stringer (illustrated in Hamer) are typical examples, although some potters work on a larger scale. Although neriage is normally made in high-fired materials, Sanders shows the making of a dish in earthenware clays.

The technique is slow and painstaking. It might be described as integrated mosaic since each element of the design is a self-contained unit that must be joined with slip to its neighbors to build the bowl, pot, or other form. One starts, as for agate, with slabs of various colored clays laid one on another and pressed together, but the layers are usually finer and thinner. The multilayered block can then be sliced through in

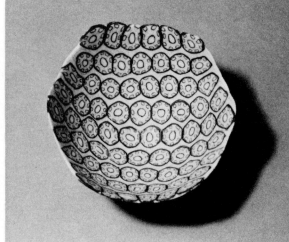

A neriage dish by Dorothy Feibleman, underwater with elephant fish. A brilliant shell-like design in its symmetrical formation. The second dish by the same potter is in a different style: a repeat "Brighton Rock" type of design the elements of which would have been sliced from a long roll of laminated clays. See also **Marquetry**.

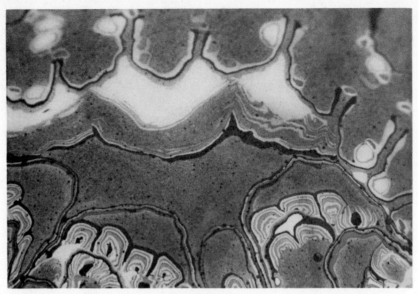

Detail of a more free-form design in neriage by Mal Magson, illustrating the variety possible in this technique and the setting of larger, plainer areas against more detailed ones.

thicknesses from a quarter of an inch or so according to the required thickness of the wall of the piece. These slabs in turn are cut into shapes or into strips to be rolled into whorls and other patterns. If the layers are left as straight lines of color, geometric patterns can be built up. The pieces are laid side by side and joined with a little slip. Frequently they are assembled in a dish or bowl mold, but flat slabs can also be used in various ways. John Dickerson, in his book, shows large-scale patterns being assembled in a big dish mold for stoneware. Feibleman lays a thin skin of white clay over the surface of her mold, over which the neriage sections are placed. When the whole form is covered and is almost dry, the outer coat is scraped off and finally smoothed over with steel wool. With dry work like this a face mask should be used. The delicate porcelain forms are fired in supporting biscuit molds. A high loss rate may be expected. Neriage can be sturdier than this as mentioned above. Clays of similar shrinkage and firing characteristics should be used and careful trials made before large-scale work is attempted.

Jewelry has been mentioned, and the miniature style is very suitable for necklaces, though they are very fragile. The technique is not a major one but exercises great fascination on those who try it.

Nickel

This is not an exciting oxide in normal conditions, giving browns, grays, and gray-greens of a muted, even muddy, nature. In reduction it can give brighter and more unexpected results—blue, yellow, purple—but is rarely used in this way. The presence of zinc will tend to increase the possibility of producing blue. Its main use, however, is as a modifier for other more strident colors, whether used as a pigment or a glaze stain. It is used as an ingredient in black glazes. It begins to be unstable at stoneware temperatures and can cause scum. It can have delicate effects on cobalt, with which it is associated in nature, being similar in atomic weight, and is probably a modifier in the Eastern blues derived from gosu. Nickel can also give pink with barium and zinc in oxidation (see recipe in Cooper, 1980) and in other zinc/barium glazes a subdued green color.

Nonceramic Surfaces

In many countries, pottery baked in bonfires or clamps may be splashed over or dunked hot into a brew of boiled plants or bark to impart a semiwatertight sheen, usually black. According to Cooper (1972), ancient American potters of the Mohica culture used a "renious paint . . . to make it water-proof." Locust beans and tree bark are used in Nigeria.

Traces of unfired pigment are found on very early Chinese pottery, while later Ming and Quing (Ch'ing) pieces were covered with black lacquer inlaid with mother-of-pearl and called, in the West, bergauté. Even stranger was the "fresco" technique of Teotihuacan. Vessels were covered with a thin film of plaster, into which a pattern was cut leaving narrow white outlines. The spaces then filled with different colored plasters and the whole smoothed flat. It proved very fragile and technically unsound. In a more plebeian way English country potters of the nineteenth century used blue wagon paint and occasionally painted in elaborate polychrome on glazed pots. A lion and unicorn on a 1737 loving cup from Halifax is an even earlier example. The patina on many old pots is the result of constant use, such as the repeated spilling of "chica," a fermented drink, over the outsides of South American cantaros (a pleasurable but not very practical technique for modern potters). Gertrude Litto tells a sad tale of Chilean potters who make a brown-to-black burnished ware. The brown, though rich and lustrous, does not attract the tourists like the black, so the potters cover it over with shoe polish!

In *Self-Sufficient Pottery* (Cunningham-Smith and Herbert) the use of wax and teak oil are suggested, applied to the pottery hot from the kiln, and polished later. The peat-fired, burnished pottery called "Jutland ware," which has continued since Neolithic

Feathers, which the pot owner can replace or alter, are slotted over fired-in Kanthal wire (see **Metals**) to decorate a simple envelope form by Irene Vonck.

A caterpillar-like construction of ceramic and wire by Gillian Lowndes.

times until today, is soaked in buttermilk "to make it non-porous" (Hamer). The usefulness or fundamental propriety of these methods is often queried. On more sophisticated wares, gold leaf has been simply glued on.

In the somewhat anarchic American scene, where immediate effect is more important than permanence, acrylics and other types of paint and distemper are used, though less frequently by top-flight potters. Kenneth Price, who "does not identify with the title 'potter,'" has used lacquer and acrylic thickly and wetly on black stoneware.

Another type of nonceramic addition is the pewter or silver lid or other covering often fitted to salt-glaze pots and beakers. Brass and other metals were used in the Near East. A more integrated finish was the copper-covered rim of Ting ware, which was fired upside-down on an unglazed rim, presumably to help keep its shape. See also at **Metals** for more details of the modern use of steel and silver in ceramics.

Notched Rim

The indented rims on pots, and especially on cooking dishes, have the practical function of compressing and consolidating the edge of the clay with the additional bonus of a satisfactory and decorative completion of simple forms. Notched rims occur occasionally on primitive ware but are most common on early English and European slipware dishes and plates of the sixteenth to the nineteenth centuries. While some appear to have been indented freehand with finger or tool, others have the regularity of a rouletted pattern (see illustration). See also **Coggle.** Some potters use the technique today, generally as a freehand pattern.

Ocher

An iron-bearing clay, "crumbly earth ores [of iron]" (Hamer). The iron is present in a semihydrated form: ferric in red ochers, ferric/ferrous in brown ochers, the yellow type bleached by lime. All are likely to turn terra cotta or brown on firing, unless the

A shard found at Lacock of a trailed but unfeathered dish with a regularly notched rim, the indentations set at a slight angle. Impressions of the rim in soft clay show the regularity of the notches and suggest the use of some kind of roulette. See **Coggle.** The illustration also shows the interesting and sometimes surprising decorative impressions that found objects can produce.

yellow color is maintained to some degree in high-lime glazes. Hakame could be practiced with ocher, and ocher washes are used in other decorative ways. Ocherous clays frequently have a high shrinkage rate, and this can pose problems. Old Seto yellow glaze is reputed to contain up to 40 percent ocher. The material was used by Leach as a dilutant for cobalt in the proportions of 98:2 cobalt, used as a pale wash on porcelain. "Red raku" is ocher-slipped before firing, the slip variegated by a charcoal technique. See **Shadow pattern.** The high shrinkage of some ochers can give crazed and broken surfaces and has been so used by some potters.

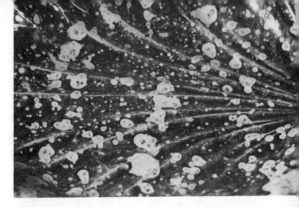

Oil Spot

Although this book is not designed to deal with glazes as such, the oil-spot effect is a unique decorative feature and warrants some discussion. It occurs on the surface of glazes with a high iron content in reduction, and occasionally a somewhat similar feature is seen on high-manganese glazes in oxidation. Oil spot can have a silvery appearance. One method of developing it is to use two layers; the first can be slip or glaze but must be overloaded with iron, even as much as 30 percent in the recipe. The top glaze is a more fluid one so that the excess iron oxide can bubble through the molten one. Frère Daniel in *Ceramic Review 69* uses a single glaze and advances the theory that ferric decomposes to magnetic iron, which is carried by bubbles to the surface to reoxidize to a red oxide against the underlying black glaze. He gives formulas averaging 0.15 CaO; 0.25 MgO; 0.6 KNaO; 0.6 Al_2O_3; 6.0 SiO_2. Variations are within certain fairly close limits. Potters interested are referred to the article mentioned. Rhodes has a third approach via slip-glaze using up to 75 percent Albany clay in the recipe with iron or ocher, spodumene, and feldspar.

Wet luster has been splashed with oil to produce a broken color on this early-nineteenth-century Staffordshire "shell" dish, while a similar technique has been used to create the mysterious markings on Geoffrey Swindell's porcelain form. On the second example, paraffin (kerosene) was splashed or dropped onto wet luster paints to break the surface tension.

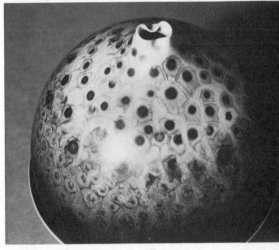

On-Glaze

As a technique which is distinct from enamels, luster, and majolica—all of which are, of course, painted onto the glaze—color can also be brushed, sprayed, or otherwise applied to a fired glaze. This can be done in conjunction with resist or sgraffito, or a

Painting in oxides onto a commercial glazed tile. The brush marks are apparent, as they always are, in this sort of decoration, but they are sufficiently controlled to add their own quality and definition to a witty image.

An industrial (Susie Cooper Ltd.) plate, hand decorated. One color has been spun on over a fired white glaze and then taken off with a brush in a flower pattern. Details added in a darker color.

Silkscreen "Op Art" decoration on a plate by Jim Jarvis, which gives a dramatic impression of three dimensions although the forms and shadows are stylized as befits the technique.

A hand-built pot by Elizabeth Fritsch on which the semigeometric decoration deliberately confuses the eye and suggests planes within the form.

pattern can be rubbed through the color to give a hazy effect. Two full firings are needed, and so it is more suitable for earthenware. The result is more permanent and integrated than enamels, but deep tones are difficult to obtain. See also **Ground-lay** for a technique that could be adapted.

Opacifiers

The principal glaze opacifiers are the oxides of **Tin, Titanium, Zinc, Zirconium.** Alumina, calcia, magnesia, and baria can also impart opacity.

Opalescence in Glaze

Certain glazes have a quality of iridescence, resembling that of an opal. A high boron content is reputed to induce opalescence. It is a feature of Chun glazes where they lie thickly. It is generally agreed that opalescent glazes, and Chun in particular, owe their bluish colors not to pigment but to the optical effect produced by glass suspended in glass. The glazes are generally high in magnesia and low in alumina. A similiar appearance occurs on raku glazes, but this more of a surface than an in-glaze effect.

Openwork

Openwork is normally cut through the wall of a plate of pot and is discussed under **Pierced decoration.** There is, however, a fragile form of openwork made by trailing or extruding a deflocculated clay (generally porcelain) into an absorbent mold, covering the surface with a web of clay strands. When stiff the form, usually a bowl, can be removed. Barry Guppy is a remarkable exponent of this technique. See illustration under **Glaze trailing.**

Optical Decoration, Optical Effect

This is a rather pointless term which has been coined to describe the work of some potters who decorate "against" the form of the piece in order to give a disturbing and disorienting effect. It is a type of optical illusion. Elizabeth Fritsch has called her work an "optical adventure"; like some of the inlay of Homoky it has strong illusory effects. See also **Trompe l'oeil.**

A three-way humorous object in which the straight and curved lines of both form and inlay give a variety of visual stimuli. Polished inlaid porcelain by Nicolas Homoky.

The ambivalent form of this "jug" by Linda Gunrussel is heightened by the spacing of the scored lines, which help to give an illusion that two dimensions are three.

"Dancing Pot" by Janice Heron. Clever geometric black-on-white decoration gives a spirit of movement to this original form.

In another sense an "optical glaze" is one that shows apparent color but to which no pigment has been added. See **Opalescence.**

Orange Peel

A common term for the pitted or ruffled texture of much salt-glaze, a surface which was responsible for shortening its life as a tableware finish in the eighteenth century— it marked silver cutlery. Today, however, this unique texture is admired and prized, especially for its effect on the iron or other coloring of salt glaze. See also **Tiger skin.**

Over-Glaze

Over-glaze normally indicates painting or applying pigment to an already-fired glaze, though it could also be applied to majolica, where color is laid onto raw glaze. See **Enamel, Luster,** and **On-glaze.**

Ovolo

A long-lasting item of ornament, from the ancient world until today. It is fundamentally a rounded or egg-shaped boss used as a repeat pattern. It was frequently used on Samian ware, for instance, and was probably borrowed from architecture.

Oxide Painting

The coloring of pots with metal oxides is, of course, as old as pottery itself, although the early work used earths or clays rich in oxides, usually iron or manganese, in a series of browns, blacks, dull reds, and yellows. The advent of glaze presupposed a technology sufficiently advanced to make possible the separation and purification of metals: copper

Rapid, free brushstrokes on a plate by Michael Cardew, which also illustrates the fading of iron oxide in the firing.

and iron originally, with tin, cobalt, and antimony evident by the first millennium B.C. The great period of cobalt painting came much later, but the oxide was used in glass and glazed brick in Babylonian times and earlier. To attain the maximum brilliance from oxides a white ground was essential, and this was attained either by the use of a white slip over the body or by a white tin-glaze. In Persia both were used; in the Turkish Isnik ware, perhaps the most colorful of all pottery, a very white ground obliterated a darker body. Pigments were painted onto the white surface and the whole covered with a clear alkaline glaze.

Today a multitude of compounded and fritted colors can be bought from ceramic suppliers for any application: underglaze, slip stains, enamels, etc., but many potters still find the use of the basic metal oxides not only a challenge but also more congenial to studio methods and aesthetics. Cardew recommends levigating oxides before use as pigments, especially cobalt, the most powerful of them all. A common complaint of potters is, however, that materials are already too finely ground and purified. The carbonates of metals tend to be of the finest grain but have the disadvantage that they are poisonous, not deadly but definitely to be handled with care. A degree of "grain" or speckle can sometimes be an asset. See **Gosu** and **Magnetic iron**.

The precise thickness of application of oxides is crucial and can only come with experience. The more powerful, as well as the more refractory, oxides can be diluted with glaze, china stone, and other materials, or with other metals oxides—for example, cobalt with either china stone or ocher. Copper will go a cindery black if laid on too thickly; cobalt needs dilution; antimoniate of lead is helped by diluting with glaze. See under the various metal headings. Mixtures of oxides do not always give a "logical" hue and will sometimes partially separate out during firing. Trials are always needed. Piepenburg gives an exhaustive list of raku color mixtures, though all such lists can be misleading, the result depending on the glaze used and a host of other factors. The

The brilliantly controlled and inimitable style of Eric Mellon. See text at end of **Underglaze** *article.*

color of the body is obviously one of these; students will paint onto a dark body and wonder why so little color eventuates. Oxides must be considered watercolors, most of them being more or less transparent. On a red clay they will therefore have little effect, whereas the same painting on a white slip or glaze can glow like the Turkish Isnik patterns. The addition of tin oxide to pigment oxides will give a whole new range, as flake white does to easel painting colors, while clay and other minerals can be mixed with oxides to form engobes that will help to sharpen the painted line and to give a more reliable coverage, although with the loss of the watercolor quality. Such mixtures have had a long and often brilliant history; the tomato reds on Isnik and a similar color

Stamped clay pads on a blue-slipped ground, on a sixteenth-century stoneware jar from Germany.

A modern Japanese teapot by an individual potter, the plum-blossom spray built up of pressed-on pads of clay, which are in turn impressed with details of stamens.

on David Leach's porcelain are basically iron oxide slips. See **Red.** Painting onto clear glazes can be disappointing, but the result will improve with experience.

Most of the above remarks apply especially to earthenware. With the generally fairly opaque stoneware glazes, their frequent saturation with iron, and the effects of reduction, somewhat different rules apply. A problem common to all oxide painting is the spreading and running of color. The inertness of tin oxide at temperatures below 1,150° C. (cone 1), together with the use of a lead/lime base glaze, helps to steady colors, as is seen in historical low-fired majolica and Delftwares. In general a viscous glaze is the key, together with careful firing. Eric Mellon spends many weeks experimenting on a single ash glaze to ensure that his painted line remains firm. Commercial colors are sometimes compounded with chrome to minimize running, but this in itself can cause problems. See **Chrome** and **Chrome-tin pink,** with more discussion under **Painting on pottery.**

Pad, Clay

Applied pads of clay in the manner of sprigs are widespread on early and peasant pottery. The more sophisticated are modeled to represent flowers, animal heads, etc., or are stamped with designs. See **Scales** for a particular use of clay pads, and also **Seal.** Tickenhall pottery was lavishly decorated with pads, possibly as early as the sixteenth century, and can stand as an example of a multitude of others.

Paddled Decoration

Wooden bats or paddles of various shapes can be cut, sawn, or carved with surface patterns for beating into clay. This method of decoration has been used throughout history in various styles and is especially widely used in Japan, where it is known as "tataki ita." A very regular pattern on a pre-Han pot is said to have been made with a carved paddle. A great variety of designs are illustrated in Sanders. The anvil-and-paddle method of making hand-built pots can result in a surface texture from the beater.

The technique almost inevitably results in some overlapping of the marks so that precise designs cannot be expected. See **Beaten patterns** and **Beater.**

Painting on Pottery

This vast subject is touched on under a number of other headings, which are listed at the end of this article. For traditional painting the absorbent nature of the surface, whether clay, biscuit, or glaze, calls for a sureness of touch, the strokes being irrevocable. The exception is the painting on fired glazes with lusters or enamels, although ironically the luster painting on **Hispano-Moresque** ware is perhaps the most direct and calligraphic that the West has ever produced. In contrast, some of the earliest enamel painting was of a miniature-like delicacy and fineness (see **Minai**), and the tradition of enamels has tended to continue in this style, becoming in many cases facile and laborious. Only when controlled by exceptional talent, as on some early porcelain of the East and West, or a strong convention—some Japanese raku, for instance—does enamel achieve the breadth of the best underglaze or raw-glaze decoration.

In the early days of ceramics, as far back as the first pottery from Jericho, painting is the commonest form of decoration, greatly helped on unglazed ware by the fact that the color, though admittedly limited in range, retained its solidarity and boldness after firing. The effects of glaze are often to dilute the color and to soften the delineation of line. Various schemes have been devised to counter these problems: the use of white

On this bold and splendid Song (Sung) Chinese pot the pattern consists of a build-up of individual strokes; the brush has been simply laid onto the surface and flicked away.

As remarkable and powerful in a different way, painted in a thick pigment or slip (it even has the appearance of glaze trailing, but this is unlikely). From eleventh-century Islam.

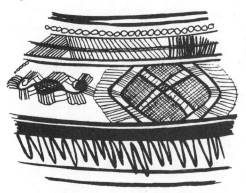

Charming fine-line slip painting on a little-known class of ware from Lodai, India.

Henry Pim decorating a hand-built form with obvious enjoyment, using slips, glazes, and lusters. The second illustration shows a completed pot.

grounds, the addition of tin to the glaze, the compounding of engobes, alkaline and borax glazes, viscous stoneware glazes. Other systems include the separation of colors by raised or incised lines, but these pieces can hardly be called "painted."

Painting normally implies the use of a brush, but fingers, rags, and other objects have been used to apply pigments. The design can also be painted in a resist material, the color being used as a background. A variation used by Leach was to paint iron brushwork in a resisted panel in a celadon glaze and then to cover the whole with another clear glaze. Painting can be combined with areas of colored glaze, as in Oribe ware, or with sgraffito through slip under a glaze. The range today is very wide: classical brushwork at one extreme; with the stabbing, dribbling, or flicking-on of color at the other. The spray can be used as a painting instrument in sensitive hands. For roughing out a design before painting with ceramic pigments, thin artist's watercolors can be used. A grease pencil (Chinagraph) is also useful. For further notes on the many

A highly decorated shell form by Jacqueline Poncelet.

The worktable of Ruth Dupre with the tools and materials for underglaze and enamel painting.

One of Ruth Dupre's original and evocative designs in underglaze and enamel. High-fired.

facets of painting see **Banding, Bianco-sopra-bianco, Bleed-through, Brush-work, Calligraphy, Color wash, Copper red painting, Enamel, Ground-lay, Iron wash, Luster, Majolica, Minai, Over-glaze, Oxide painting, Resist techniques, Slip painting, Spraying, Tin-glaze,** and **Underglaze colors,** as well as at the various oxides and tools, such as **Brushes.**

A bottle by Shoji Hamada with asymmetric panels separated by trailed glaze.

Formal paneling on a teapot enhanced by light and dark glazes with resist and enamel. See detail under **Enamel.** *By John Maltby.*

Ron Nagle's famous if somewhat mistitled "Cups" are variations on a theme, and all have a colored panel, sharply defined, which looks as if it has been wrapped around the form. Holes at the corners intensify this effect. The panels are applied as "china paints" (enamels), sometimes needing many firings—ten to fifteen have been mentioned.

Paneled Decoration

Hamada and Leach often divided their dish and pot surfaces into panels within which to place their decoration. Flat areas on beaten thrown pots were used, often in reserve, and the walls of slab pots frequently quartered. Paneled areas were a feature of Chinese Qing (Ch'ing) ware, and Islamic potters would divide plate surfaces into panels with self-contained patterns. Some Oribe and earlier Japanese designs were more loosely paneled. Ancient Greek painters of the Geometric period would isolate a space for detailed drawing against a plain or abstractly decorated ground. Today a number of potters emphasize the angles of cut or beaten pots by the contrast of setting a plain dark glaze or slip against a lighter decorated rectangle. John Maltby is especially successful, but the style is not common. Ron Nagle's "cups" show a contrasting angular area around the "handle" as if a panel had been wrapped around the form.

Paper Resist

The bold, clean patterns of ancient American pottery often suggest the use of a resist material, and there is evidence for the use of paper or similar material on twelfth-century Chinese (Chi-chou) ware. Margaret Medley asserts that the leaf and cut-paper designs on these dishes are the burnt remains of applied material, but the edges are so sharp and contrasted with the background that suggestion of a resist technique is strong. A few country potters have used resist, but its incidence is not widespread in any period. A combination of paper and wax resist was used at the beginning of the nineteenth century at Longport. A paper pattern was pasted onto the piece and the whole waxed over. The paper was removed and color applied. The method was used

Paper resist on porcelain with colored slips, by Sally Somerville. The tiny "leaks" on the black edge are clues to the technique.

for luster but could well be adapted for other applications where it is required to resist the background rather than the design elements. Today a number of potters decorate stoneware and earthenware with paper resist, sometimes with the additional use of the brush, trailer, or spray-gun. Jane Hamlyn and Michael Casson have written articles on the method in *Ceramic Review 6* and *55*. Leach has warned that it can "easily lend itself to meritricious effect, but this depends on the person who employs it." He himself has used it on his "Pilgrim" and "Mountain" dishes, which are more fully described under **Cut-paper resist.** Paper resist is one method of making silkscreen designs.

Paper patterns tend to be characteristically bold and open. This quality, together with the possibility (rare in ceramics) of reconsidering and altering the composition before committing to the dish or pot, make it very suitable for beginners. One disadvantage is that comparatively large areas of paper that look adequate when cut and laid will appear as uninteresting blank spaces in the finished design. There are a number of ways of getting around this weakness: (1) The surface of the piece can be slipped or otherwise colored before applying the paper; a coarse dryish brush in the manner of hakame would give interest and contrast. Unfired pigment will be disturbed by the paper and an engobe is recommended. (2) A second series of paper shapes can be used with a second slip, color, or glaze. (3) The sheet of paper can be pierced with shapes that will break the blank area. (4) The shape, say of a fish or leaf, can be·sliced into several sections laid slightly apart, giving an "exploded" form. (5) In a more realistic way the veins of a leaf or the joints of an animal can be cut away to give finer lines within the shape. (6) The resisted areas can be treated as reserve panels within which or across which to use brushwork, trailing, or other decorative schemes. Other ideas will come with practice. See also illustrations under **Latex resist.**

A thin, pliable paper, the sturdier types of tissue, or typing copy paper are used, generally on leather-hard clay. Newspaper is also suitable but can give a false impression. Casson even suggests a stiff paper used on soft clay with the edges pressed into the surface to give an almost molded appearance. Whatever paper is decided on, it should be soaked in water before use and any drips shaken off. Judicious cutting and

This combination of cut and torn paper resisting a black slip shows the variety that can be obtained by using sections of paper leaving fine lines between. It also illustrates the effect of a thinnish slip that has been partially "absorbed" by the glaze (an earthenware honey-colored glaze). Slight striations in the body of the dish have also become apparent.

Thin-paper resist was used to develop this wave-like pattern on a dish by Eileen Lewenstein. Various colored slips are brushed over and one or more glazes are applied.

overlapping are necessary on a curved surface. The paper must be firmly adhered to the surface and the edges pressed down onto clay with a fingernail or a wooden tool. Where slip is used as the covering coat, it must be poured on evenly and steadily; pigment is brushed over with broad, even strokes on large areas of resist, the strokes made from the body of the paper outward. Dipping and spraying are also possible, the latter having the advantage that the paper need not be firmly adhered (see illustration under **Airbrush**). When the resist is used on biscuit an adhesive may be needed. With great care the method can be used between glazes, the lower one mixed with a siccative to advantage.

A design in cut paper will obviously have a clear, sharp outline. This can be softened if necessary by tearing the paper to produce a more fluffy edge (although limiting the control of the shape), or the paper can be removed when the slip is still damp and the outline softened by rubbing with the finger. The paper is best removed before firing. As the clay dries it will crinkle the paper, making its position more easily detectable. Tiny areas of paper are difficult to find under slip.

Pate-sur-Pate

A slow and tedious, though highly skilled, technique of laying one layer of porcelain slip over another until a relief pattern is built up. It was related to the Classical style and to cameo glass, even though it appeared at the end of this phase. It was developed at Sèvres in the mid-nineteenth century and introduced into England about 1870 by Solon at Minton's, where he continued to work for thirty-five years. Although the technique was taken up by most major European factories, the Minton work remains the best known. Leach is scathing: "It would be difficult to find a better example of what should not be done with clay." Much of the work was done on a darker ground so that the varying levels of translucency could become more apparent. Whatever its artistic merit, the skill was phenomenal. For a more rapid and spontaneous slip modeling, see **Barbotine**.

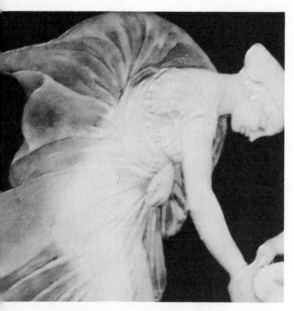

The incredible effect of building up layer upon layer of a translucent Parian clay on a dark blue ground, typical of the work of the industrial potter Louis Solon, who came to England to work for Mintons for twenty years during the latter part of the nineteenth century.

A highly stylized pattern of bulls on a Cypriot bottle, ca. 1250 B.C.

Pattern

It has been pointed out in Leach (1940) that the word *pattern* really means an original motif in the sense of an exemplar and not necessarily its repetition. The *Oxford English Dictionary* gives *patterning* as an arrangement of patterns, but the word is seldom used. In general *pattern* is commonly if loosely used to describe a repeat motif, as in "building up a pattern," while *design* or *composition* indicates the whole concept.

Peach Bloom

A soft peachy pink with patches of a deeper hue developed in China (K'ang Hsi) using copper in a high-alkaline glaze with careful control of the kiln atmosphere. "The bloom results from incipient devitrification of the glaze surface" (Dodd). Tou Lung was a "red bean" variety, Kuo Lung an apple red.

Pen

It has been suggested that the vital, calligraphic luster on Hispano-Moresque pottery may have been applied with a quill pen, and the shapes of many of the strokes are certainly similar to modern lettering. A square-ended brush, however, would have been more practical. Sanders describes a reed used like a quill pen with thin iron slip by Taroemon Nakazoto, giving "decoration of great sensitivity and strength."

On a more mundane level, underglaze felt-tipped pens are now available for line drawing on ceramics. Pigments also include on-glaze gold and silver. Several pottery suppliers list such pens.

Pencil

Graphite pencil marks usually burn out, but sometimes a faint line remains on stoneware biscuit. Pencils impregnated with ceramic colors can also be obtained for per-

A

Fine and broader use of the ceramic pencil or crayon as underglaze color. A. by Jacqueline Poncelet and B. by Alison Britton.

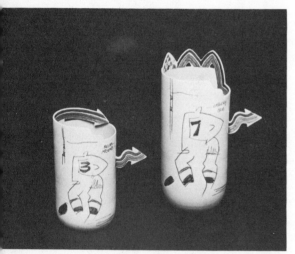

Decoration freely drawn with ceramic underglaze pencils, by Ruth Franklin. See more illustrations under **Crayon**.

B

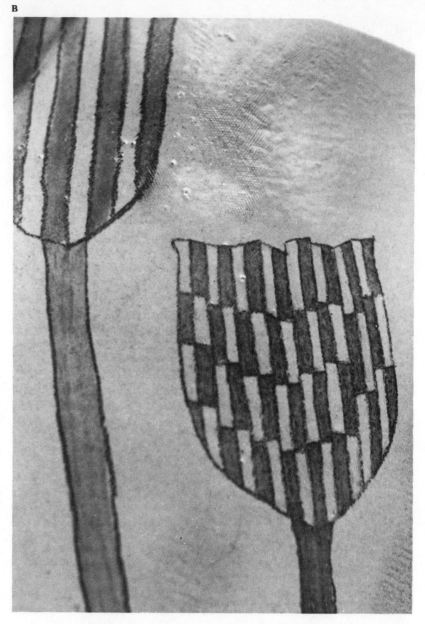

manent line drawing. Ruth Franklin uses ceramic pencils for line drawing on porcelain biscuit, sprayed over with white semi-matt glaze.

A pigment pencil or crayon can be made by mixing a stiff clay/color/glue paste and rolling it into a pencil shape. A covering of paper will render it more rigid and practical.

Persian Colors

A name given by William De Morgan, in the late nineteenth century, to colors painted onto a white slip under a clear glaze, which would more accurately have been called

"Turkish colors," the technique resembling that used at Isnik in the sixteenth century. Blues, greens, and turquoise were dominant.

Petit Feu

A European term for the low-temperature firing of enamels.

Photoceramic Processes

There are a number of processes whereby photographic images can be developed on ceramic surfaces without an intervening transfer. One system, which unfortunately seems to have been abandoned by Kodak in England, sensitized the ceramic surface so

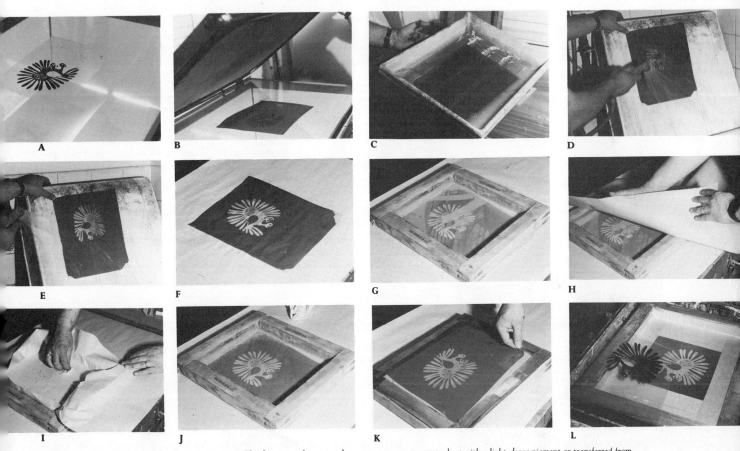

The photographic preparation of a silkscreen image. A. The design is either painted onto a transparent acetate sheet with a light-dense pigment or transferred from a bold image onto acetate by a commercial photocopier. The sheet is shown laid onto the glass screen, emulsion side up, of an ultraviolet light-box.

B. The acetate is covered by a sheet of indirect photostencil such as Siracol or other proprietary make and exposed according to the particular instructions of the makers of the lightbox.

C. The exposed photostencil sheet is immersed in a solution of water and hydrogen peroxide (bleach) for about a minute. This will soften the unexposed areas.

D. E. F. The sheet is held vertically against a suitable surface and sprayed with warm water, which washes away the unexposed image.

G. H. I. J. A screen is laid onto the damp sheet, covered with a flexible paper (newsprint is suitable), and the fabric rubbed firmly onto the image. This will adhere it to the screen. The pressing should be done twice to ensure that adhesion is complete.

K. When dry the acetate backing is peeled away leaving the stencil on the mesh.

L. This picture shows the original image and the "negative" on the screen, which has been squared and blanked off with adhesive tape ready for printing onto a tile or transfer paper. See **Silkscreen** *and* **Decal** *for further stages.*

173

that degrees of stickiness were developed according to the amount of light falling on it through a transparency. Pottery color dusted on resulted, when successful, in a tonal reproduction. The transparency needed to be in direct contact so that only cylinders or flat surfaces were suitable. It was called the Cermifax process and is mentioned by David Hamilton, but he quotes the not very encouraging success rate of one in ten. The suffusion of the image when the negative is moved farther away from the ceramic is a quality that could be utilized by the studio potter. Gerry Williams in his excellent *Studio Potter Book* gives details of two other Kodak techniques known as KOR and KPR (ortho- and photo-resist). The pigments are mixed with an n-butal acetate developer. A drying oven and a safelight, together with a degree of photographic experience, are essential. The details of this rather complicated process are given by Williams. Oxides, underglaze colors, or enamels are suggested, with a preference for enamels. KPR is for use on more or less flat surfaces; in KOR the image is projected onto the emulsion and can therefore accommodate shaped surfaces although distortion will obviously occur. Dodd mentions photosensitive glazes but gives no details.

Conrad deals at some length with photosensitive processes, and the reader is referred to his book. He also suggests Kodak booklets AJ/5 and P79 (Eastman-Kodak, Rochester, NY, 14650). A system known as Picceramic embodies an emulsion that can be painted or sprayed onto a ceramic surface in a darkroom. An image is either projected onto the emulsion through a positive transparency with opaque blacks or laid on directly. The areas not to be exposed must be masked off. Tests must be made as exposures vary with circumstances from ½ to 8 minutes. The appropriate ceramic pigment is painted onto the moist emulsion, which is then bathed in a fixer. The silver and surplus pigment is washed off under running water. The chemicals are toxic. Another type called Kallitype is not ceramic and requires protection with acrylic or similar lacquer.

In the industry, photographic realism is common but is normally on a white ground, whereas modern studio potters have combined it with the textures of hand-building or the effects of impure materials such as iron spot. It would be possible to use it less realistically to produce areas of texture or broken images, which could be mysteriously suggestive. Eric Grenborg uses black and white photo-decals and adds color in the normal way. An Alan Pirie plate in *Ceramic Review 63* shows a landscape built up from photographic transfers. It is obvious that without some subtlety of approach photo-resist can easily degenerate into art at its most "applied." Photo systems can also be used to produce screen prints of images. See illustrations.

Phototrophy

A phenomenon quoted by Hamer in which the color of a glaze may change with the amount of light falling on it. The change can be noticed when part of a surface has been covered, for example, when lifting a cup from a saucer. It can be induced in glazes by the addition of 15 percent of titania and rutile. The glaze darkens in bright light. Not exactly useful decoratively except, perhaps, as a party piece! Potters will be familiar with the changing color of glazes as they are unpacked hot from a kiln.

Pierced Decoration

Early potters saw little point in cutting away the walls of pots laboriously built up, except for such uses as colanders, presses, or incense burners. The decorative value of the pierced holes, however, even in these practical objects, was often exploited, as in the primitive burners from Europe and the much more sophisticated sieves with delicate bird and human designs on elaborate backgrounds found in ninth-century

A strange little pot from Bronze Age Britain, reputedly used as an incense burner. The piercing is combined with incising as on the modern plate by Ian Godfrey.

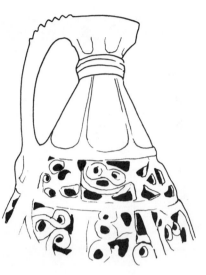

Charmingly pierced water strainers have been made at Fostat in Egypt since the ninth century. They sit on or in the necks of drinking vessels. The cutting is greatly varied: birds, fish, flowers, beasts, and, in this case, a seated man.

The outer case of this Fatimid Dynasty (Egypt, twelfth century) turquoise-glazed ewer is pierced, as mentioned in the text. Within the pierced wall is another vessel, which actually holds the liquid. It may have been purely decorative or some kind of cooling system.

Fostat (Old Cairo). More purely ornamental were the twelfth-century Rayy open-work designs on the outer cases of double-walled ewers. Chinese Ming cups and bowls had finely cut patterns called "devil's work" or Ling tung, often in unglazed trellis designs. Many other examples include the Persian Gombroon wares, the extensively cut Co-medians plates from Italy, and English Leeds ware. Small-scale piercing (see also **Rice-grain pattern**) covered over with glaze enhanced the translucency of later Chinese porcelain, as it did for the Near Eastern imitations of porcelain. The Rhages twelfth-century "transparencies" were sometimes covered with a deep blue glaze.

Cutting through stoneware in a free and broad style by Ian Godfrey, which stems historically from Leeds and other pierced-rim wares of the eighteenth and nineteenth centuries.

Like the little incense burner shown above, this cut cylinder by Sybil Houldsworth has been pierced for a purpose: to hold a nightlight or candle. A variety of hole sizes, grooves, and shallow stamped circles ensure decorative as well as useful qualities.

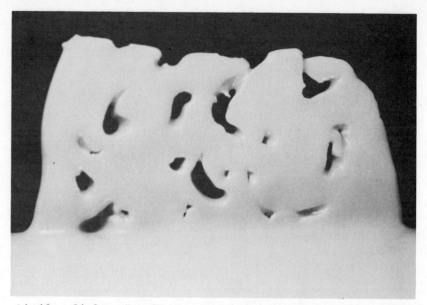

A detail from a Colin Pearson "winged" pot in porcelain, which would be blank and less interesting without the piercing. The design is also reflected in the carved edge.

In the eighteenth century the outer skin of double-walled stonewares from Nottingham were pierced to give an appearance of lightness, a technique known as "carving." A similar system was used in Worcester "Persian" porcelain, and several craft potters, including David Eeles, have cut patterns in the outer walls of double pots. Various styles have been adopted by artist potters. Ian Godfrey's plate rims, cut in the Leeds tradition, sometimes have more space than substance; Eeles, as mentioned, returns to the Rayy style in open-work outer walls of flasks, but the technique is most popular on porcelain, enhancing the sense of delicacy and translucency. Alan Whitaker sand-blasts porcelain with great skill into convoluted bands and segments of apertures; Irene Sims cuts walls of cylinders into the most fragile of tree and landscape designs; Dorothy Feibleman produces networks of porcelain sometimes combined with neriage, Sheila Casson a rather more sturdily pierced porcelain. Many others develop fresh aspects: Peter Voulkos pushing rough holes through a series of slashed and beaten plates; restrained slots in Richard Devore's stoneware forms; and so on.

Two drilled and incised bone china forms by Angela Verdon, the natural translucency of the material heightened by the pierced wall. The potter uses a dentist's drill for this exacting work.

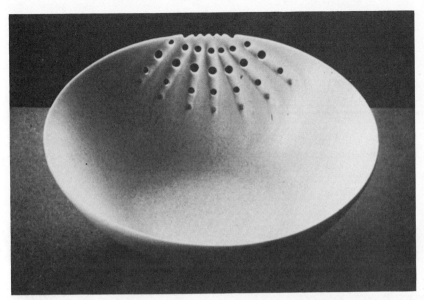

A graduated, shell-like pierced design that focuses the eye and gives point to an otherwise plain half-sphere. By Hazel Johnston. Note that the lowest row of circles is not quite cut through and that the serrated rim continues the design.

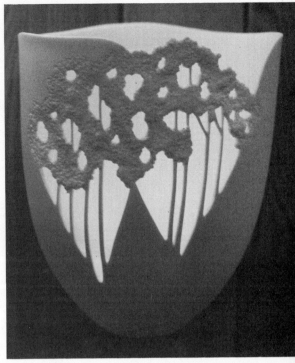

Porcelain delicately carved and textured with great skill by Irene Sims.

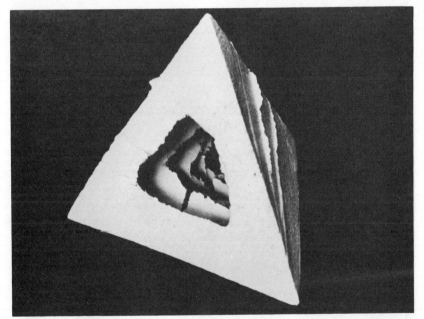

It is impossible to separate the decorative piercing from the overall form of this pyramid by Janice Heron; one is integral with the other.

Piercing must, of course, always stop short of the point where serious warping or even the collapse of the material may occur. Cracking during drying is often a development of strains imposed during the cutting rather than the piercing itself, although a line of weakness can also occur through a line of adjacent holes.

While a thin knife is the favorite tool, teapot grill cutters or small shaped cutters used in other crafts and even pastry or biscuit stamps can be useful. Angela Verdon drills lightly fired bone china with a dentist's drill.

Pigment Oxides

A term used in this book to denote the oxides of metals that directly impart color to

An intriguing texture somewhere between pinholing and crawling. The underlying body is probably well-grogged and contains some pigment with a refractory, high-surface-tension glaze. By Lucie Rie.

ceramics. The principal oxides are of copper, chrome, cobalt, antimony, iron, manganese, and nickel. Rutile is an iron-stained titanium. Compounds of silver, gold, platinum, together with cadmium, selenium, praseodymium, uranium, and vanadium, are less commonly used, and mostly at low temperatures. All are dealt with under their respective headings. White pigments are listed under **Opacifiers.**

Pinholing

An aggravating glaze fault which can only rarely be turned to decorative advantage.

Pink, Rose

The commonest, somewhat unsympathetic pink is derived from chrome (see **Chrome-tin pink**). There was an extensive use of rose-pink on Famille Rose painting in eighteenth-century China. This was enamel, where the color is more easily attainable. Purple of Cassius is such a color, and the Chinese enamels were developed from colloidal gold. A pink luster can be obtained from a thin layer of **bright or liquid gold** on a tin glaze. In high-fired magnesia glazes, cobalt can give pink flushes. Pink crystals may form in dolomite glazes with up to 10 percent of rutile, and Emmanuel Cooper (1980) has a recipe for a nickel "shocking pink." There is also a zirconium/iron pink that can be used at high temperatures.

Plumbago

See **Graphite.**

Poinçon, Punch

An archeologist's term for the figures and other items of design used to impress the molds of Arretine and **Samian ware.** The modeled pieces were biscuit fired and then used to impress the inner surfaces of soft clay thrown molds. Minor parts of the composition—flower stems, etc.—were hand incised. The poinçon left a negative impression that provided a relief design when a bowl was made in the mold. This was all part of the intensive mass-production of Samian ware, especially from the Gaulish potteries that provided pottery to most of the empire in the second century. The stamps were curved to fit a standard bowl size and were often of a high standard of craftsmanship. There are possibilities for the application of the technique to modern pottery.

Polishing

The Chinese sent over polished red stoneware teapots with early supplies of tea in the later seventeenth century, and the material was imitated by Bottger, who polished hard stoneware on a lapidary's wheel, as did the Elers brothers in England. It was compared to porphyry. Today fine, eggshell-like surfaces are achieved on biscuit porcelain by rubbing with a wet-and-dry (silicon-carbide) emery paper ("flour" grade) after firing. Nicholas Homoky's inlaid porcelain is treated in this way. Angela Verdon polishes bone china, and Martin Smith uses a lapidary's wheel on his sculptural red earthenware forms.

In a very different way, some primitive bush-fired pottery is given an organic polish, which is long-lasting. A few modern potters apply polish to raku, etc. See also **Burnishing, Gloss ware,** and **Nonceramic finishes.**

This painted and inlaid piece in biscuit porcelain by Nick Homoky has been polished with very fine wet-and-dry emery paper.

Decoration consisting of spots of slip on a typical Roman form. A light slip is laid over a darker body. First century A.D.

Poppyhead Pots

The name given to a type of bulbous beaker with rows of small embossed dots on the shoulder, mainly of Romano-British and Roman Empire manufacture. The bosses were often arranged in squares and appear to be dropped or trailed on.

Potassium Dichromate

A soluble and toxic compound used at low temperatures (around 900° C./1,650° F.) to obtain a bright red in high-lead glazes. At higher firing temperatures, it will change first to an orange and then to a yellowish color. Small additions of ferric oxide will help to maintain the color at the higher temperatures.

Pot-Lid Pictures

Vast numbers of small, flattish containers for potted meats and fish, hair pomades, creams, etc., were decorated with figures, scenes, and other designs in gay colors in the mid-nineteenth century, primarily to stimulate sales but incidentally brightening the whole range of industrial ceramics. They exploited the bright hues of the newly developed multicolor printing of the 1840s. They are sought after by many collectors. Potters today also make shallow boxes mainly for the decoration on the lid, not so figurative as in the past, though this will surely come.

Pouncing

The process of scattering finely powdered charcoal through pinholes in a sheet of paper or stretched silk was used to trace an outline design onto the surface beneath. The finely dotted line guided the painter's brushstrokes and ensured a certain uniformity. It was widely practiced on Delft and other tiles. The "pricked" design was not, however, slavishly followed in the heyday of Dutch tin-glaze: "Although the tile painters borrowed some subjects from engravers and laid out the composition with pounces and pricked paper, they became fully their own simply by much repetition" (Caiger-Smith). Parts of separate engravings were used to build up a "new" design on some English wares, and these would have been pounced. A Bristol Hotwell plate illustrates this process; a figure appears from quite another context—and somewhat out of scale.

   An alternative system in which the design was executed on tracing paper in charcoal, and from which a number of faint impressions were taken, is reputed to have been used on the unfired body of blue-and-white Chinese porcelain of the Ming and Qing (Ch'ing) dynasties.

Poured Glaze

The act of pouring glaze over a pot, even though the intention is merely to cover the surface, usually affects the decorative finish through runs and overlaps. The rough runs and pours on medieval pots were probably more the result of haste and economy than conscious design, attractive though some of the results are. In the Near East, bowls were poured with alternate colors from center to rim in a purely ornamental way. Glaze poured over the neck of a pot as it slowly turns on the wheel will run in rivulets. This style was popular in the early days of studio pottery, used by Chaplet, Delaherche, and others, and in our own time by Janet Leach in a restrained manner. By turning the wheel faster while pouring, spirals as well as runs will occur. The sixteenth- and

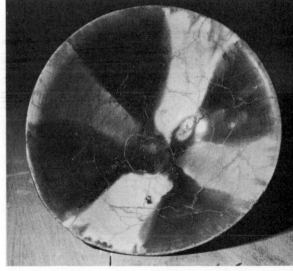

Green, blue, and white loops of glaze on a twelfth-century Persian bowl.

A seventeenth-century baluster pot found in North Devon, with a lively double pour of dark glaze down the side. It could have been accidental from emptying the glaze from the interior, but it looks more conscious.

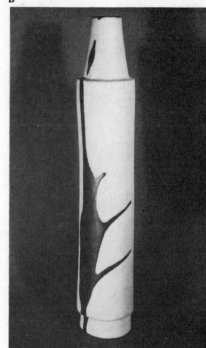

Three potters' approaches to glaze pouring on a pot. A. A skillful twist has directed the running glaze around the base of a pot by Janet Leach. B. In this piece by Dan Arbeid a rather rigid shape has been softened by the freely run glaze, probably poured from the base in contrast to the previous examples. C. Lastly, a more traditional straight pour from the rim over the broad belly of this fine hand-built pot, large swags contrasting with finer dribbles. By Ruth Duckworth.

seventeenth century Oribe potters poured their green and buff glazes in swags and loops, dividing a dish between contrasting colors and decorating the lighter one with brushwork. The Chinese, with their more precise and considered designs, rarely used the technique after T'ang times.

The pouring of glazes over the necks and sides of pots is one of the main glazing techniques of today. Tony Birks (1974), however, is of the opinion that glaze runs can have a disruptive effect on the form and profile of a pot, and that they should be limited to strong and simple shapes. Ray Finch and others attain a well-defined design by making several pours from the center line across a dish toward the edge, leaving a holly-like shape in the center (this is glaze over glaze). Decorative pouring is more often used on earthenware and stoneware than on porcelain. Lines of white glaze can be poured onto flattened bottles and "pebble" shapes, the glaze whipped into sideways runs by a sharp shake as it pours down. Memmott illustrates pouring glaze from a jug onto a revolving wheel as mentioned above, giving chancy spiral and centrifugal effects. Free-form patterns can result from pouring contrasting glazes side by side or over-lapping. Sylvia Hyman pours intense and brilliant colors across square dishes in this way. Various colors can be derived from some glazes simply by the varying thickness of the glaze. Dry ash glazes are useful for pouring over the more rugged types of slab pots, etc.

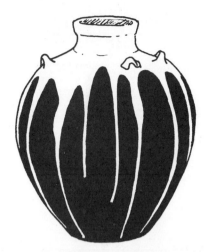

A stoneware jar by Donald MacKenzie with poured glaze which, in contrast to the Duckworth example, has run in narrow lines that break the form into interesting shapes.

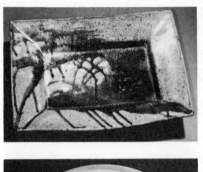

Glaze pouring on plates. The first three by Raymond Finch: one dribbled in a semicontrolled way, the other two clear-cut and poured in swags from the center outwards. The last example is by Hamada, glaze on a vitrified biscuit and probably poured from a ladle.

Powdering, Powder Blue, Powder Brown

Dodd describes a technique of mixing color with an oily medium, brushing it onto glazed ware, and then dusting dry powdered color on top to achieve a stippled effect. The reference is to industrial pottery, but it could be adapted to studio use. Powder blue is a specific effect obtained by blowing or dusting cobalt (or smalt) onto the body or glaze. "The action isolates the blue as specks on a white ground, which gives luminosity to the color" (Hamer). A form of powder blue incorporating resist was used in the Qing (Ch'ing) dynasty and later in many tin-glaze potteries. There are English Delftware (*ca.* 1740) pieces with reserved panels on backgrounds of powdered-on manganese dioxide, and also of blue and a specific "powder brown" in imitation of the Chinese "dead leaf brown." The use of powdered color or frit in this way leads to a possible health hazard, and if practiced by the studio potter a mask should be worn.

A number of glazes have been dribbled, one over another, giving a subtle but dramatic effect over a heavily grogged body. By Ian Auld.

Praseodymium

A pigment oxide which will produce yellowish stains with zircon. The color is rather weak but will stand quite high temperatures.

Press Molding

Although this is primarily a forming technique, the surface of a mold can be cut to give compositions in relief to the cast piece. This is dealt with under **Molded relief** and **Poinçon.** In tiles a vast range of Spanish, German, and English work was relief molded by pressing, for either outlining colored glazes (**cuenca**) or glazing-over with a single color. In modern work the dishes of El'Nigoumi are outstanding. His script, birds, and other designs combine his own tradition with that of eighteenth-century English slipware.

Slabs of clay can be pressed onto cut or other irregular surfaces to produce textured slabs for pots, etc. An example is the patterned slab illustrated in Rhodes.

Pricked Decoration

On a number of primitive pots the design is delineated by a series of pricks or small depressions, and in others they are used to build up a textured surface within a cut line. "Stroke ornament" consisted of separate jabs instead of a continuous line (fourth millennium B.C., Northern Europe).

Printer's Type

The impressing of clay with printer's type, either wooden or metal fonts, has been practiced at least since the seventeenth century and probably earlier. The impression is often inlaid with a contrasting slip. In most historical examples (see exception under **Lettering**), type is used for its natural purpose of spelling out a name or rhyme, but in modern work various-size blocks have been used to form compositions purely for their decorative qualities. Type is more commonly used on slab pots, tiles, and the like rather than on thrown ware.

A straightforward use of impressed typefaces; quicker and cheaper than cut stone and almost as permanent, if less elegant. As this Foundation plaque is in the Stoke-on-Trent Museum, it has obviously outlasted the market it commemorated in 1835.

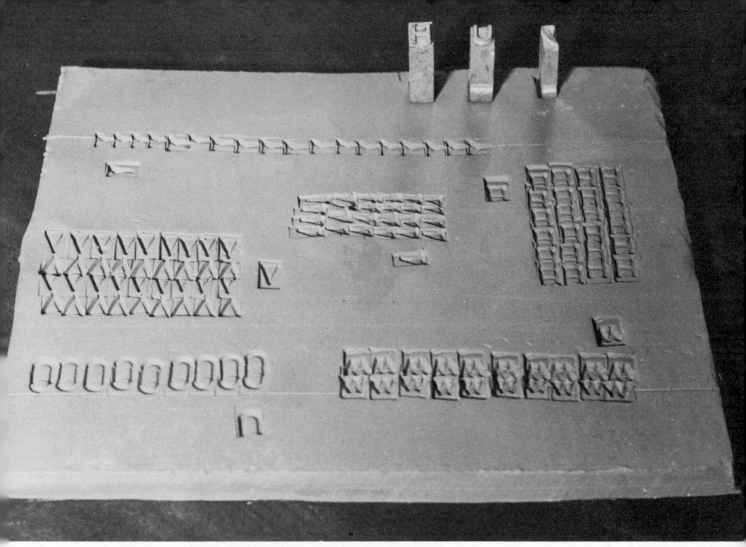

The impressions made by metal and wooden typefaces can be combined and repeated to form patterns only indirectly related to the letter used, as seen in the progressing darts of the Y, for instance, at the back of the slab.

Printing

See **Transfers** for this aspect of printing, and also **Bat printing, Cut brick, Cut sponge, Lithography, Photoceramic processes, Silkscreen,** and **Stamping.**

The transfer of color from a cut block of material to a ceramic surface is comparatively modern. The later fifteenth-century tiles are reputed to have been "printed" in white slip from a wooden stamp, the resultant image being shallower and less hard-wearing than the truly inlaid type. In the industry today printing of one sort or another is paramount.

A form of printing with polyurethane foam blocks is described by Michael and Harriet Cohen in Williams. The broad design is marked out on the form and the main outlines cut with a knife. The areas not required to print are then burnt away with a soldering iron or hot wire. The potter must wear a mask and use a fan to blow away

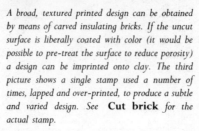

A broad, textured printed design can be obtained by means of carved insulating bricks. If the uncut surface is liberally coated with color (it would be possible to pre-treat the surface to reduce porosity) a design can be imprinted onto clay. The third picture shows a single stamp used a number of times, lapped and over-printed, to produce a subtle and varied design. See **Cut brick** *for the actual stamp.*

the noxious fumes. The printing is done with appropriate pigments onto the raw, damp glaze surface. Glaze-on-glaze effects could also be tried. Paul Soldner "prints" glaze and color onto raku with his fingers and palm, but this is stretching the meaning of the word to its limit! See also **Rubber stamp.**

Procès Barbotine

See **Barbotine.**

Punch

See **Poinçon.**

Purple of Cassius

A precipitate of chlorides of gold and tin, or a mixture of colloidal gold and stannic acid, discovered by Andreas Cassius of Leyden around 1685. The color results from finely divided gold on SnO_2 particles. It was the basis of one of Bottger's first enamels, which preceded the rose-pinks of Famille Rose of China. It assumed a mulberry-purple tint at Vicennes, a lilac at Sèvres, and a crimson-claret at Chelsea. A pink from gold was used extensively at Leeds early in the nineteenth century. It was later supplemented and in most cases supplanted by **chrome-tin pink,** a less pleasant color. The over-firing of gold enamel on tin glaze will often produce a rose-purple.

Rainbow Effect

Spectrum light effects are seen on lusters derived from silver, bismuth, copper, and tin. The thickness of the metallic layer with its reflections from both the upper and lower surfaces is just sufficient to break white light into spectrum colors when viewed from certain oblique angles.

Raku

A pottery technique of some antiquity, originally associated with the tea ceremony of Japan, its history described in many books including those by Reigger, Piepenburg, and others. Its modern manifestation in the West is noted for its often dramatic surface

Mottled white glaze against the darker body of reduced raku. By Elspeth Owen.

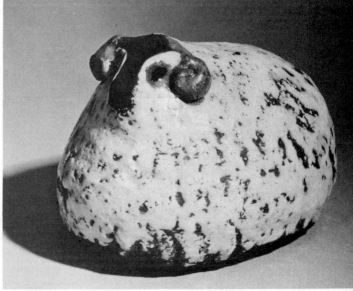

White tin-glaze on reduced raku, cleverly and simply applied, give detail to the modeling, with a combination of dabbing and crawling to give a strong suggestion of wool. By Rosemary Wren.

appearance resulting from carbonization and reduction at the red-hot and cooling stages. A distinctive feature (the earlier Japanese raku was aircooled and had a different purpose and aesthetic) is its black or dark gray variegated body color combined with a coating or splashed areas of crazed and stained glaze, often originally white, and frequently with a lustered or iridescent surface. The rapidly, often crudely, formed and textured small pieces—thumb pots and the like—of a few years ago are being replaced by larger, sometimes very large, smoother, and more sophisticated pots and bowls, or hewn, modeled, or beaten sculptural pieces. Some of the original fragility has also been overcome by higher firing and special, less grogged, bodies. In England one of the major

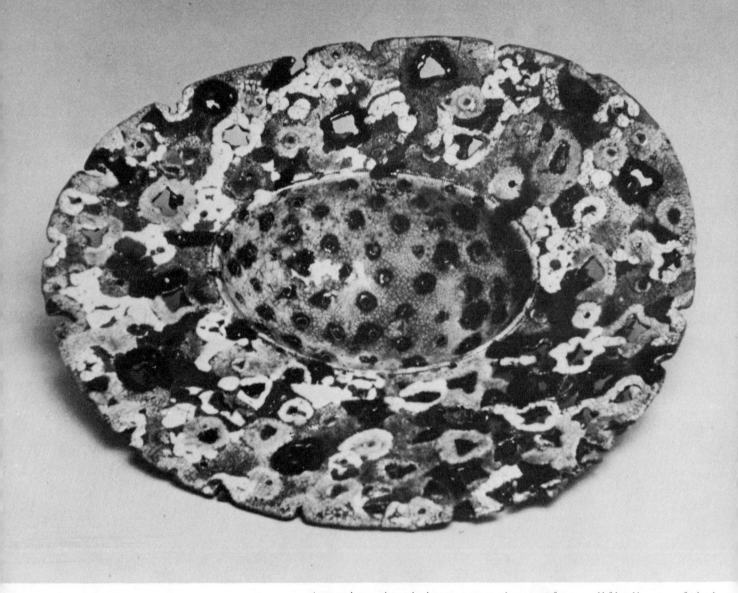

An unusual approach to raku decoration, covering the entire surface in a wild fabric-like pattern of colored glazes and enamels. By Ian Byers.

moving spirits in the change has been Robin Welch, who has applied the clean, almost mechanical lines of his stoneware to raku, dealing with a single substantial and carefully considered piece at a time. Rhodes' dictum that "a raku pot is in no way different from any ordinary pot except that it is underfired, soft, and bears the marks of tongs" has been overtaken by the creative talents of many potters especially in the United States, but also in Europe and England. It is no longer necessarily underfired, nor are tong marks often in evidence. Martin Smith even removes his pieces from a top-hat kiln with asbestos gloves and carefully controls crazing by a rapid wipe while hot with a damp cloth. Most decorative techniques described elsewhere may be used, but, even discounting the body color and glaze qualities, they will be transformed by the unique medium of reduced raku.

The typical pitted and crazed surface of sawdust-reduced and water-dunked raku. The cut facets show the variations of color and texture to good advantage. By Sybil Houldsworth.

Reactive Glazes

Glazes of different characteristics—for example, a shiny glaze under or over one compounded near to the formular limits—can give broken surfaces and other reactions. These are dealt with in a number of technical books on glazes.

Red

Before the advent of chrome, cadmium, selenium, and uranium in the nineteenth and twentieth centuries, pottery reds were derived from reduced copper in the Far East from the fifteenth century and more brilliantly in the seventeenth and eighteenth centuries; from gold in enamels (see **Purple of Cassius**) in eighteenth-century Europe; and worldwide since the earliest times from iron oxide. Many of the iron reds are nearer to brown. The gloss wares of Ancient Rome and some slips on pre-Columbian American wares are a good terra-cotta red, and there are isolated brighter examples such as the thick **bole** used at Isnik. Red glazes are even more difficult, and United States potteries attempting them in the late nineteenth century were reduced to bankruptcy. On stonewares the Oriental **kaki** approaches red, but Hamer states that "a bright colour requires complete oxidation." Iron in large proportions in an oxidized ash glaze can certainly give a hot red, but not always a sympathetic one. David Leach uses red clay in a similar way to the Isnik potters, but on porcelain and in reduction. He trails a 50:50 mixture of red clay and nepheline syenite and calcined red clay onto the raw glaze. Colin Kellam exposes the body in small areas under a clear glaze to give a coral-red, the rest of the pot being obscured by an opaque glaze with brushwork. A cherry-red from Armenian bole was used on Caffaggiolo majolica, and ruby-red lusters were fired at Gubbio. Red enamels are easier to compound from iron oxide and have been in use since the thirteenth century. A bright red can also develop from chrome with lead at low temperatures. See **Potassium dichromate**. Iron in bodies and slips may be rust-brown but it is generally referred to, perhaps hopefully, as red. At low temperatures a fairly bright orange is possible.

It will be seen that the true ceramic reds are at the lower end of the temperature scale, with the exception of reduced copper and the spots of pigment mentioned above, although modern technology has produced coral colors that will stand stoneware temperatures. See also under the various metal oxides mentioned.

Red-Figure Ware _____

See **Black- and red-figure painting**.

A comparatively rare example of lettering on a red-figure kylix from Ancient Greece, looking like a modern cartoon "balloon."

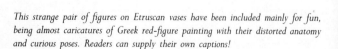

This strange pair of figures on Etruscan vases have been included mainly for fun, being almost caricatures of Greek red-figure painting with their distorted anatomy and curious poses. Readers can supply their own captions!

Red Ocher

See **Ocher.**

Reed Brush

There is an old tradition at Karatsu of painting in thin slip with a reed, similar to the American cattail plant, cut like a quill. This would give results like Western lettering or like much of the painting on Hispano-Moresque ware.

Reeding

A term often applied to closely set horizontal grooves cut into a pot, it indicates a semicircular groove, like the markings on a reed. Examples are found on Roman and other early, generally thrown, pottery and occasionally on medieval pots. It is common in a more rigid style on industrial wares. On creamware it was related to the prevailing Neoclassicism and to silverware. The modern potter uses reeding sparingly, sometimes between the neck and spread of a shoulder of a jug or pot, or as a break in form of a beaker. See also **Turned decoration.**

Relief Decoration

The various techniques of relief decoration are dealt with under **Applied decoration, Barbotine, Carved molds, Chatter, Embossing, Frilled cordon, Molded relief, Pate-sur-pate, Poppyhead pots, Ribbing, Rope decoration, Roulette, Rusticated slip, Seal, Slip trailing, Sprigging, Stamping, Strip decoration, Studs, Throwing rings,** and **Tube lining.**

Turquoise-glazed low-relief on a Persian Sultanabad twelfth-century bowl, very probably molded.

A superb stork reserved, probably resisted, by the nineteenth-century Japanese potter Nin'Ami Dohachi.

Reserve

The word is used in its meaning of "unaltered." A reserved area or pattern is one that retains its original surface and color while the background or surrounding area is painted, covered, or otherwise differentiated. This can be done freehand, but more often a resist material is used. See **Cut-paper resist, Latex resist, Paper resist, Stencil,** and **Wax resist.**

Resist Techniques

Various materials can be adhered to the surface of a ceramic piece before the application of slip, glaze, or pigment in order to retain areas or designs in reserve. Wax is the most popular, but liquid rubber, leaves, paper, and other materials can be used. In the nineteenth century, china clay mixed with honey or glycerine was used to resist luster colors; see below. Resist can be used to produce a design in many combinations: between biscuit and glaze; raw clay or biscuit and slip; clay and color; biscuit or glaze and color; glaze and glaze; glaze or biscuit and enamel. With most resists the reserved area will be plain—the color of the underlying material—but wax will often retain small drops of color that remain after firing. The wax itself can be colored with pigment, a technique used at Hornsea Pottery, where the pattern is applied through a silkscreen with a mixture of oil and pigment. This resists the glaze, leaving the design in a colored matt finish. For a similar effect, brushstrokes can be covered with wax resist before a second coat of glaze is poured over, a system used by Henry Hammond.

The simplest resist technique is to rub the clay or biscuit surface with a candle, which may be scraped to a point for better control. This is most suitable for pigment; it will barely resist slip or glaze. Janet Leach (see *Ceramic Review 51*) has used resist almost in reverse, reserving the background and leaving irregular lines of dark glaze on

A dramatic resist pattern, enhancing the break in the rim. By John Ward. See also **Masking tape.**

An interesting approach to what might be called "negative" resist, that is, the background resisted rather than the items of pattern. Warwick Parker.

a pale biscuit. See more discussion under **Cut-paper resist, Latex resist, Leaf resist, Paper resist,** and **Wax resist.** A special resist is required for oil-based pigments such as enamels. This is a water-soluble gum, arabic or dextrin, or a proprietary brand. The on-glaze color is sprayed, painted, or laid on (see **Ground-lay**), covering resist as well. Immersion in water or holding under a tap and gently easing the resist with a sponge will dissolve it away, together with the applied color. The glaze surface must be grease-free in applying the resist, a condition helped by wiping over

A twentieth-century commercial tile that employs the type of resist used by the studio potter.

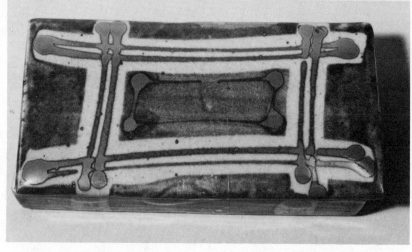

Resist combined with trailing by David Frith.

This is, strictly speaking, a form of fluting but the impression is of swirling, diagonal ribbing. By Kathleen Pleydell-Bouverie.

with whiting. A very sharp resist line can be obtained by using masking tape, usually on a fired-glaze surface.

Rhodian Red

A tomato-red color found on Turkish Isnik and given the somewhat inaccurate name "Rhodian red" in the eighteenth century. See **Bole** and **Red.**

Ribbing

Relief ridges on pottery. Ribbing has occurred widely on pots and bowls, especially since the development of the potter's wheel, which made it possible to form horizontal ribs during throwing. The cylindrical forms and models of Japanese Haniwa (third to fifth centuries), however, are strongly ribbed although hand-built, perhaps to hide or strengthen joints between slabs or coils as the Cretans had done some 2,000 years before with their vast storage jars. Roman pottery was often ribbed during throwing or turning. It is not so common on the smooth, flowing lines of Chinese pottery; where they do occur they are usually rounded and softened, a mild punctuation of the profile. A single ridge may accentuate a shoulder on Islamic ware, and ribbing is even more rare on European tin-glaze. Fluting will sometimes, in effect, form vertical ribs, as on the splendid bottle illustrated in *Ceramic Review 50.* Pleydell-Bouverie has used subtle ribbing on pots and bowls under a thick glaze. The carinated profiles of Karen Karne's pots often amount to ribbing. A round-toothed comb can be used for parallel ribbing. See also **Cordon** and **Frilled cordon.**

Rice-Grain Pattern

This consists of small perforations in the wall of a piece resembling or formed by inserted grains of rice. The holes are then usually covered over with glaze. Persian Gurgan and Rayy ware show this type of decoration as early as the twelfth century, used as an aid toward an effect of translucency, which their lower-fired bodies barely achieved. The best-known Far Eastern type is that from the Ch'ien Lung period in

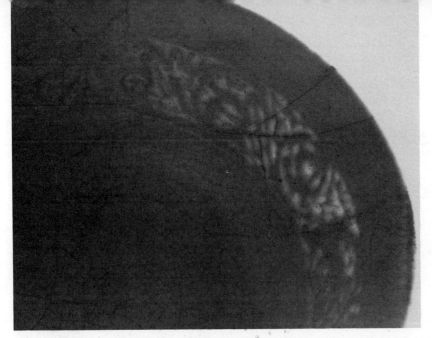

A section of a Rayy (Rhages) eleventh- or twelfth-century bowl showing light shining through the quite intricate design made up of small apertures in the "rice-grain" style, covered over with a translucent white glaze. The body, though looking coarse and rough at the foot, is, in fact, a slightly translucent frit/clay mixture.

A modern industrial and very regular version of the rice-grain style.

China, whose potters are believed to have copied it from the Persians, although their thin translucent porcelain would have hardly needed its aid. It is still turned out in great quantities in Japan and the Far East. Modern potters often use perforations to enhance the qualities of porcelain, but rarely in this particular style.

Rilling

Parallel horizontal indentations or cuts made around a pot. *Rill* means "stream," hence a cut channel. Similar to reeding.

Two turned grooves or rills give a minor emphasis, continuing the line of the lower handle junction, on this sturdy jug by John Leach.

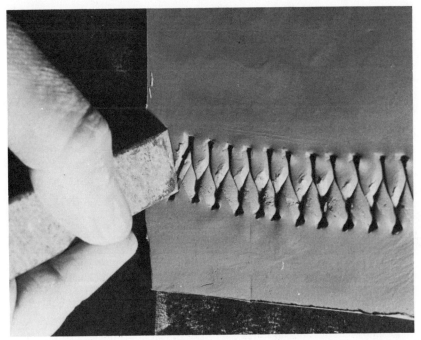

Rocking an ordinary square-edged tool (a steel sorting tool in this case) and giving a forward twist at the end of each movement has produced this striking ornament on fairly soft clay. Historically it was often used on the shoulder of a large pot and the technique, a rapid and lively one, could well be revived.

Rocker Tool

This is described in Bray and Trump as a tool with a straight or curved edge which is moved across soft clay by pivoting on alternate corners. Neolithic Mediterranean and pre-Classic ancient American potters are presumed to have used the system. Hamer states that the regular zigzags of dots on Beaker Folk (second millennium B.C.) pottery was made with "a notched rocker tool," in this case perhaps a single roll for each line. Barton, however, calls similar marks "impressed cord." One can envisage a number of uses for rocker tools for designs and textures on modern pottery, thrown and hand-built.

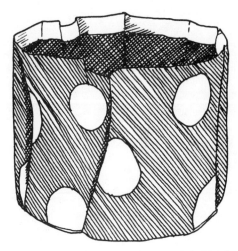

Balls of porcelain clay were rolled onto a stoneware body slab before building this "polka dot" bowl. The simplicity of the design has been given added interest by the folding and overlapping of the wall. By Johan Van Loon.

Rolled Inlay

A method of laying strips or shapes of clay onto a slab of a contrasting color and rolling one into the other with a rolling-pin. The technique gives somewhat ill-defined patterns but has potential. It is discussed at greater length under **Inlay**. Virginia Cartwright and Johan Van Loon have used rolled inlay, Van Loon for a polka-dot design to which it is well suited.

Rope Decoration

From Jomon pottery onward, rope-impressed ornament—as a simple linear indentation, as an overall texture obtained by a length of rope around a core being rolled over the surface, or by beating with a rope-wound paddle—has been fairly common. See **Beaten patterns, Cord impressions,** and **Paddled decoration.**

A bowl hand-built from a slab of red clay inlaid with porcelain by rolling. By Virginia Cartwright. The softness of the outline of the inlay is typical of this technique.

Stylized rope pattern on a large Late Minoan (ca. 1500 B.C.) storage jar. The rope motif often indicates a seafaring culture.

Relief decoration of twisted or pattern-impressed rolls of clay resembling rope appears on many pots—on the fine jars of Knossus; on Syrian and other glazed pottery; and occasionally on modern studio pottery, for example, the rather severe forms of Anita Scott.

Rouge Flambé

An exuberant, sometimes vulgar, on-glaze streaked copper red found on some industrial art wares. In China the term is synonymous with certain types of **sang de boeuf.**

Roulette

This is usually in the form of a small wheel on a spindle, the circumference being carved, stamped, or cut with a pattern, a name, or simple notches. The wheel is rolled over the surface of soft clay, impressing a repeat design in a raised line on a depressed ground. It is a widespread and ancient technique, especially on semi-mass-produced wares such as Roman Empire ceramics. Although most frequently found on wheel-thrown pots, it also occurs on hand-built pieces; Ladi Kwali roulettes the shoulders of her coiled and stroked jars, for instance. It is seen on proto-Yueh jars, pots, and dishes. Rouletted dashes were spiraled onto the surface of some T'zu Chou lidded pots with a black-and-white finish. Margaret Medley's description of a white slip covered by a black one does not quite explain the sharp delineation of the roulette marks. Possibly the black was spun onto the white after the roulette had depressed the pattern into the surface; or the roulette could have been cut to give a raised pattern, the black coating being subsequently scraped from the ridges while turning on a wheel. These guesses are suggestive of modern treatments a potter could invent.

Country potters impressed the name and address of their potteries around pots, or used the tool to provide a quick and simple pattern. Leach asserts that the notched edges of baking dishes were rouletted. See **Notched rim**. Nottingham salt-glaze with its thin glaze was particularly suited to rouletting, sometimes used to draw stems and flowers with close dots or indentations, as was also done on Derbyshire "brown wares." In a more elaborate fashion, tiles were all-over impressed with animals, reptiles, and plants from carved rollers almost too wide to be called roulettes. The

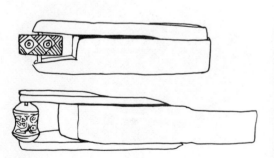

Two roughly made roulette wheels from early-nineteenth-century Virginia. Barber calls them "coggles."

An unusual curved roulette "cylinder seal" from Uruk, ca. 3750 B.C.

198

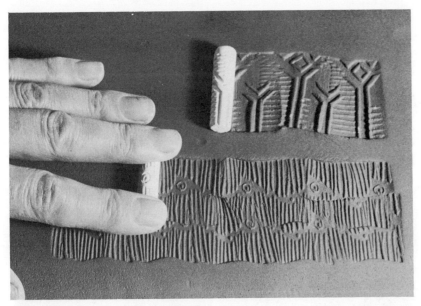

Carved sticks of blackboard chalk used to produce quite elaborate patterns by rolling them over soft clay. Their disadvantages are a short life and a liability to break.

Using a simple cog-like roulette wheel of fired clay to produce an overall pattern or texture by running it first vertically and then horizontally on a leather-hard clay surface.

Japanese include the roulette with rolled cord or cord-wound sticks under the heading "nawame." Lathe rouletting has been used a good deal in the industry.

The simplest form of roulette is a stick of chalk that can be carved and rolled over the clay surface, but true roulette wheels made of biscuit fired clay, cut or molded plaster, carved wood, or even metal are mounted on a wire spindle set in a wooden or wire frame. The raised print of the hard plastic tape of hand-embossing machines could be mounted onto a wheel—unfortunately, unless the back or a cast was used the letters would be reversed. Rouletted impressions do not have to be in the traditional horizontal line but can be used as on the Derbyshire pieces mentioned above, or arranged and repeated to form overall textures or more formal compositions.

Rubbed Color

Incising, combing, and similar techniques—even a well-grogged body—can be enhanced by rubbing pigment into the depressions. This can then be sponged, scraped, or sandpapered from the surface where not required.

A textured area of pot surface has been rubbed over with color to give contrast and to emphasize the form of this thrown and altered pot by Hans Coper.

Rubber Stamp

To make a rubber stamp it is possible to cut a reverse design in a small slab of plaster and build a wall around it, or cut the motif at the bottom of a shallow "box" cut or molded in the slab. Fill with liquid rubber after coating first with varnish, and then coat with a thin smear of soft soap to ensure that the rubber when set will come away cleanly. The stamp should be mounted onto thin foam rubber and then onto a wood block to serve as a handle. See also **Printing** and **Stamping.**

Ruby Luster

Where a copper metal luster has a copper-red background, its color tends toward a rich purple-red. The copper either can be incorporated into a very soft glaze (below 1,000° C./1,830° F.) painted onto a harder glaze containing copper with a little iron, or it can be painted onto a fired glazed surface as a copper/clay mixture. Reduction is carried out during cooling in the 750–600/1,300–1,100 range. An excellent entry on ruby luster giving more details appears in Hamer.

Run Glaze

See also **Poured glaze.** The most famous potters to turn run glaze into a distinctive art form were the T'ang Chinese, their brilliantly colored earthenware glazes splashed and painted onto rich, rounded forms. This riot of mottled color has never been equaled. A few Islamic potters used a similar idea and nearer our own times Staffordshire figures and other pieces were decorated with run mixed glazes. The French pioneer studio potters used the technique of run glazes in the nineteenth century. In Cooper (1972) a bowl from nineteenth-century Vermont is dabbed with circles of glaze that have run toward the center, uncannily similar to a Samarra bowl of 1,000 years earlier. This sort of glaze treatment is rare.

The running of a viscous glaze into luscious rolls and drops at the base of a glaze line is another story, and generally a happy accident. China clay replacing flint to increase the alumina content is a way of making glaze more viscous. A spun iron-painted line is also reputed to help.

T'ang Chinese earthenware made full use of running colored glazes, perhaps out of necessity, to produce strongly contrasted but soft-edged patterns. The lower edge of the glaze is also usually irregular and run to complement the designs. On the spouted bowl, simple blobs have taken on feathery shapes; in the detail from the side of a horse model the glaze colors have run in an extreme fashion and it is surprising that they stayed on the vertical surface at all.

 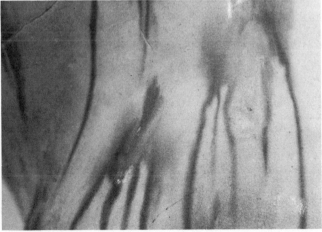

Viscous drops of glaze at the foot of an Islamic fourteenth-century turquoise glazed earthenware pot. Luscious droplets like these usually occur on stoneware but we also find them on T'ang lead-iron glazes.

A black glaze allowed to creep into the white produces a striking pattern. Bowl by Lucie Rie.

Detail of a remarkable platter with poured and run glazes. By Neil Moss of California.

Run Slip

When blobs or dots of slip are trailed onto a contrasting coating they can, while both are liquid, be induced to run into patterns by judicious tipping or shaking. Laid along one side of a triangular dish they will run inward toward the opposite corner, giving a quite lively and pleasant pattern (Fournier, 1977). More elaborate and controlled designs are also possible. With all run slip restraint is called for if the result is not to become marbling. It is a comparatively neglected technique today partly due to the eclipse of earthenware, although slip can, with modified recipes, be used on stoneware.

Probably one of the earliest examples of what is known as "splash and trickle" decoration. From Ancient Crete.

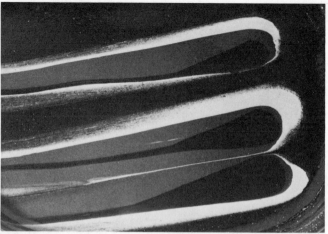

A run-slip dish and detail by Sheila Fournier. Blobs of slip were laid on one on another, black on red on white, the whole on a wet black slip base. They were then shaken from one end of the dish to the other. The detail shows the black slip burning slightly through the white layer above it.

Bright contrasting slips, black, buff, and red, poured from a spoon or trailer enliven this piggy bank by a schoolchild. Colors have been superimposed one on another.

Rust

Iron rust is a hydrated oxide and can be used to give speckle in bodies and glazes. Rust color is achieved in stoneware glazes by saturating with iron oxide, 8–12 percent of the recipe. A reasonably thin layer of glaze is recommended. Saturated glazes may develop a matt or crystalline surface. Oxidation during cooling is essential.

Rusticated Slip

A sort of "roughcast" decoration found on some Romano-British York wares and others. Thick slip appears to have been patted with a bat or paddle (or the hand) just as it is beginning to stiffen in order to bring up a coarse texture. It is not often practiced today, but some modern styles could make use of it.

Rutile

A titanium mineral with some iron. Alone it gives opacified broken creamy colors to glazes as seen in commercial tiles ad nauseum. Hamer states that 15 percent of rutile can produce a glaze that alters in tone when light falls on it. See **Phototrophy.** High iron rutiles are the ilmenites. Rutile is useful in developing a crystalline glaze. It can be reduced to blue. It is most commonly used to modify other colors and for its effects on glaze colors and surfaces.

Saggar Firing

See **Fuming.**

Salt-Glaze

Though it is not in itself a decorative technique, the surface textures and colors of salt-glaze are very beguiling, varying from thin, almost clear glaze to large brown leopard-skin blotches. Paul Soldner has used salt in a raku kiln to produce flashings of various-colored "rich surface marks" (*Ceramic Review* 76), but most firings are in the high stoneware range. David Davis uses washing soda in place of salt, the pots having sprayed-on copper and iron. A number of salts are used to produce colors and glazes of varying characters. The Pennsylvania German potters used engobes under the glaze to change its color or as a ground for decoration. Iron decoration blends well with salt-glaze, but the wide use of cobalt on many German and nineteenth-century American pots never quite blended with the general character of salted ware.

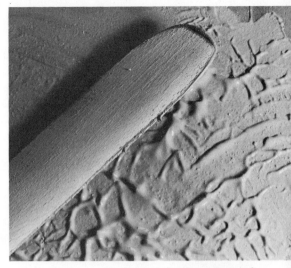

Patting wet slip with a paddle, a method of producing the type of "rusticated" surface found on some Romano-British pots from Yorkshire. The broken texture would be suitable for modern forms. The precise thickness of slip can be used to control the degree of lift.

The traditional salt-glaze surface, varied and broken not by artifice but as a result of quick, skillful handling of the materials and the fire. See also illustration under **Incidentals.**

Two pot lids in a salt-glaze by Wally Keeler showing the decorative effect of different body and glaze recipes combined in this case with highly expert turned spirals.

Jane Hamlyn has widened the scope of salt-glaze decoration with incising, combing, trailing, and stamping to add to the inherent attraction of the orange-peel finish, although how far one can go along this road is controversial, especially in conjunction with the strong "leopard-skin" effects developed by many potters.

High silica slips or bodies tend to give a bright, smoother surface; less silica a more mottled, broken texture. Fluxing, especially inside vessels, may be assisted by a coat of feldspathic glaze. The early New England potters used Albany slip for this purpose. Red clay or cobalt-stained slips, traditional on salt-glaze of the past, are used by studio potters today. While many still rely on the natural attractions of the glaze surface, there is also a tendency toward more elaborate and explicit decoration using slip trailing and other technique at

Samian Ware

A type of Roman gloss ware, usually with relief decoration. See also **Burnishing** and **Gloss.** Historians, on the strength of a contemporary reference, ascribed it to the Isle of Samos, hence the name, though manufacture there has never been confirmed. It is possible that the clay came from Samos. See also **Terra sigillata.** The term is now used loosely for any red-gloss ware from Italy or the Roman Empire, except the more sophisticated Arrentine ware. As early as the second century, *Samian* was used by contemporary writers to mean simply "made of clay." The work was done by specialized craftsmen, a mold-maker, a presser, and so on, in what must have been extensive "factories." Most work was pressed into biscuit molds with the top section thrown on. See **Poinçon.** The finest Samian is orange red and glossy, but the potting in various parts of Europe varied in quality through the five centuries during which Samian ware was made. As well as molded decoration, Samian was incised, slip-trailed, or used applied (sprigged) ornament. See **Barbotine** and **Sprigging.** There are black and marbled Samian pieces. The technique was never fully developed in Roman Britain.

Sand-Bed Reliefs

Storr-Britz suggests that, for large decorative reliefs, a bed of damp sand with a surrounding wall can be modeled, combed, or otherwise marked out with a design. If grogged slip is carefully poured in and allowed to dry, a decorated slab of clay will result. The slab can be cut into sections before being removed.

Sand-Blasting

The cutting of patterns into fired ceramics by directing a stream of refractory particles—for example, silicon-carbide grit of about 300 mesh—by means of a special "gun" at a pressure of about 160–180 pounds per square inch is practiced by a few potters today. The flying "sand" is obviously highly dangerous to the eyes, skin, and lungs, so the whole operation takes place in an enclosed box containing armholes connected to rubber gloves and a window. It is used mainly on porcelain to effect a texture or to cut through fired, glazed pieces. Alan Whitaker applies plastic tape to those areas he wishes to leave unaffected and may take two hours to achieve his filigree patterns. Zinc sheeting can be cut and used as a stencil. Ann Mortimer cuts indentations and holes through slip-cast spheres. Peter Starkey finds that he cannot really see what he is doing and asserts that there is no real control, although he claims "fantastic potential" for the technique, which is borne out by the examples mentioned above. A potter would need the resources of a large art college or a factory to make the experiment economically feasible.

Sang de Boeuf

A red, reduced-copper glaze, the term applying especially to examples from the Chinese Qing (Ch'ing) dynasty. It is glassy with minute bubbles and has often run to form a welt at the base of the glaze line. It is a blend of tiny red patches, sometimes streaked with gray, clear glaze, or green. "Sang de pigeon" is a more liver-red type.

Much experimental work went on at the turn of the twentieth century in England and Europe, and by Hugh Robertson in the United States, to imitate the Chinese glaze. It was found that some tin oxide assisted the color. In the form of **rouge flambé,** flame-like streaks of blue and purple appear. The effects have been luridly imitated by on-glaze methods on industrial porcelain. A number of studio potters produce reduced-copper glazes of this type successfully. Some early work by Gerry Williams, shown in the film *An American Potter,* is very striking. Derek Davis combines the red with a white glaze and other colors. See also **Copper red.**

Sawdust Firing

Today this is practiced almost entirely for its decorative effects: lustrous black, mysterious mergings of blacks and brown, or, on porcelain bodies, blacks, grays, and smoky whites, sometimes with white spots resembling the stars in a night sky. The colors are mainly from impregnation with carbon (see **Carbonized ware**) and possibly some degree of reduction. A degree of control can be exercised by lifting the piece partially from the burning sawdust as soon as it shows above the surface (sawdust is burned from the top downward). Judy Cunningham-Smith remarks that the resin from pinewood "sometimes produces beautiful blue and silver markings." Many potters insist on grog or sand "filling" for the body, but straight red clay or porcelain can be used to produce a smooth finish. In all cases there is a risk of cracking, and pots and bowls are better lifted from the "kiln" when exposed rather than left until the sawdust has completely burnt away. A still, warm day is almost essential.

Since the purpose is decorative rather than a return to primitive methods for their own sake, there can be no objection to prebiscuiting at about 1,000° C. (cone 06) or whatever temperature gives some physical strength while retaining full porosity, which is probably necessary for the typical carbonized effects.

A skillfully carbonized design in a sawdust-fired dish by Sebastian Blackie. See also **Carbonized ware**.

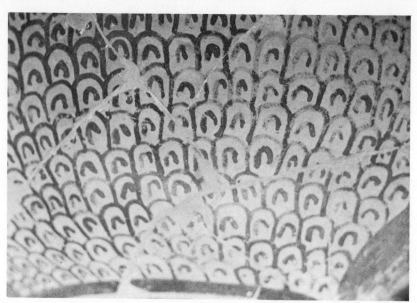

Detail of a 1350 B.C. Rhodian pot of which a large area is covered with painted scales and interior hoops.

Scales

Overlapping semicircles resembling fish scales appear on pottery from many parts of the world: incised scales on Chinese Chou-dynasty owl figures; overlapping finger-flattened pellets of clay on fine Gaulish beakers in Roman times, the scales pointing upward; on medieval jugs and pots, again laid from the base like a pineapple; an

Rising scales, made by pressing pads downwards with the finger, on a thirteenth-century London jug. It may be coincidental that there is a resemblance to the pineapple, which became a favorite decorative motif in England and abroad.

Finger-pressed pads of clay around this sturdy little teapot by Ian Godfrey overlapped to form lappets or scales acting as terminals to the diagonal scoring of the body.

ambitious aquamaline in the form of a ram covered in small scales to represent wool; and many other examples. Downward-facing painted scales appear on a Nubian second-century flagon, one of the finest pots ever made (illustrated in Charleston). Painted scale patterns are frequent on the rims and other areas of Meissen, Worcester, and Vienna porcelains. Scale patterns are not common today except occasionally as applied clay (see **Applied decoration** and **Pad**), but the idea should be retained as a small item in the potter's decorative vocabulary.

Scratched Decoration

Over a wide area of Neolithic Italy and France pottery was decorated by scratching lines with a flint or other hard point into the burnished, fired surface. The ragged line was then filled (inlaid) with ocher or a chalky material. With a sharper tool it is possible to engrave fired pottery, but the line is still frequently broken-edged.

"Scratch blue" was used in the eighteenth century on salt-glaze and even on creamware. A fairly deep line was incised into leather-hard clay and cobalt oxide rubbed in. After the glaze fire, a blue line with a faintly fuzzy edge resulted due to the fluxing of the color. The almost white stoneware body developed in the mid-eighteenth century invited scratch blue. Some may have been made at Liverpool. It also appears on nineteenth-century U.S. folk pottery, where leaves, fish, and other patterns are also tinted with a stippled blue. It does not appear to have been taken up by modern potters, but there are possibilities in the technique and its variants. Hughes mentions a historical variant: the body coated with blue and then covered with a white engobe, which was then scratched through to the blue beneath. See also **Flow blue.** The main technical difficulty is getting rid of all traces of cobalt on the surface, but even this could be turned to advantage, leaving a faint wash or stipple texture.

Screen Printing

While silk is the normal material for screen printing, nylon or organdie can be used or coarser materials, even perforated zinc, can be experimented with to produce textures or designs on pottery. By its nature all direct screen printing must be received by a more or less flat surface. The scope is widened if the image is printed onto an intermediate material such as transfer paper. See **Silkscreen** and **Transfers.**

Scroddled Ware

An American name for **agate ware,** also called "lava ware." It was made at Bennington Pottery, but its expense limited it to a comparatively small output. Brown and reddish clays were streaked with gray and cream bodies.

Seal

The commonest use for a seal in ceramics is, of course, to impress or stamp the potter's name, symbol, or production details usually under the foot. But even when hidden, a good seal is always a decorative bonus and can warrant a position on the face of a dish, perhaps a major or the only item of decoration. It can be impressed straight into the clay but more effectively on a small pad, giving the effect of a wax seal.

Stamped seals appear on a few ancient pots such as Roman Samian ware, impressed into the mold. Earlier Egyptian scarabs in "glazed frit" and other items were often cut with a seal beneath, presumably as an official's mark for use on wax or similar material. Large applied seals showing a figure, a lion, and a wheel adorn a medieval York jug

A typical scratched and crosshatched design on a pale salt-glazed body. There is no perceptible spread of the pigment, as sometimes occurs. See also **Flow blue**.

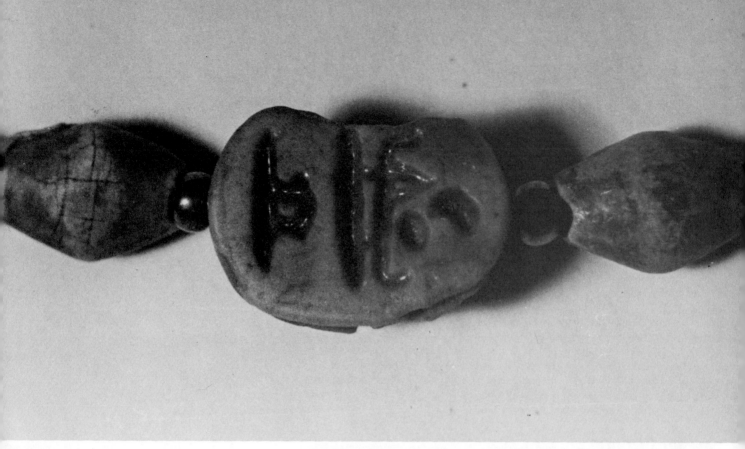

A 3,000-year-old seal on the underside of an Egyptian frit-paste scarab. Probably used by an architect or government official.

A roulette and its pattern from Susa, Mesopotamia, ca. 3500 B.C., sharply and cleanly cut and called by archeologists a "cylinder seal." See also **Roulette**.

A large stamped seal forming part of the decoration of a casserole by David Leach when he was working at St. Ives, carefully placed under the curve of the lug handle.

The pronounced raised seal on a hand-built bottle is the sole decoration apart from the slightly mottled texture of the glaze.

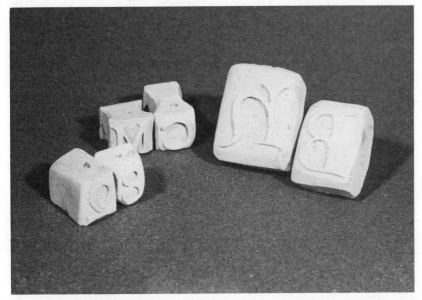

Initial and date stamps for Henry Burger and Michael Cardew at Winchcombe Pottery, 1930–1939. These would have been used for sprigs as well as stamped seals.

under a green glaze, and on another jug an elaborate sprig was applied with the lettering "Thomas me fecit"—but backward! Initials also appear, though rarely, on medieval and seventeenth-century pots and on at least one example the potter again forgot to reverse the letter. Official seals were used to identify Japanese pottery types: plum flower for Koishibara; chrysanthemum for Onda. Initials occasionally appear on Greek pots, but through the ages the potter has generally remained anonymous. Seal-stamped ware is, therefore, comparatively modern, and even today its value is disputed.

Attractive and interesting seals impressed into the base of a pie dish.

Seals are normally of biscuit pottery but can be of wood or plaster. The last will quickly deteriorate if not strengthened. The design must, of course, be reversed and will give better service if fairly bold and simple. It can be intagio or relief: an incised stamp giving a relief seal is perhaps more effective; the reverse can be inlaid with pigment to give it more character. Two unusual methods of making name or initial seals have been suggested by readers of *Ceramic Review*. Letters in metal type can be bound or glued together and used either direct or via a plaster or clay cast; a seal of

At an inaugural party to launch a new pottery, we prepared a dish for each visitor decorated with our seals under a stoneware glaze. The visitors painted their own initials in gold, which was then fired during the party in the manner of the original raku.

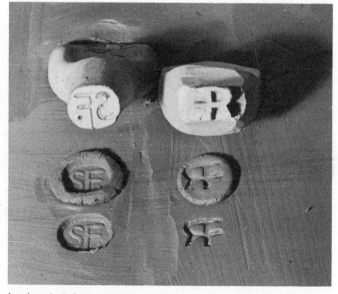

Intaglio and relief potter's seals with their impressions on clay pads, set directly into the clay surface.

a full name can be taken from the raised letters on a credit card. Usually the potter will carve his own monogram or sign; if cut into plaster, several clay casts can be taken. As mentioned above, detailed cutting will soon be worn away and a broad, well-defined design will have a longer life. See also **Roulette** and **Stamping**.

Seaweed

Strands of seaweed wrapped around a pot before firing can leave glossy imprints on the biscuit. A remarkable, bright red stringy pattern of a type of glaze from seaweed is illustrated in Sanders. The salt content is an operative part of the reaction. Salt-soaked rope or cloth can also leave ghostly glossy images. See also **Fire cord.** Joan Campbell uses seaweed to give surface markings on raku (Lane, 1983).

Secret Decoration

Called in China "an hua," this was either fine engraving or low-relief molding on white porcelain. It is possible to discern it only by transmitted light, when it resembles a watermark on paper. While not so consciously "hidden," types of formal decoration by modern potters rely on the effects of light picking out degrees of translucency controlled by various thicknesses of body. See also **Lithophane.**

Selenium

A modern material for use at low temperatures. Red results from mixtures with cadmium. Maroon, orange, and red enamels are produced by various compounds of these materials, but their volatility causes difficulties. Selenium can be toxic and should be used with care. There are now some doubts about its use on tableware.

Sgraffito, Sgraffiato, Graffiato

Sgraffito is the cutting-through of one layer of color to show a contrasting one, often the body color, beneath. The term is sometimes widened to cover all scratching or cutting into clay, but this tends to make it meaningless. Other techniques of cutting into clay or removing the surface coating are discussed under **Combing, Engraving, Finger combing, Incising, Scratched decoration,** etc. The slight variation of the word—sgraffiato or graffiato—is used to denote a design in which the background is more or less cut away, leaving the main elements of the composition in the surface color. Further cutting can delineate the reserved areas. This is a useful distinction.

Sgraffito does not often appear on very early pots. The cutting and white filling of lines on some primitive pieces look at first glance like sgraffito but are in fact inlay. The Greek black-figure potters, however, drew details of muscles, features, and clothing through their dark slip silhouettes. The Chinese excelled at the method; the fluidity and verve of line on some T'zu Chou and other wares has rarely been equalled. As with many other cultures, the Chinese were not always "pure" in their techniques, combining sgraffito with brushwork, stamping, etc., and they cut with equal facility through pigment, slip, and glaze. Japanese Shino combined reserved slip with sgraffito and brushwork under a feldspathic glaze. Korean potters combined it with **mishima.** Naive but lively work appears on early Islamic ware, later to develop into graffiato designs of great power. These were often a white slip on a lightish red earthenware body with a honey-colored, green, or manganese brown glaze over. Colored slips were also used: black, blue, and green. A certain unity was achieved by covering some pieces with a turquoise glaze, which had the effect of turning the cut-away areas almost black.

Two aspects of Chinese Song (Sung) work, the first cut in an almost scribbled fashion through the powerful blocks of color on a dragon-decorated jar; the second is firmer and at the same time more delicate, the background darkened by combing in the style of sgraffiato (see text).

Block sgraffito or "graffiato" on an eleventh-century Chinese "pillow." The marks left by the tool in cutting away the main white area can be seen, and they add an extra dimension to the design. Brilliant contrast is achieved through the fine sgraffito on the bear's head and on the rope.

The so-called silhouette wares of twelfth-century Persia were of this kind. The strictness with which the later converted Turks translated Koran edicts was not evident in the earlier Islamic wares and figures; animals and any subject that came to hand were exploited. Byzantine and Cypriot potters continued the traditions and produced strongly cut figures, birds, and animals. In general "the ware as a whole must be regarded as a kind of peasant pottery" (Hobson), although magnificent work was done. Peasant-work sgraffito has tended to remain a feature of folk pottery worldwide. It paralleled the great tin-glaze epoch in Europe, though the majolica potters did not use it to any degree. Some luster painting was scratched through to mark details, such as the planking on the magnificent Hispano-Moresque ships, while faces, hair, and clothes were suggested by fine lines, which revealed the white glaze beneath. Of some Italian sgraffito, Honey says, "The grace and strength of the drawing are characteristic of Italian Renaissance Art." Surprisingly (because it demands more artistic skill) most peasant potters preferred the brush to the engraver, but it had a place in all peasant

214

Building up textures by means of long and short sgraffito lines, an original approach on a twelfth-century Byzantine dish from Miletus.

An entertaining fourteenth-century English tile employing the graffiato technique (the background cut away) with details cut into the blocks of white slip. There is a wealth of comment in the positions and expressions of the characters, Jesus and his tempters.

communities, especially in Europe. In Hungary, sgraffito would define an area of design that would then be filled with slip or color. It is comparatively rare in English medieval pottery—some tiles and jugs—and was little practiced until the seventeenth century. In the English West Country, the line was free and curvilinear; in Devon, the background would be cut away to leave the slipped surface in slight relief. A reversal of the normal white slip took place in Staffordshire; a dark slip on a buff body. In the later nineteenth century, potters would sell raw (unfired) slipped pots to would-be decorators who would return the finished pieces to be fired and glazed. Such were the

A traditional pot from Ceylon (Sri Lanka), with variety obtained by crosshatching, closely cut lines, etc.

A Staffordshire sgraffito dish of 1720, cut with a precision and rigidity that would suggest a later date.

Rapidly cut sgraffito on a wet hakame surface by Michael Cardew.

Unlikely creatures on a jug by Fishley Holland.

Impressed and sgraffito decoration by the Hungarian Stephen Gonda, somewhat confused and obliterated by brushed-on color oxides.

humble beginnings of the modern artist potter, comparable to the decalcomania craze in the nineteenth-century United States. Rhymes and tags were often scratched through slips, even as early as 1733 in the United States, usually then and for the next hundred years in the German language. See **Inscriptions.** Pouncing was used to aid repetitive work in many potteries. Sgraffito began to fade in the early nineteenth century as brushwork became more popular.

Sgraffito remains a favorite with student classes in ceramics; like paper resist it does not require quite the speed and assurance of the brush or slip trailer. The simplicity of the technique can make it a very direct form of expression, although it can also lead to finicky and lifeless work. In one form or another it is widely practiced by the professional potter through slip, color, and glaze. The early work of Hans Coper shows combing and scratching through a self-glazing black slip to a white body—strong and stark. Lucie Rie's sgraffito lines are so fine as almost to constitute a texture; in contrast, Cardew cuts brush-like strokes of great simplicity. There is a fine bird-and-clouds dish by Leach. Peter Stoodley combs through vitreous slips on garden pots of majestic proportions. In a very different style, Val Cushing emphasizes the form of a globular body by reserving circles on a sgraffito-textured background. A similar formal emphasis is achieved by Peter Voulkos with his drawing of a head on a round-bodied bottle. Other potters cut through glazes and enamel.

Two block sgraffito designs by schoolchildren, the first through color, the second through slip. Note the instinctive, more delicate detail on the spiral plate at the center and rim.

For slip, the cutting is generally done with a flat-ended, slightly angled bamboo tool. This can be fine or broad, an average of about ⅛ inch across. V-gouges and many other tools are also used, but too sharp a point will cut too deeply and can also give a broken line. The quality can vary from spider-like scratches to wide, sweeping strokes, using the tool like a wide quill pen. Cutting into leather-hard slip will give a clear line, the waste clay coming away cleanly. On wet slip a plough line will result with a slip build-up on each side. This can be attractive, but the danger of deep cutting and

"Block" sgraffito by Hans Coper, strong, economical, and impressionistic, the large eye giving dramatic emphasis. Note the texture left in the cut-away areas.

dragging is always present on a wet surface. Dry clay will break away each side of the stroke; and, though a fine line is possible, it will rarely be a smooth one. Combing, the use of a stiff hogs'-hair brush, finger sgraffito, and other methods are dealt with under the appropriate headings. The depth of the cut should be sufficient merely to remove the slip and not to cut into the body. Any burr on the line is best left until quite dry, when it can be rubbed away. For sgraffiato a knife or other broader tool can be used to remove the background slip. If this background is left with flecks of slip still adhering, they will give interest and weight. Counterchange can be a potent element in sgraffito design.

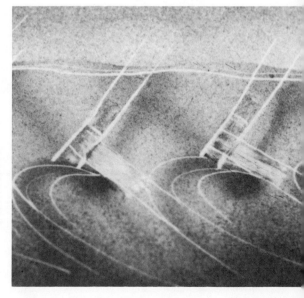

Two contrasting styles of sgraffito line: geometric cutting through a matt black glaze to a porcelain body by Julien Stair; and the mysterious, evocative drawing of Alan Pirie.

219

A burnished dish by Siddig El'Nigoumi. Variety of weight and interest is given by varying the distances between the radial lines and contrasting these with the greater mass of the camels. Note the clever use of one animal walking in the opposite direction, giving a circular movement and containing the whole design within the dish.

Free and fantastic slip cutting by David Toresdahl. Blocks of dark slip with incised details.

Detail of a figurative design on a sculptured ceramic form by Rudy Autio. The free lines are balanced by the black areas and the hard outline. If there is discernible influence it is the rapid sketches on pottery by Picasso.

Sheila Casson working at one of her sgraffito landscapes. See **Landscape** *and* **Stylization**.

Remarkable, painstaking sgraffito through sprayed-on colored slips to porcelain. By Bill Brown.

Pigment sgraffito can be done on the raw clay, on the raw glaze as Caiger-Smith does with a porcupine quill, or on the fired glaze. Glazes can be cut through from one to another or through to the body. As mentioned above, details of drawing on luster can be cut through to the white glaze beneath. At Crich Pottery they pour colored glazes in lapped sweeps and then cut through them, drawing landscapes and other patterns from one glaze to another or through to the biscuit. A final glaze is sprayed over the whole surface. The interaction of the glazes produces interesting color effects (article in *Ceramic Review* 56).

Shadow Pattern _____

Black and gray markings on ocher-slipped "red raku" are achieved in Japan by a special firing of previously biscuited pots. Pieces are piled into a fireclay box or saggar with a perforated base under which a wood fire is burned. When it is well alight, small blocks of charcoal are dropped among the pots, staining the ocher slips in a random fashion. Later a thick glaze is applied. It is an allied technique to **fire cord.**

Shavings can be produced in various ways, as byproducts of turning, cutting, etc., and each will have its own character. In the illustrations a block of leather-hard clay is rubbed over a Surform blade to produce curled fragments. These are shown being lightly beaten onto a thinly slipped slab pot in a controlled shape. Color, slip, or glaze can be brushed or sponged over at appropriate stages.

The complicated texture on this cylinder by Eileen Lewenstein was built up of coarse wood ash (the bits which would not go through a 40s sieve) with leather-hard turnings thrown on. The ash also contained sand and gravel.

Shavings

Clay shavings from turning or scraping can be beaten into the damp clay surface to produce a somewhat "rustic" finish. The decorative whorls from pot-turning can also be utilized. The unglazed, burnished Shudei ware of Tokoname are treated in this way with pressed shavings. Small pellets of clay cut from the surface with a round-ended tool can be turned over and gently beaten-back to provide a negative/positive of the same shape. See also **Texture** for a nineteenth-century American example.

Shell Impressions

The serrated edge of a cockleshell was used to decorate prehistoric Mediterranean wares, known to archeologists as "cardium" decoration. Used with discretion, many shells could be used to give characteristic impressions. Murex shell impressions appear on 1250 B.C. Mycenean pottery.

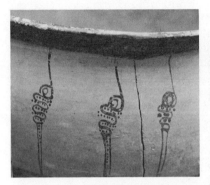

The murex shell transformed into an abstract design on a Mycenaean pot of ca. 1250 B.C.

The base of a hand-built bowl by Ewen Henderson with shells imprinted into the clay.

Shot Clay

An extreme technique from Hungary is described in *Ceramic Review 79,* where Imre Schramml fires at soft clay cubic porcelain forms with a gun to transform them "by perforation, collision, penetration, into dynamic and variable form." "Variable" would be right!

Shoulder

The shoulder of a full-formed pot is the focal point for the eye, and the most significant decoration usually occurs here, as a band or pattern, as free brushstrokes, or a more localized emphasis such as the mask on Bellarmine bottles. The throwing spiral is also often at its most significant at this point.

Sienna

A hydrated iron/manganese ochrous earth. It is used in easel painting but could be useful in ceramics. It may need to be calcined. Similar natural compounds were probably used in early slips such as those from ancient South America.

Silhouette Wares

The Greeks worked mainly in silhouette with details in a fine sgraffito line, but "silhouette ware" usually refers to a twelfth-century Persian group whose solid designs were painted in black pigment and covered with an off-white or turquoise glaze.

Detail of the silkscreened plate shown under **Optical decoration**. *A line, block, and mesh pattern typical of the technique.*

Compositions of leaves, script, etc., were also cut through a slip or pigment, leaving a light-colored background in the graffiato style. Leach and other modern potters have used silhouette often through the medium of paper resist.

Silkscreen

Fundamentally silkscreen printing is a sophisticated form of stencil. It was used extensively in the pottery industry by Maw and other tile factories.

The simplest form of screen is a wooden frame over which is stretched a silk bolting cloth. Silk itself is now more rarely used, being replaced by man-made fibers. Cheap throw-away screens are also made. Other materials, even wire mesh, have also been used. The screen is marked out with a design, and the areas not to be printed are varnished or otherwise made impermeable, for example, by covering with tape or paper. Varnishing may be done freehand or by means of stencils. The screen is applied to a flat surface such as that of tile or a slab pot, and color rubbed through. Screens are also used to print on a special paper to make decals. A squeegee is normally used to press the color through the screen. Oil-bound enamels are most commonly used, but glaze, slip, and other pigments can be used with suitable mesh screens. For curved surfaces the indirect method of first printing onto decal paper is used. Large areas of color which would be difficult or impossible with a brush are possible with screening. The "cushion edge" of many modern commercial tiles can spoil the effect of screening.

Geometric, sharp-edged graphic designs are often screen printed. The rigid lines and

A Port Merion Pottery silkscreen design called "Magic City," with a variety of tone achieved through dots and lines.

Silkscreen transfer decoration on a pyramid by Matthew Hancock using smaller elements of design than the last two examples.

squares of Glenys Barton's constructions are screened onto bone china. Glaze can be screened on as a pattern, or, if a print is made with an oil-based medium, glaze poured over will run from the printed portions and the fired piece will appear to have the glaze cut away to show the color of the printed image. Any color or screened material must be matched to the mesh size; if it is coarser or contains larger particles it will not penetrate properly.

A variety of resists may be employed. Lacquer or a hard-drying glue can be used according to whether the pigment is water or oil based. The design can be painted in liquid latex and then "reversed" by coating all over with glue and then peeling the latex away. Paper can be adhered to the underside of the screen. Very clean lines are obtained by the use of lacquer film that is supplied with a paper backing: a cut is made

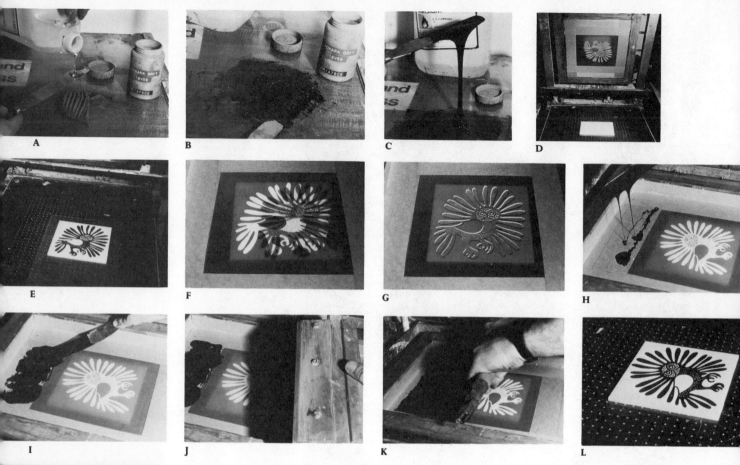

A series illustrating the basic technique of silkscreen printing.

A. A quantity of pigment, in this case a dark gray enamel, is laid onto a glass slab (no other surface is suitable) and a small pool of oil medium poured onto a spatula.

B. C. The oil and pigment are ground together on the glass until a treacle-like consistency is obtained as shown.

D. The screen, traditionally of silk but now often of other man-made fibers (see **Photoceramic processes** for method of transferring an image to a screen), is fastened into the hinged section of a press and a tile laid onto the bed. There must be a fractional space left between the screen and the tile (or paper) to be printed when the screen is closed onto it.

E. F. G. To obtain accurate registration on the tile the original image, which has been drawn or photographed onto a transparent acetate sheet (see **Photoceramic processes**), is laid in place on the tile. When the screen is closed down, we can see (in illustration F) that it does not line up with the positive image, and the tile must be moved until the two correspond as in G.

H. I. The acetate has been removed from the tile and the screen lowered onto it, leaving a slight gap as mentioned above. Pigment is dribbled onto the end of the screen and evened out with a square spatula.

J. K. A squeegee made of a strip of rubber mounted on wood is used to pull the color across the screen and to press it through the mesh onto the surface below. Firm, even pressure and steady movement are essential.

L. The printed tile after lifting away the screen.

M. The tile drying on a rack, which can also be used for support while firing the enamel.

with a knife that penetrates the film but not the backing. After cutting the design, the elements to be printed are removed and the sheet adhered to the underside of the screen with sparely applied thinners. The paper is peeled away when the film has dried on. Sharpened wire loop tools can be used to cut narrower lines. A thicker type of film is used for slip printing.

Finally, there are involved systems of photoresist utilizing a photosensitive emulsion that becomes water-insoluble under the effects of light. Contact negatives, projections, even natural objects can be used to control the design. Certain screens can develop half-tones. A series of illustrations showing the use of the light box in the making of a screen stencil may be found under **Photoceramic processes.**

The basic technique of printing is seen in the illustrations accompanying this article, and there is an associated series under **Decal.** As mentioned above, glazes and slips may be screened using a coarse mesh. Other techniques, including direct glue painting for non-water-based pigments, are described by Conrad. Screen-printed slabs may be used for building into pots. Cylindrical, conical, or angular shapes are possible by this method. Thin, fairly soft decorated slabs can, with great care, be stretched and formed over curved molds. Most printing via decals is, however, done on biscuit or glaze.

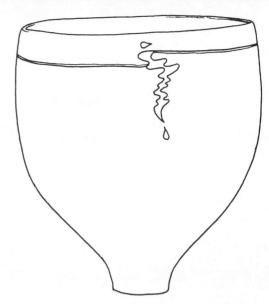

Silver

Silver metal used alone for luster will tarnish. Tomimoto added gold and platinum to silver to prevent blackening. Later he omitted the gold. Modern commercial silver luster is made from platinum, sometimes with gold addition. True silver is warmer in tone. Silver sulphide can be used with ocher for luster in reduction at about 750° C. (Cone 017). Copper and silver compounds will give orange-red to yellow lusters. A touch of liquid gold mixed with the silver will help to prevent tarnishing as mentioned above. See also **Luster,** and for the use of silver as a metal under **Inlay** and **Metals.**

Silver metal has been inlaid into this bowl by Debbie Pointon. The piece was soft-fired and smoked prior to the inlaying of the silver band and motif. The incising was done at the leather-hard stage and a rubbing taken; this was transferred to a sheet of sterling silver, which was cut and filed to fit.

Sintered Engobe

See **Engobe.**

Slide-off Transfer

A design may be silkscreened onto litho, also called thermo-flat, paper and covered with a plastic medium or cover coat. The decal is soaked in water until the image, fixed to the cover coat, will slide from the paper. The residue of the gum will adhere the image to the ceramic. See diagram. The plastic coating fires away. There is a series of illustrations on preparing a slide-off transfer under **Decal.** The making of transfers, however, often needs professional expertise, materials, and equipment, and there are a few suppliers in Europe and America who will prepare short runs for potters. See also **Transfers.**

Slip-Cast Relief

Slip casting with relief patterns is essentially an industrial technique, and millions of pieces have been so made. Inevitably the intaglio of the relief is seen inside the pot. The method is used for studio porcelain by Jacqueline Poncelet and others where the outer relief or formal alteration and its inner "negative" both have value. Undercutting is obviously a greater danger than in smooth-surfaced molds, and several pieces may be necessary, with attendant seam-line problems. Most industrial relief is cast by the jigger and jolley system so that the inside surface is smooth.

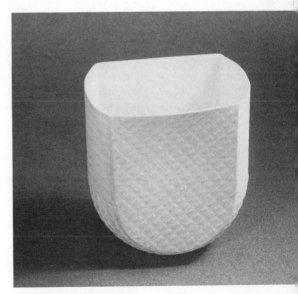

Cast bone china by Jaqueline Poncelet. Note the negative of the pattern inside the form.

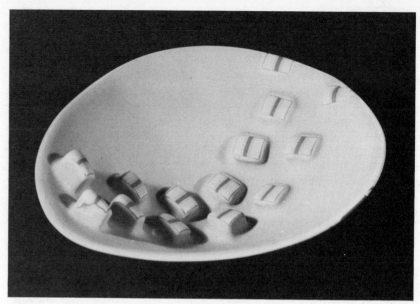

A curious use of slip casting. The neriage-type blocks were placed in the mold and the form cast over them. The surfaces were then cleaned down to the pattern. By Kathryn Lawrence.

Slip Colors

Early potters used natural iron- and manganese-bearing clays, sometimes, as is reputedly the case with Greek red and black ware, aided by reduction. Deliberately colored slips, using a light base clay, were in general use in East Persia in the eighth and the ninth centuries, probably developed to prevent pigments from running excessively under the glaze. Precise and lively calligraphic brushwork resulted. Even white slip over a black ground was achieved. The manuals by Rhodes, and many other books on the materials of ceramics, deal with the practical aspects of colored slips. Their advantages lie in their ability to provide a flat all-over color; in the fact that the clay fixes the color when both are dry and so avoids smudging; and in their ability to react with glazes to provide interesting results. Resist, sgraffito, combing, marbling, and other variations are possible, and one slip can be laid over another. A heavily loaded slip will give a deep color with less tendency to run than pigment alone. The main snag to their use is the shrinkage during drying, which can cause peeling and crazing. Methods of avoiding this include compounding refractory slips, deflocculation, and application at just the right leather-hard stage of the body clay.

Most of the oxides can be used in slip, although the most common are iron, cobalt, copper, and manganese. Commercial slip stains are available but are expensive if used in quantity.

Slip Cup

Trailers in the form of cups, often with a depression on each side to fit fingers and thumb and with holes for goose quills, were common in the eighteenth and nineteenth centuries. A single quill would be used for lettering or outlining figures, but for feathering and other designs up to seven nozzles would be employed at one time. Barber illustrates several. See also **Blow bottle** and **Slip trailers.**

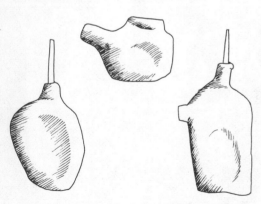

Three roughly made but doubtless effective pottery slip cups (trailers) in use in Virginia around 1800. Note the recessed sides for ease of holding.

Slip Dipping

The simplest method of slip decoration was practiced in nineteenth-century English country potteries, where a red clay pot was dipped neck down into buff slip, sometimes merely covering the rim. There was an element of hygiene since the light slip not only was of a finer grain than the red clay but would also show up any lack of cleanliness. The only aesthetic consideration lay in the depth of the slip, usually about one-third or two-thirds of the way down the pot. Although one might suppose slip dipping to be common in workaday pottery of the past, it is surprising how seldom one finds examples. Guiland does not illustrate a single dipped pot from American folk pottery. Brears, however, calls dipping the "simplest and earliest" method in most countries from the sixteenth century on. Some were slipped overall or with a "bib" as a ground for sgraffito.

Today dipped slip, or **engobe,** is used on beakers and other tableware to vary the glaze quality either from the inside to the outside or over part of the outer surface. A high-iron slip, for instance, can be used over a stoneware body, the whole covered with a pale glaze. Plates and bowls can be either dipped from the rim or partially immersed side and side about. Sam Haile bib-dipped jugs or just touched the belly of a pot in black slip, giving an oval ground for trailing. See also **Dipping.**

Slip Glazes

Apart from the recognized slip glazes such as Albany slip, mixtures containing about 50 percent clay plus pigment and a flux such as feldspar can be used as painting colors. Mary Rich applies sometimes minute and delicate slip-glaze ornament to her teapots under a thin salt-glaze. Most slip glazes are on high-fired ceramics. Some Song (Sung) glazes are of this type. There is a wide field for experiment using slip glazes of various types. They help to stop the running of the color and can give a solid block where this is required. They can be used without a glaze cover, especially on nondomestic ceramics, and a certain degree of relief can be obtained that will vary the surface quality. See also **Slip painting.**

Slip Painting

Perhaps a majority of all pre-industrial pottery was decorated by the laying-on of slips. The limitations of slip painting became apparent only with the introduction of glaze. The earliest decorated pottery in the West, from Jericho, is painted in clay earths with a skill, variety, and verve that are astonishing at the very birth of a difficult and revolutionary technique. Painting in red-browns, blacks, and yellows continued through the pre-Dynastic cultures of Egypt, and reverse painting, white on a dark ground, was also done. It is found, swirling and brilliant, two continents away in China; it became sophisticated and realistic in Crete and was finally used as a high art form by the potter/painters of Classic Greece. The slips used were sometimes so high in color content—iron, manganese, etc.—as to warrant the name "pigment," although all were likely to have been discovered naturally in the earth and not compounded from clay and purified oxide as is done today. The coming of glaze altered all this, and slip came to be used more thickly as a poured-on cover coat, although generous brush applications under a thin glaze was fairly common in the Islamic period and has continued in peasant pottery until modern times. Some rough white strokes of slip are found on medieval jugs and pots.

The prime slip painters were, however, the peoples of Central and South America, using an unsurpassed variety of design and a varied polychrome palette. Every creature

Some of the world's finest slip painting came from Peru, and this highly economic and powerful bird design has rarely been equalized, suggesting all the ferociousness of a bird of prey without resort to realism. From the Mochica culture.

An attractive design on an unglazed Roman Empire dish (from Fasano, Apulia) with three lively perch and limpets in white, brown, buff, and black.

A powerful bird and totem semigeometric design on an Ancient American Nazca pot, painted in natural slips.

A different and more gentle bird trailed and painted in slip from tenth-century Sari in northeast Persia. The slip has remained fairly solid under the thin alkaline glaze.

An example of the slip painting of twelfth-century Persia, a splendid arrangement of simple shapes and spaces.

from man to insect was portrayed, together with flowers and magical/abstract geometric and other compositions. Most were burnished to a dull gloss. There is a wealth of information on modern South American work in Litto's book *South American Folk Pottery,* and Val Barry in *Ceramic Review 28* has an interesting description of modern Pueblo pottery. They tell us that a fine-grained local clay is soaked in water, and, when it is smooth and of a consistency to drop slowly from the finger, four to six layers of a light slip are applied to the clay body with a cloth and then burnished. Yellow,

*A brightly colored kaleidoscopic pattern in stained slips on a burnished earthenware pot by John Ablitt. The type of finish ensures the maximum crispness and brilliance of the slips. Compare with the effect under a glaze under **Slip trailing** and elsewhere.*

An unusual approach to slip painting was adopted by Anne Turner on this slip-cast form. The slips were laid onto the surface of the mold before the form was cast, being transferred to the pot during the process of casting.

orange, and red-brown clays are then used for painting onto the slip base. Black is made by boiling down the stems of plants—tansy and guaco are mentioned—with the addition of natural iron or manganese-bearing earths. The end fibers of the Yucca plant are cut and chewed to form a fine brush-like point, and this is used to paint on the slips. "Only designs which recognise the curvature of the pots . . . and are conscious that only part of the decoration lies in the field of vision at one time are successful" (Barry)—a basic truth of all pot decoration which makes it different from and more difficult than the styles used on the insides of bowls. Bands of slip are sometimes applied with the fingers alone. Painting onto burnished surfaces are sometimes left matt as a contrast. Slip painting is not widely used today, but Fritsch's "optical" designs, for instance, resemble colored slips.

For glazed pots, where a full stroke of natural clay slip is required (as distinct from the rough striations of hakame), a soft, thick brush is needed in order to lay on a sufficient coating. A thinner application may disappear under the glaze, which utilizes

Irene Vonck lays thick slip onto her slab forms with a knife, impasto. The slip colors are varied with glaze stains and applied as a slurry rather than a true slip. After bisque firing, glaze is sprayed on and then wiped away or thinned out in areas, using a sponge.

part of the clay surface for its own purposes. This is especially true of lead glazes on earthenware. Long lines are therefore difficult, and blobs of slip reflecting the shape of the brush are more successful. The Chinese built up flower and other patterns in this way. The fading of the slip can be a virtue in the grading of color from the center outward toward the perimeter and the end of the brushstroke. Special slips or engobes with more opaque or strongly colored characteristics can be made up to counter

233

Andrea Gill's "Face Vace," lowfire slip and glaze.

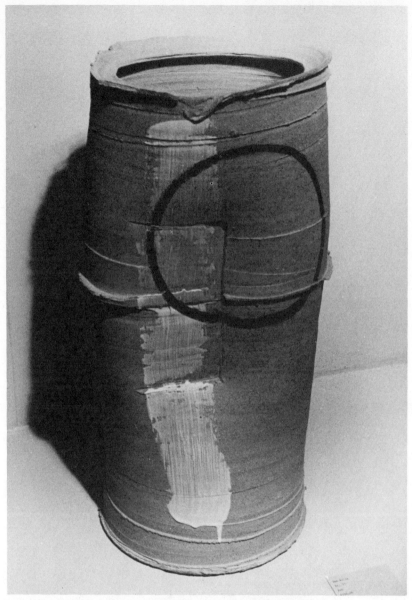

Simple but striking decoration in brushed-on slip on a beaten pot by Dan Kelly.

slip-fading under a glaze. Slip can be thickened with acetic acid to assist a firmer coating. See also **Slip colors.**

Slip Patting _____

At Onda and elsewhere in Japan a technique has been developed whereby a wide, flat (hake) brush is loaded with slip, which is then patted rapidly onto a slowly revolving dish or bowl, giving a radial, slightly raised pattern in the wet slip. The result is intriguing, and the technique can be seen in action in the film *Potters at Work.*

 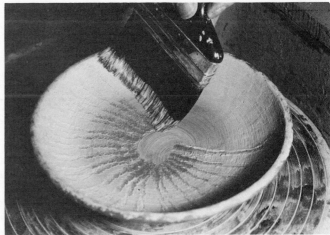

Those lucky enough to have seen the fine film "Potters at Work" will know what I call "slip patting" should really be like. Attempts to reproduce the shell-like pattern, however, were less than wholly successful. Two of the results are illustrated, using a multiple Chinese brush which seems too soft and a stiffer house-painting brush. The latter gave a more interesting whorled pattern but without the definition of the Japanese work. The dish should, perhaps, have been flatter to give a more regular lift to the slip over the width of the brush. I probably also made the mistake of covering the bowl with slip first; patting straight onto the clay with a loaded brush might have been more successful.

Slip Pouring

Decorative swags of slip can be poured over pots and plates, perhaps to be further embellished by brushwork, sgraffito, etc. Slip poured from a jug onto a revolving wheel will give horizontal spirals with overlapping runs. In *Ceramic Review 54,* Ruth Karnac mentions a Chinese method of pouring slip into the center or along the radius of a plate or bowl when it is spinning on the wheel to give an even, overall coverage by centrifugal action. The shallower the bowl, the slower should the wheel turn.

Slip Techniques

Individual techniques are discussed under **Burnishing, Combing, Feathering, Hakame, Inlay, Lift-off slip, Pate-sur-pate, Resist techniques, Sgraffito, Slip painting, Slip patting,** and **Slip trailing.**

A minor technique not previously mentioned is to cover the surface of a pot fairly thickly with slip and then to texture it (see **Rusticated slip**), or to induce rings and dribbles with a finger or tool while it is spinning on a wheel.

As general advice on the use of slip, there is the obvious danger that water absorbed by the pot from the slip will soften it to a dangerous degree. The wall thickness of a thrown pot should therefore be as even as possible, and the piece should be slipped at the stiff leather-hard stage. The slipped pot should be put where it will not be moved or shaken for an hour or more. Handles are especially vulnerable and may need support. A mold is often necessary for flattish dishes; a few pads of clay are not enough, as the dish can break across them. Some potters slip the insides of bowls before turning them, the base being thicker and more able to stand up to the softening effect. The disadvantage is the possible damage to the slip surface, which can then never be

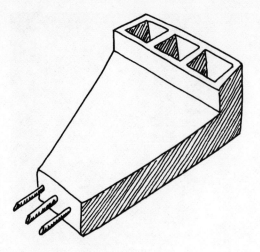

A compartmented Stoke-on-Trent slip trailer that could draw three parallel lines, if necessary in three different colors. From Stoke Museum.

adequately repaired. Thrown plates usually stand up better to slipping than do molded ones.

Slip Trailers

A great variety of containers have been used as reservoirs for slip trailing. The simplest is a paper cone; the commonest today is a hard or floppy rubber bag. A section of a bicycle tire inner tube with a cork inserted is suggested by Clark (1984). Although cows' horns and other esoteric containers have been used, the earlier slip potters normally made their own pottery vessel either as a slip cup or as a closed-over container with a hole at the top for filling and also for controlling the flow by covering with the thumb. Multicompartment trailers allowed the use of more than one colored slip to be applied at the same time and reservoirs with up to seven outlets are known. In 1811, Richard Waters was granted a patent for making cloudy, or Welsh ware by using a number of pipes to distribute the color rather than one as formerly. It is likely, however, that multiple trailers predated this patent. *Welsh ware* simply meant trailed or marbled pottery. The slip pots were designed for comfort and ease of holding; they would often have depressions to fit fingers and thumb or were shaped to sit easily in the palm.

Nozzles have been made from any natural material that provide a rigid tube: bamboo in the East and goose quills in the West were the most common. Today they are of glass or plastic. A very individual "trailer" in the form of a ladle with a hole in it was used by Hamada for rapid, free trailed/poured slips and glaze. It is interesting that the sweeping movement was always toward his body.

Slip Trailing

Although slips were the basic decorating materials throughout the first 6,000 years of ceramic history, the trailing of slip through a nozzle onto dishes and pots appears only rarely. There are a few Roman bowls with white trailed lines in regular patterns, and the incredible **barbotine** relief figures and animals are built up from very thick slip indeed. The Castor potters must have reveled in their emancipation from the tight

A simple and well-contrasted pattern in white slip on a near-black ground. The little breaks in the sweeping lines are an object lesson in design. Castor ware from Roman Britain of the second and third centuries A.D.

On this Tamba bottle, white slip has been trailed onto a black glaze into which it has to some extent become embedded during firing. For this unusual mixture of materials it is obvious that careful experiment would be necessary.

An amusing motif from an early-eighteenth-century slip-trailed plate.

molded designs of much Roman gloss ware. It was not until the thirteenth century, when trailing began to be used on the ubiquitous medieval jugs, that it became at all widely practiced. From that time on it was part of the stock-in-trade of the peasant potter and reached a high point in late-seventeenth-century England and Europe. Examples are also found in eighteenth- and nineteenth-century U.S. folk pottery, where the tulip was the favorite motif, probably imported from Germany.

The trailed line is sometimes left as sufficient in its own right, but it more often acted as a defining limit for washes or brushed-over areas of slip. An additional ornamentation, developed on seventeenth-century slipware, was to apply dots, usually of white slip, along the line giving a jewel-like effect. Another curious development in Pennsylvania was to beat the slipped line into the surface with a "batter." This could only be done on the flat sheet, and the dish would be made after the decoration. It was considered that battering prevented the design from flaking under heat or wearing with use. Special unbattered pieces were made for display only. Country potters continued with slipware until their recent and almost complete extinction. The partial eclipse of earthenware over the last thirty years has reduced the number of studio potters who decorate with slip, though a few have continued in the traditional manner. Bernard Leach had used it in 1917 in Japan and later at St. Ives. There was a short-lived but lively resurgence in the 1950s in England with David Eeles, William Newland, and others, and Sam Haile used it in an individual way a decade earlier. It has been used

An English traditional pie dish enlivened with flicks of trailed slip on the dry body.

An unusual design on an English country-ware dish, probably from the early nineteenth century.

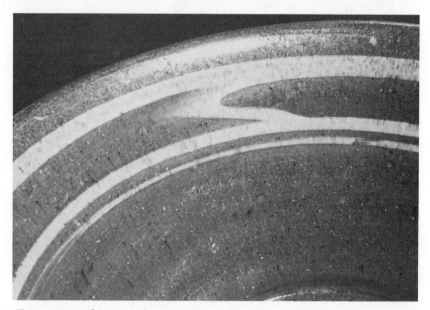

The country potter of the nineteenth century could not spend time decorating his pieces, and in this case, rather than lift the trailer from the bowl between one line and the next, he has made a swift and entirely effective transition with the slip still flowing. Note also the intuitive design sense in the lower fine line which gives balance and a sense of completion. A Welsh dough-mixing bowl in traditional style.

on stoneware, and its application has been widened to include the rather wild spurting of slip over surfaces, trailing onto spinning pots, and other variations.

There are two main slip types: that trailed onto a leather-hard clay ground, as was generally used historically for figurative designs; and the use of a wet slip base, essential for feathering and marbling and favored by many modern potters for its fluid quality. Spontaneity and boldness are the hallmarks of good trailing. With great insight, Tony Birks describes trailing as midway between the work of the cartoonist and the folk artistry of the cake-icer. The physical act of trailing is a simple one but capable of great

An unusually wild and free piece of slip trailing from Crete, covered with a thin amber-yellow glaze. Probably from the late nineteenth or early twentieth century.

variety. Modern work rarely achieves the lively immediacy of much eighteenth- and nineteenth-century trailing, naive though these often were; speed and confidence can only come with long practice.

Essentially different effects will result from wet and dry grounds, as mentioned above. Dry ground is naturally harder in style, but much of the admired work of the past was done in this way, the enclosed areas being filled by means of a trailer or a large slip-loaded brush. The line will be in visible relief under the glaze unless battered. This sort of work is most effective on large surfaces. Birks recommends covering the surface with slip for "wet" work but letting it dry to a tacky state before trailing. This would give better adhesion. For wet-ground trailing, the dish needs to be leather-hard (unless trailed first in the flat state) and to be supported by clay rolls or a mold. The point of the trailer should be held only just above the newly slipped surface, and the slip should be applied with a smooth but brisk movement. If noticeable pressure on the slip bag is necessary to extrude it, then the slip is too thick. The old pot-and-quill trailers relied on gravity alone, and this should be your guide. See also **Blow bottle** and in Fournier (1977) for illustration of a "blow pipe" trailer by Peter Smith, a version of the baby-bottle type that has been used. The hard-rubber bulb trailer is less likely to result in a free and spontaneous line than other types. In Pennsylvania the potter used an open cup and controlled the flow by raising and lowering the quill spout. In England the container often had a hole in the top, the flow controlled by means of a thumb over the hole. With wet-ground work, if the finished dish or slab is raised an inch or so on one side and allowed to drop back onto the bench, the line will become more

Sam Haile started trailing in a lively but more or less traditional way but developed a very individual style as shown under **Bib**.

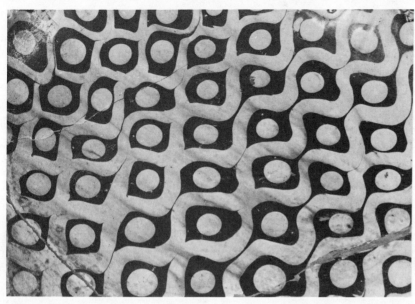

Detail of a dish by Bernard Leach showing how the spaces between the lines and dots form attractive designs in themselves.

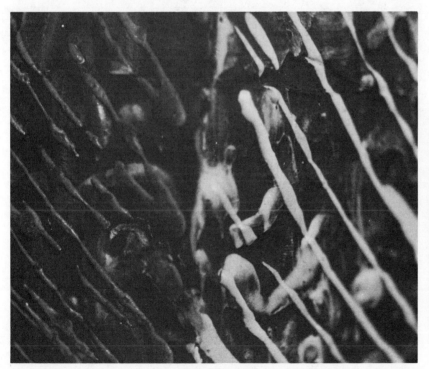

A detail from a form (similar to that shown under **Painting on pottery**) by Henry Pim, illustrating a modern approach to slip trailing.

A pie dish by Maureen Koppenhagen. The slip trailing and filling are in the Toft style but also have overtones of the later molded line. The whole is covered with a transparent green glaze.

Vigorous and free trailing on a stoneware dish by Takeshi Yasuda.

integrated with the ground. Stop well short of marbling, however, and it is not advisable to do this to trailed lettering. Mary Wondrausch (*Ceramic Review 79*) works with very liquid slip from a well-filled trailer, and the line sinks into the base slip. She then "jewels" the line with white slip. Work is done on the thrown dish before turning. Watt, Blake, & Brears TWVD is the trailing clay.

Leach used a combination of line with areas of colored slips to give contrast and mass to a design. The result is something of a hybrid but can be more dramatic than simple trailing, which gives quieter and more relaxed satisfactions. Another interesting variation is to slip the whole surface and then to sponge away an area or areas before trailing. This can give bold and varied effects. The eating-away of slip by glaze will also alter the appearance of a design that looks solid when raw, and some potters, for example, Peter Dick, use the effect to give interest to standard wares. On upright surfaces the pot may usefully be held at an angle, or a more informal cascade may be trailed on by holding the trailer still and revolving the pot (or dish; see illustration) on a wheel. The thickly modeled barbotine Romano-British beakers have never been

Clean asymmetric trailing on a thrown bowl and saucer by Margaret Carr; and a detail of similarly asymmetric lines trailed onto lightly brushed slip (hakame), the trailer moved as the bowl revolves on a wheel. By Sheila Fournier.

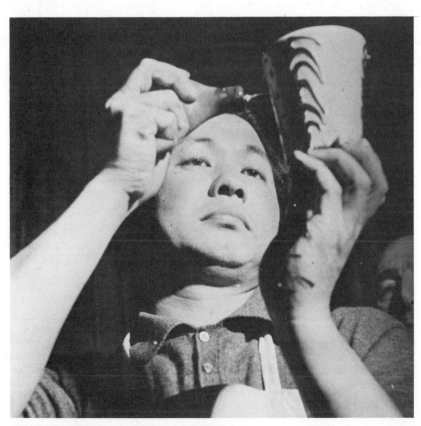

Kenji Funaki trailing the side of a beaker—held upright!

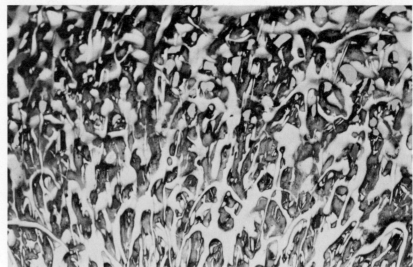

Porcelain slip trailed into a hollow mold has become the bowl itself; decoration and form have, indeed, become one. A remarkable technique by Barry Guppy.

reproduced, the nearest being the laborious **pate-sur-pate.** At the other extreme a design can be built up of dots of slip, as is seen on peasant pottery of Eastern Europe and the attractive and distinctive trailing in this style by David Morris.

Prepared slips made of refractory, low-shrinkage materials are sometimes trailed onto biscuit. At Tambo, Sanders shows a lengthy piece of calligraphy that was trailed onto unfired glaze to become an imbedded white-line slip in an almost black glaze after firing.

Smalt

A fused mixture of cobalt, sand, and a flux used especially in European tin-glaze work. It was the finer of two ceramic blues, the other being zaffer, and was developed in Saxony in the mid-sixteenth century. See details under **Cobalt.** A certain Christian Wilhelm expressed interest in manufacturing smalt in 1620. In the United States it was supplied as early as 1787 from East Haddam, Connecticut. Smalt is often mentioned by Storr-Britz in indicating any pigment/flux mixture, not merely of cobalt. She suggests mixing the frit with a little clay and recommends it for banding.

Smear Glaze

Mentioned by Boger (1971) as a technique of wiping the insides of saggars with glazes so that a thin deposit is induced on the surface of enclosed pieces. She says that it followed salt-glaze and can be confused with it. It is, in effect, a controlled form of flashing. Hughes calls it "an almost invisible glaze displaying a suggestion of a dull polish." Cups of glaze and other volatile materials were introduced with the pottery into tightly sealed saggars. Joanna Constantinidis today achieves very striking results from a similar technique. See illustration under **Fuming.**

Smoked Glaze

If a reducing atmosphere or smoke is present in a kiln at temperatures below 1,000° C./

1,800° F., carbon can stain the raw glaze and fail to burn out even at stoneware temperature. The cloudy marks can be decorative but are rarely intentional.

Snakeskin Glaze

A decorative effect caused by high surface tension. Dodd gives a formula for firing at 1,140° C./2,085° F.—0.3 PbO; 0.3 MgO; 0.2 CaO; 0.2 ZnO; 0.2 Al_2O_3; 1.5SiO_2. Hamer, however, recommends a double glaze layer, the undercoat a good well-fitting dark glaze possibly strengthened with a binder, and the top layer a high-clay recipe that will crawl over the lower one. The under-glaze may be soft-fired first. Also called **lizardskin glaze.**

Sodium Compounds

See **Flashing** and **Salt-glaze.**

Solution Color

Color imparted by certain pigment oxides dissolved in a glaze and having the same hue by transmitted and reflected light. The majority of common colored ceramic glazes fall into this category.

Spangles

A coarse iron oxide. See **Magnetic iron.**

Speckling

Speckled glazes may result from iron impurities burning through from the body, especially under reducing conditions. See also **Bleed-through.** In oxidation the use of dried and crushed red clay in the glaze recipe, even though passed through an 80 sieve, can produce a fine speckle. Iron spangles is also used but is more difficult to keep in suspension.

A flashed, speckled stoneware bowl, biscuit outside, glazed in, by Gwyn Hanssen. Some natural clays will develop speckle, especially in reduction, but it can also be induced artificially by the addition of iron spangles, etc., in the body.

The speckle on this oxidized buff stoneware ash glaze has developed through the inclusion in the recipe of hard-dried and resoaked red clay passed through a 60s sieve.

Mary Rogers, who is "fascinated by speckled and dappled things—the speckles on trout, inside of flowers, birds' eggs, and broken shadows on water," builds up her textures with tiny spots of pigment that merge and unify in the firing. One can also speckle with a coarse spray or by using unground pigments (see also **Iron**), although the results are not always aesthetically desirable.

Spiral

See **Circle and spiral** and **Throwing rings**.

In one of the most ancient pottery cultures, the Naqada of pre-Dynastic Egypt, the spiral, closed at the outer limit, is commonly featured.

Details of two types of "endless spiral," one design surrounding a Cretan (Minoan) jar of the seventeenth century B.C. The second is a detail from a tall, squared Late Jomon (Japanese Neolithic) vessel, three vertically arranged spirals on a crosshatched ground.

A beautifully drawn endless spiral on an ancient pot.

A "catherine-wheel" of painted spiraling lines giving an effect of continuous movement. Thirteenth century, Mamluk period. The alkaline glaze has given great control of the color.

Splashed-on Glazes/Colors/Slips

Roughly poured or splashed mottled colors have a long history: a Cretan pot *ca.* 1600 B.C. in the British Museum with "splash and trickle" slips; the T'ang Chinese work to which the name **tiger skin** is sometimes applied; early Persian (eleventh-century) pots and bowls with splashes of pigment over sgraffito; some pieces from the Yuan dynasty (illustration in *Ceramic Review 54*); the Japanese pottery of Onta; and modern "action" techniques. Historical examples are often combined with more controlled elements, such as the sgraffito fishes of Yuan. The name "hu-p'i" (tiger skin) is applied in Japan to both T'ang and later K'ang H'si wares. There are also some Derbyshire salt-glazed pieces with splashed-on glaze, dark on a grayish background. Today the styles are often literally hit-or-miss affairs, but if practiced with sensibility they can be lively and releasing for the potter.

Sponce

The paper on which a design was pricked out for **pouncing** was known as a sponce.

Sponged Color

The **blue-dash chargers** of the seventeenth and eighteenth centuries were sometimes blue-sponged on the rims. The application of cobalt or manganese with a sponge was used to indicate trees, etc., and fur or hair on cats and other models in the nineteenth century. A group of dishes and plates made for the U.S. market by Staffordshire potters, mainly in the period 1820–1850, are described by Boger as "a rather coarser [variation of] Prattware," but they have a charm and peasant simplicity combined with an excellent grasp of composition and weight. They were of birds, flowers, and buildings with such names as Red House School, Star, and Peafowl. They combine easy brushwork with sponged-on color to depict foliage or a general background. The style is called "splatterware" by U.S. ceramic dealers. A not dissimilar ware was also made in America in the nineteenth century. The modern potter Yeap Poh Chap has used bold

On this charming tin-glaze plate, probably from Bristol, eighteenth century, the foliage has been applied with a sponge.

sponged decoration on plates, but it is not common today. It is a useful technique for students, to encourage free decoration, and it is one of the few ways of getting an overall mass of color in pigment. The pores of coarse natural sponges can give interesting patterns. See also **Ground-lay.**

Spraying, Airograph

Potters have mixed feelings about sprayed glazes and colors for aesthetic, technical, and health reasons. Birks' (1974) advice is to forget sprays. He mentions the difficulties of recycling the extensive waste material and the fact that hand-held sprays cope badly

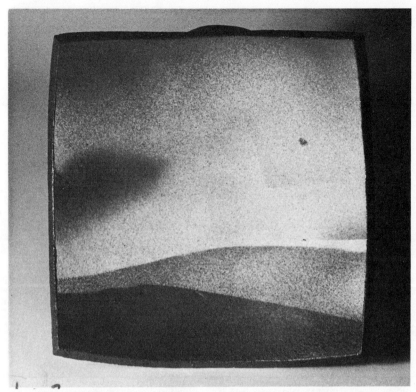

An impressionistic landscape sprayed onto porcelain slip over a stoneware body. For the sharper lines a card stencil or template was used. The textured color is typical. By Sheila Fournier.

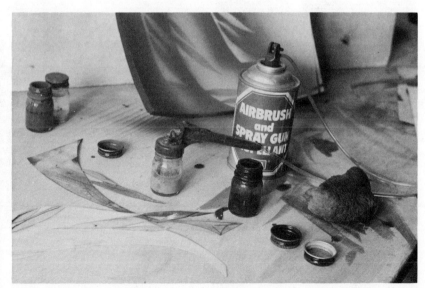

Simple spraying equipment, fairly expensive in use but valuable for trials and short runs. Templates are shown in the foreground. The various bottles of color ready at hand ensure a rapid turnover from one oxide to another. See method under **Stencil**.

with concave and irregular surfaces. Certainly one can spray a large pot with a small amount of glaze, but it is difficult to assess thickness, and it is wasteful in that so much misses the pot itself. It can also increase the risk of pinholing in glaze. On the other hand, it is almost the only way to achieve subtle gradations of tone by overlapping and merging, although these effects are usually reminiscent of the graphic artist and must be carefully controlled if they are not to appear slick. Spraying is useful for glazing once-fired pottery and is used by Colin Pearson for his "winged" forms. Glaze spraying over underglaze colors is not so likely to damage them as dipping would.

Spraying is a comparatively modern development. Cooper (1972) mentions elaborately sprayed ware of the 1880s from the Rookswood Pottery of New England, giving subtle changes of brown, yellow, and green described as "Rembrantesque." Spraying for technical reasons is common in the industry. Today Ian Pirie combines incised lines and brushwork with spraying for his landscapes; Sheila Fournier sprays oxides onto a porcelain slip over a stoneware body to bring out the brilliance of the colors; and others use the technique in many ways and for a variety of reasons.

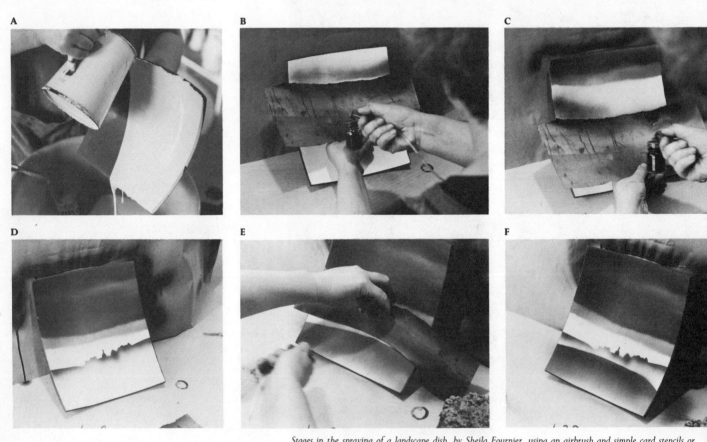

Stages in the spraying of a landscape dish, by Sheila Fournier, using an airbrush and simple card stencils or templates.
A. Covering the clay with a porcelain slip. This will help to ensure adhesion of the pigments and give a slight gloss after firing. B. Using a torn soft edge of stiff paper when the first sky color is sprayed on. C. The same stencil used to build up a skyscape. D. A more elaborately cut edge used to give a village skyline. E. A harder edge of card produces a roll of hillside. F. The landscape completed. The undefined area immediately above the hill suggests mist.

There are several types of spray-guns. The simplest is powered by the breath of the potter, the type of blow-gun used to cover drawings with varnish—take care not to inhale! In the late nineteenth century, in Cincinnati, Laura Fry was granted a patent for the application of underglaze colors using a mouth-atomizer, but it was not upheld in a later court case against Rookwood Pottery in 1898. The basic powered gun is an aerosol with a spray nozzle attachment, obtainable from potters' merchants, with various-sized apertures for glaze and for different types of color. For example, a commercial underglaze color uses a special nozzle. (See **Airbrush** for illustrations of the use of spray-guns.) It is a fairly expensive way to do the job but is useful for experimental work. A paint spray-gun can be fitted to an electric drill or to a vacuum cleaner according to the type of mechanism; it is rather noisy and liable to clog. Larger-scale set-ups are available, with a booth and exhaust fan, both of which are essential for general work. Hand-pumped sprayers, such as those used for insecticides, can be utilized for coarse work, but a reservoir type is preferable for better control. Carbon dioxide cylinders, available for making carbonated drinks, may be utilized. It must be stressed that even when using sophisticated booths with extraction units, there is a health hazard with all spraying, since chemicals become suspended in tiny droplets that hang in the air. A mask should be worn and not removed until the spray has settled.

Practice is needed in deciding distance, pressure, and the type and amount of color. Gradations of tone are natural to the technique, as is a somewhat fuzzy edge, although sharper results can be obtained by the use of card or paper resist or stencils. Storr-Britz suggests a pigment/water/methylated spirit mixture for on-glaze (enamel) spraying. Turpentine and linseed oil (the latter for larger areas) are also mentioned.

Sprigging

This is the application of small bas-reliefs or medallions, usually from a mold, onto a ceramic surface. Although sprigging is usually associated with German salt-glaze, especially the Bellarmine bearded masks and the countless Wedgwood cameos in jasper ware, the technique was used much earlier. Much Roman Empire Samian ware combined sprigging with molding and barbotine. There are Han animal masks and a third-century proto-Yueh group (with leaping horses and figures) apparently sprigged, while some slightly later pieces are elaborately covered with flowers, tree forms, and

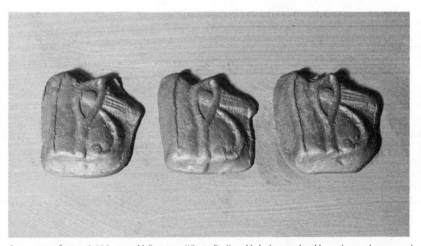

Sprigs taken from a 3,000-year-old Egyptian "Osiris Eye" mold, looking rather like seahorses this way up!

Unusually high-relief sprigging on a Bow (London) eighteenth-century beaker in soft-paste porcelain.

The mold and resultant sprig on a beaker from Winchcombe Pottery, England, 1930–1939. This does not appear to be a true sprig but a circular slab of clay stamped to produce the stag design with the edge impressed with a tool onto the beaker.

lappets. Others are more restrained, with charming decorated bosses set between handles. A type of Ming ware had fish and dragons laid onto raw celadon, which fired to a reddish biscuit set in the glaze. Medley aptly calls this "floating relief." The German potters of the fourteenth century were dedicated to applied reliefs that showed well under the thin salt-glaze. In the sixteenth and seventeenth centuries, entire surfaces of large flagons were adorned with swirling vines, oak leaves, and medallions. On others a single mask was sufficient to concentrate the eye and accentuate the form. Curiously, in spite of much German immigration, the early New England potters only rarely used the sprig. Simple decoration is occasionally found on medieval pots and more frequently on later English ware. At Onda and elsewhere in Japan, applied carved motifs have been used for many years. The technique is known as "haritsuke." Sprigging is rarely suitable for tin-glazed wares and does not figure largely in the great spread of decorated pottery from Islam through Spain and Europe. Sprig molds were brought to South America from Iberia, where they are still used on elaborate peasant pieces. Apart from Wedgwood it was quite commonly used in England; the Astburys applied white pipe-clay sprigs on colored grounds. Although there is a great deal of freely applied decoration today, the more or less self-contained sprig is less in evidence. Seals pressed onto a ball of clay have the appearance of sprigs and are discussed under **Stamping.**

The sprig mold can be of clay, cut in reverse, of course, and biscuit fired; of carved plaster or wood; of plaster or clay cast from another form; or, as used in the industry, of metal. Though the design is usually cut by the potter, it is also possible to press a wad of clay over any object—a doll's face and other images have been used—removed, dried, and fired; or a plaster cast can be taken. The design must be free of undercuts. The individual sprig is normally restricted to a width of about two inches, though larger areas are possible. The essence of a true sprig is its well-defined and self-sufficient character.

On a suitable open shape—the shoulder of a pot or the wall of a cylinder—the sprig can be dampened (not slipped) on the back and applied directly to the surface by

A large, commemorative sprig by Gordon Cramp. The technique is particularly useful for runs of this kind.

rolling it onto the pot and lifting the mold away. Dry, porous molds of biscuit or plaster will release their sprigs easily, but wood and metal need light oiling with a thin lubrication or olive oil. Alternatively the sprig may be removed by pressing a spatula or palette knife onto the damp surface, which will then adhere sufficiently to lift the sprig from its mold. The pot surface must be moist enough (a thin coat of water rather than slip can be brushed on) for the sprig to slide into position. Press onto the damp surface with a wooden modeling tool using the hollows of the design. The method of applying the sprig directly to the surface from the mold is apparent on some historical pieces. The mold-applied sprigs have a mark around them where the mold has come into contact with the soft clay surface, sometimes leaving an impression of the mold wall around the sprig when the pressure has been too great. This could be used to advantage as a "frame" for the sprig. At Soil Hill in Yorkshire and other country potteries a thin coil of clay was sometimes stuck around the outer edge of the sprig, forming a frame and preventing it from lifting off during drying and firing. Building up a design from smaller motifs rather than large sprigs will ease the problems of complete adhesion and the trapping of air. These remarks apply to the traditional sprig, but the technique can be treated as a starting point for further treatment, which may alter or partly obliterate the original motif. But, as Soldner points out, "this is a different ball game."

Spun Color

The spinning of lines or bands onto a pot is dealt with under **Banding,** but larger areas or whole surfaces may be covered by spinning the pot under a loaded brush. A totally even coverage is impossible by this means—the pigment may even run out before a full circle has been completed. This limitation must therefore be turned to an advantage. As the loaded brush touches the wall or surface, a thicker layer will be applied than through the rest of the stroke. The illustration of a Murray Fieldhouse bowl shows how dramatic this can be. The spiraling of the stroke may also be a decorative feature if done with speed and sensitivity. Color on glaze should be applied while it is still damp; if bone-dry, bubbles or bare patches may result on some glazes. High-clay recipes and those containing siccatives may be exceptions.

Detail of a plate decorated by Sheila Fournier, pigment spun over wax resist. The thicker color shows up the resist, the thinner or lighter color gives variety and contrast.

Square Liner

A long-haired brush with a square-cut end. It is designed for painting bands but can also give interesting strokes of a calligraphic character.

Stain

The term usually indicates a very finely ground, often fritted pigment as distinct from the metal coloring oxides themselves. Stains are, of course, made from the usual range of oxides but are not only stabilized and blended with other minerals to produce a given color (though sometimes only in a given glaze) but are also prepared so that the raw, unfired color has some correspondence to the final fired hue, whereas many oxides are black or change during firing. This is a decided advantage in pottery painting or designing, but the colors tend to have the stamp of the factory on them and they are less likely to induce experiment or lead to understanding or individuality. They are rarely used in reduction, and many are prepared for earthenware firings only.

Stained Clay

Most clays are to some degree naturally "stained," generally with iron oxide. Natural manganese-bearing clay deposits are not uncommon. Most of the early slips, and in South America these are of five or six distinct colors, were probably natural clay-like deposits. Today potters use a red or a pale clay with controlled additions of pigment oxides and various tempering materials, or they use prepared industrial body stains that are more sophisticated and finely ground versions of similar materials, which are usually fritted or sintered. Oxide additions will not only color a clay but will alter its behavior; 2 percent of cobalt carbonate in a porcelain body, for instance, may well cause it to bloat. Many pigment oxides are chemically basic and therefore make a slip more fusible. The 10 percent or so of manganese dioxide in a black slip will lower its melting point, and as a result glaze will often take more thinly than on the rest of the piece.

The browns, blacks, and occasional green of seventeenth- and eighteenth-century slips were revolutionized by Wedgwood and others who produced both bright and pastel colors from their "improved" white clay bodies. Jasper ware was made in blue, lavender, sage, olive, pink-lilac, yellow, and black but proved too expensive in pigments and was replaced by jasper dip, a stained slip over a near-white body. Barium was an ingredient of the clay. Other producers reverted to slipping the body clay, but for sprigging, modeling, jewelry, neriage, and agate work a stained body must be used as the only method of obtaining self-color and as such is widely employed today. Stained clays are used by Audrey Blackman for coiled and modeled figures and by Garry Wornell-Brown, Dorothy Feibleman, and others for **neriage, inlay,** etc. Its use does not appear to be so widespread in America.

Stamp

See also at **Seal.**

Stamping

Stamping can mean either of two distinct operations: the impressing of a motif into the material of a pot, or printing onto the surface by means of a relief design impregnated with color. The latter can be done with a cut sponge or other material that will hold pigment (potatoes have been used) and a design built up from repeated motifs. See also

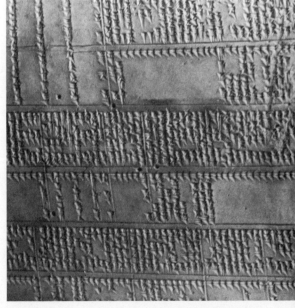

In contrast to the densely covered roll shown under **Impressed decoration**, *this cuneiform tablet has a more open and decorative style. It is a type of dictionary arranged under subject.*

255

Two rare stamped or impressed fishes in the center of a Han Chinese plate. The lead glaze has largely disappeared.

Printing and **Rubber stamp.** In *Ceramic Review 75,* David Morris describes stamps cut from polythene foam with which he applies a blue bentonite/glaze mixture to which a little water-based emulsion has been added. This results in a thinner glaze take-up on the decorated areas.

Impressed stamping can be separated from general impressed decoration in that it is done with a specially prepared tool so that each impression is complete in itself. The commonest stamp is the potter's name or sign. These are dealt with under **Mark** and **Seal.** Very early examples of stamped hieroglyphs are found on Egyptian blue-glazed flasks; circles are stamped on Haniwa figures; occasional "advertising" stamps or

Small star and "caterpillar" stamps and roulettes build up a simple pattern on a Romano-British Castor ware bowl. Fourth century.

The background to the calligraphy on this Song (Sung) T'zu Chou sgraffito bottle is made up of repeated stamped circles such as may result from impressing a hollow key end or a fine tube, probably in this case hollow bamboo.

exhortations such as BIBE (drink) appear on Samian ware; rather crude S-stamps called "duck" patterns were used on 200 B.C. English pots. In Korean Koryu and Yi wares the starry stamped patterns were usually inlaid, as are Seto and other Japanese styles. Rosette stamps are found on third- and fourth-century New Forest pottery and on medieval cooking pots. The seventeenth- and eighteenth-century pottery at Wrotham (Kent, England) was decorated with applied reliefs stamped into white clay on a red body. Rosettes, fleur-de-lys, stars, and masks were motifs used. It is often called

A Chinese pottery stamp, probably for impressing the surface of molds for bowls and other items. See note on a similar Roman technique under **Poinçon**.

Examples of the use of tile stamps in medieval times. The top line shows a recessed design and one from the same stamp but inlaid; the lower shows colored and plain examples of relief patterns.

A fourteenth-century pottery stamp for pressing onto clay pads for relief decoration.

A wooden stamp used for the decoration of tiles in the seventeenth and eighteenth centuries, Devon, England.

*Here "stamping" is used in the sense of **printing**. Random flowers stamped onto Delft (tin-glaze) balls used in the game of carpet bowls. Seventeenth and eighteenth century.*

"slipware," but this is not quite accurate. Stamps impressed into applied pads of clay resemble sprigs, and it is difficult to tell them apart on some early pottery. Often the potter has failed to reverse the stamp. Nottingham stonewares are often stamp decorated, as were some slip-trailed pieces of the Toft type. Cantonese potters have a collection of tools suspended at their waists for notching and stamping of applied strips of clay. In some modern Peruvian villages a single potter will specialize in producing double-ended stamps for the rest of the craftsmen, with curvy leaves at one end and sun and checkerboard at the other. A cluster of circles represents grapes. All of these

Relief decoration from intaglio stamps on clay pellets. Note the flattening effect of the stamps. By John Huggins.

259

A slab-built cylinder pot that has been impressed with a large and a smaller stamp. By Bernard Rooke.

are traditional patterns. It is asserted by a number of ceramic historians that many medieval tiles were stamp-printed with wooden dies dipped in slip, but I cannot imagine slip behaving in this way and have been unable to reproduce it.

Stamps are usually of biscuit or plaster, the latter being made more long-lasting with epoxy resin, though this involves fumes and the heating of the plaster. Follow instructions of the makers of the resin. Sharp edges will quickly wear, even on biscuit-fired stamps. Wood is a possible material; metal will need oiling before use, and the clay

A wooden Indian fabric printing block used as a stamp. The whole block has been pressed into the largest tile but, in the other two, separate motifs from the same block have been used to build up patterns by repetition. The impressions are deeper than they need be in order to show up clearly in a photograph.

should not be too soft. Both carved artificial sponges and soft insulating brick have been used, the latter giving a distinctive granular edge.

Large, six-inch-square stamps are sometimes used for tiles to produce either relief or indented patterns. These are especially liable to damage, and one of the very hard modern plasters, or wood, should be used. Because of the problem of distortion of the damp clay during stamping, the design should be pressed onto a sheet of clay and trimmed later, or the clay should be confined in a frame. Stamped tiles of this sort have a long history, culminating in the many thousands that must have been made through the medieval period for churches and the great houses. Hamilton suggests an interesting variation by means of positive and negative images made by casting one stamp from another and using the tiles alternately in a spread. The same idea could be used for pots and dishes. The great advantage of stamping is that designs can be quickly built up from simple motifs placed in conjunction. Printer's type is a great source of material. See also **Bat printing, Impressed decoration, Lift-off slip, Printing,** and **Seal.**

Stamp Varnish

Varnish or gum can be used with rubber and other stamps to print onto ceramics. When the printed gum is almost dry, powdered color can be dusted on and the surplus removed when quite dry. See also **Ground-lay. Lettering** can be applied in this way. The varnish should be evenly spread onto a glass slab to attain an even coating. Lacquers can be used.

Standard Black

Four percent each of the oxides of cobalt, manganese, and iron in a slip or glaze will generally give black, but the industrial standard black (as in Dodd) is 30 parts cobalt; 56 red iron; 48 chrome; 8 nickel; and 31 alumina.

Stannous, Stannic

See **Tin oxide.**

Steel Engraving

Printing onto ceramics from steel engraving via transfers (decals) or sheet gelatine from steel engraving has been used. To prepare the plate, the steel is covered with an asphalt lacquer and the required design is cut through the lacquer. The exposed steel is etched with a 1:2 dilution of nitric acid and water. Great care must be taken with the acid, and the room should be well ventilated. The etched and cleaned plate is warmed and color is rubbed into the lines, which is then taken off as a print on transfer paper and hence to the ceramic.

Stencil

This is a form of reusable resist that is laid on or held close to the surface of a dish or other piece to control the shape and extent of applied color, slip, or glaze. It can be of card, plastic, thin metal, etc. It can be a solid area or have apertures cut into it. See also **Cut-paper resist** and **Paper resist.** It is usually used to prepare large, bold shapes of contrasting color for further detailed treatment and is especially useful for sprayed work. If a brush is used, all strokes should be away from the stenciled edge. With aperture stenciling, such as that commonly used for lettering, the color needs to be sprayed, sponged, or splashed on, or the once-only paper resist used. Interesting effects result from moving the stencil, giving double images or gradation of color. As with other semimechanical methods it can lend itself to meretricious effects. One can use the positive and negative cutouts from the same stencil as shown by Paul Soldner in his broadly drawn figures.

 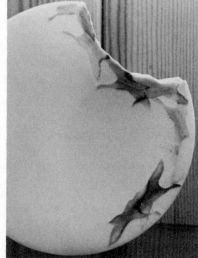

Two repeated stencil patterns: the first as items in the build-up of an evocative seascape by Alan Pirie; the second on a broken-circle form in porcelain by Irene Sims.

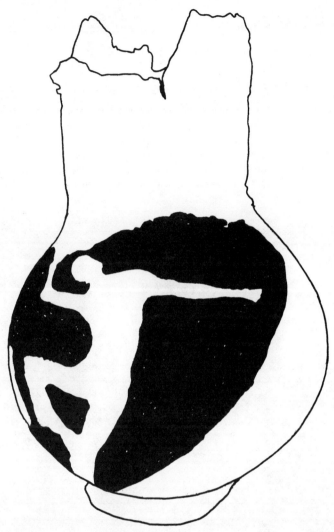

A stenciled figure (cut from a Vogue magazine) on a typical asymmetric and ragged-edged raku pot by Paul Soldner (1971). Iron, copper, and rutile stains were used.

Stones

Some small stones or rock chips will explode on firing, and these have been used in Japan to cause craters in the ware as a decorative feature. In pieces from Asahi the stones explode under the glaze to leave peaks, a somewhat esoteric finish. Other rocks will stay whole or will alter in the firing; those incorporated into Iga wares are given several firings to develop qualities that include "stones like stars." Occasionally surprising colors will result from stones that have been beaten into the surface. I once had a ruby red develop from coarse sand beaten in but never managed to repeat it. Experiments in a saggar or small kiln are obviously essential. "Stone inlay" is mentioned in connection with the Pueblo Martínez family, and a pot is shown in *Ceramic Review 68* with small white inlays round the neck.

An assembled form by Eileen Lewenstein, the clay rolled in coarse sand and gravel, glazed whitish buff, and fired to 1,250°C.

Straw-Rope Firing

A Bizen technique discussed under **Fire cord**.

Strip Decoration

A form of applied decoration using strips of clay which has been common throughout pottery history. There are many examples on medieval English jugs, for instance, some being fine enough to be confused with trailing. The strips may be left plain but are more often impressed with the fingers or with a tool. Plants and trees are often represented, as are abstract patterns, using contrasting clays. It is not often found today but is a useful addition to the decorator's stock of techniques.

An unusual and charming Chinese pot with an "offering" niche modeled in applied strips or coils of clay, tool-impressed to suggest hangings of cloth and rope.

Studs

Small pellets of clay stuck to the surface of pots, sometimes stamped, modeled, or altered, are found in all cultures and in various degrees of sophistication. See also **Boss.** A thirteenth-century Islamic bottle is decorated with studs all over the shoulder; they are used to break the line of a bold rim on Chinese "bulb bowls"; hundreds of studs in fan-shaped lines cover the surface of a Peruvian Chimu bottle; and so on. Although, in general, primitive man liked his tableware smooth, the single stud will

Small studs add to the decorative lower handle junction on this jug, which at first sight appears to be medieval European but is, in fact, Parthian, some 1,000 years earlier. It is coated with a now partly decomposed turquoise glaze.

Studs pressed on so that the edges have split, a simple but effective element of decoration. By Anthony Sterkx.

sometimes point up the form of a vessel, and some curious small cups from Bronze Age Europe are covered with small pellets worked into the form. A number of potters use studs as decorative features today.

Stylization

"To represent or design according to a style or stylistic pattern rather than according to nature," according to *Webster's Dictionary,* and "to conventionalise," according to the *Oxford English Dictionary.* A degree of simplification is also implied, with the eradication of unessential or incidental elements. Stylization occurs widely on ceramics as a matter of both preference and necessity. Designing on absorbent surfaces with a brush or with a trailer does not lend itself to naturalistic detail, although much skill and painstaking labor have been wasted on attempts at "realism," especially in nineteenth-century industrial ware.

All the great decorative periods have used "stylistic pattern," simplifying and imposing their own view of the visible world and sometimes hinting at an invisible one. The type and degree of the stylization of seen objects in different cultures set them apart from one another so that it is easy to distinguish a group of pots from one time and place from another, though a single odd fluke piece can be apparently out of its time.

Leach's desire to capture the essence of a bird in some twenty brushstrokes (see **Brushwork**) is one example of stylization in modern pottery; the ragged scratched line and dabbed and brushed color of Rudy Autio's "Three Ladies" is another. Both potters are consumed with the search for essentials but from the points of view of two different cultures, with something of a chasm between. In the last fifteen years, and in Great Britain especially, landscape has been used as a subject for stylization. The airy suggestions of hill and cloud and tree have been evoked through spraying, carving, painting, even through the medium of mocha. Sheila Casson, for example, reduces moonlight, rolling country, and ploughed fields to a series of sgraffito lines of great simplicity and effect, which come close to the point where the stylization of nature

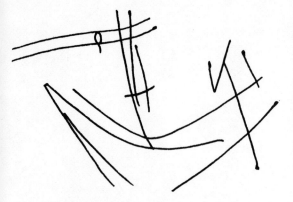

A brilliantly schematic incised representation of a ship from the third millennium B.C. Indus Valley culture of Mohenjo-Daro.

This figure from Persia of 5,000 years ago shows stylization of the highest order, the figure subjugated to the design in a way that foreshadows those of Moore and others.

The simplification of a bird form to a few brushstrokes has been a common exercise among potters for several thousand years, but few have excelled this unknown painter of tenth-century Persia. Compare with the equally stylized but very different characterization of the Mochica bird under **Slip painting**.

The ultimate simplification of a ploughed field landscape into a sgraffito design, by Sheila Casson.

ceases and pure pattern or geometry begins. Such a progression has occurred in all cultures. The simplest device can illuminate the style of thought and approach to life of past peoples: the meandering magic spiral of the Ancient Egyptians as opposed to the hard, precise circles of the early inhabitants of Greece is a prime example: one can almost be thought of as a stylization of water, the other of iron.

Swastika

The swastika, though given notoriety in the twentieth century, was originally considered to be a solar symbol and was widely used on early pottery, especially from the Mediterranean area.

Detail of a Greek lidded bowl showing an early use of the swastika motif set among elaborate geometric designs.

What might be called a double swastika decorates this highly modeled Etruscan cinerary urn.

Tan Bath

A nonceramic surface, but one of considerable longevity. A solution of boiled oak bark is splashed over a pot that is hot from a bush firing or similar primitive kiln, which colors it, increases the burnish, and affords a measure of imperviousness. Similar finishes are found all over Africa and elsewhere, including "sago starch" in Borneo.

Tarsia

An Italian woodworking technique resembling marquetry which has been adapted to ceramics. A pattern is cut away from a sheet of clay and the same stencil is used to cut the pattern from a contrasting colored sheet. The second is inlaid into the first and rolled flat.

Tea Dust

A technique used in the Qing (Ch'ing) dynasty, green enamel being blown through a fine gauze onto a brown or bronze-colored ground (Medley).

Tear Marks

Raised streaks of glaze usually running toward the rim on some Chinese bowls, especially Ting wares. These may have run in the firing but were more likely to have occurred in the act of pouring the glaze.

Template

In ceramics, a mask or stencil, usually in the form of a fairly rigid material such as thin card, that is held on or near the surface of a piece to reserve an area or outline. Used especially in spraying. Frequently only one edge of the template is used. (See illustration and **Spraying**.)

Tenmoku, Temmoku

A widely used dark or variegated high-iron glaze that has been known in a number of forms since Song (Sung) times. Hamada used mashiko clay and wood ash, but there are many recipes. An early form was called "purple ting," and there were also **oil spot** and other effects, the latter called in Japan "yuteki tenmoku." Black raku is another variant.

Terra Sigillata

A term applied to a type of red-brown, glossy-surfaced pottery from Greece and Rome, especially from the latter, which is also known as Samian or simply red-gloss. The word derives from "terra," meaning clay or earth, and "sigillata," seal, from the fact that many had relief or impressed decoration. The surface coating is generally considered to have been made from the finest levigated particles of red clay. See **Burnishing** and **Gloss ware.** A deflocculant can be added to the slip to assist suspension. Rhodes recommends a specific gravity of around 1.2, that is, a thin slip. The firing is low. A final burnishing will improve the shine, but the highly modeled surfaces of the original Arretine and other Roman wares seem to have precluded this treatment. The slip can be dipped, sprayed, or painted onto slightly damp ware. It will probably have a high shrinkage, and the layer must be kept thin if it is to fit most bodies. Behrens suggests a recipe of 40 clay; 100 water; and 4 soda ash. Some degree of imperviousness is imparted but usually not complete watertightness. The term is often used in the United States to describe the modern work of Woody Hughes and others where an oxide painted or self-glazed surface is used, sometimes in combination with other finishes. Some pieces may be burnished.

Tessha

A rust-and-black stoneware glaze, a variety of **tenmoku.** The rust patches are of crystalline iron which has reoxidized during cooling.

A sprayed landscape of the type shown under **Spraying** *for which simple cut-card templates have been used, a curve for the earth and sky and a more elaborate profile for the outline village.*

A modern adaptation of the terra sigillata technique by Fiona Salazar. Hand-built.

Textile Patterns

See **Cloth patterns**.

Texture

Any surface variation that can be sensed by touch constitutes texture, a term allied to *textile*. The surfaces of the majority of pots are fairly smooth and have little texture in the true sense of the word; potters have always tried to make their surfaces as bland as possible by burnishing and, later, glazing. All surfaces, however, have their own subtle character: glassy, unctuous, or dry, and it is interesting to feel a pot with one's eyes shut. The texture—the degree of sandiness or "bite" in the body of tableware—has long been in contention among studio potters, but there would seem to me to be no argument in favor of a body that will damage a table surface. More obvious tactile qualities, however, occur in hand-built "sculptural" ceramics with the addition of sand, grog, metal, stones, and other materials in the body or those beaten into the surface. Alternatively the clay itself is roughened, scratched, cut, and beaten to provide surface variation. Various grades and colors of grogs can be used. Pretextured clay can present difficulties in slab building, where the edges will show a different character.

In Clark and Hughto's excellent book on American ceramics, a note from Mary McLaughlin, writing in the late nineteenth century on the women potters of her time, reads: "Two vases, while still wet . . . have been rolled or peppered with fragments of

A textured background from Song (Sung) China stamped with a tool, probably of bamboo, like a hollow punch. It effectively isolates the powerful calligraphy.

270

Detail of a pot by Lucie Rie where texture is obtained by the crawling and pinholing of the glaze.

A striking disc by David Tomes with spun-combed texturing of the grogged body. There is also the contrast of the steel inset.

A diagonally textured pot by Julien Stair given added interest by variations in oxide staining.

Coarse mesh used to provide surface texture on a porcelain form by Peter Simpson.

Variations in texture are the sole decoration of this large and powerfully coiled form by Ruth Duckworth.

The surface of this ceramic form, "Gull Variation 1" by Gordon Baldwin, has been roughened and scored with color rubbed in and scraped away. Several firings were necessary to achieve the precise desired result.

A variety of surface textures on a piece by Peter Hayes. A form of combing has been used, but the overall character arises from the rolling of a fairly dry clay surface so that it splits into fine fissures.

Texture from sand and gravel slip on the surface of a cylinder, which collapsed under the strain, assuming a unique form. By Eileen Lewenstein.

dry clay until their surfaces were the texture of nutmeg graters." She was not amused! Clay can be rolled onto fabric, textured wallpaper, or netting for surface interest. Sueng Ho Yang (Korea) applies a powdered clay/feldspar mixture to the pot surfaces during throwing to give a broken, rough surface of a highly individual kind (*Ceramic Review* 76). Various common organic materials can be beaten into clay to produce textures when they have burnt away: coffee grounds and wood chips have been suggested. Glazes can be induced to crawl over slips, etc., to give a broken surface. See also **Beaten patterns, Impressed decoration, Scratched decoration,** etc.

Thermotophy

Many potters will have noticed that the colors of pots on opening a kiln that is barely cool enough to touch will be different from the cold color. White glazes appear cream and the quality of browns and reds is altered. The only point in including this phenomenon is that some glazes, notably those containing titania, will reverse the process if subsequently heated. This can cause some surprise when withdrawing a casserole, for instance, from an oven.

Throwing Rings, Spirals

Most potters throughout the history of ceramics have carefully removed overt evidence of processes, including that of throwing. There are a few exceptions: the fine Nubian-Roman amphoras from the fifth century; the occasional Liao Chinese tall vase; the

A

B

C

Three contrasting variations on the throwing or turning spiral. A. Subtle marks on a beaker by Bernard Leach, just sufficient to throw slight shadows but with no enhancement of color or glaze. B. A heavily knuckled spiral rounded over by the thick crackled glaze, its color and texture shown to advantage by varying reflections. By Kathleen Pleydell-Bouverie. C. A sharp, close spiral that alters the color of the glaze on the ridges. Staite Murray.

Siegburg Jakobanne jugs; a splendid Thetford cooking pot with a clean spiral on the belly and shoulder; and some medieval baluster jugs; but examples are rare in comparison with the whole output. Horizontal ribbing is more in evidence, but this is more often turned or added. The true throwing ring is always a spiral groove, sometimes overlapping where the potter has taken a fresh hold. This gives the examples mentioned above their vigor in modern eyes. The deliberate search by the Japanese Tea Masters, however, for rugged "naturalness" often supported very direct, even crude throwing and throwing spirals, and these are common on such wares, especially on those from Imbe (Bizen). Today rings are accepted as natural evidence of throwing and are sometimes used decoratively by brushing color over strong grooves either to give a broken and varied effect or to give interest to a glaze as it breaks and usually darkens on the ridges. By no means do all pieces benefit from or need these ridges, and many potters return to the habits of their forebears and smooth the surface with a rib. On other than tableware the spirals can be used in many ways. Karl Sheid slashes downwards to give a triangular vertical break through the rings, which is very effective. Potters have used sections of thrown shapes to build new forms, and the knuckle marks can be an important element. A spiral thrown on a flat disc can be utilized in decorative tiles (John Lawrence in *Ceramic Review 51*) or on pots as applied ornament. See also the cover of my *Illustrated Dictionary of Practical Pottery*. The illustrations show ways of using spirals on slab pots. Large discs have also been used as free-standing forms, cut and joined one to another, as in the work of Glen Hugo.

Tiger Skin

This is often applied to a variety of splashed-on or mottled glazes such as the T'ang earthenwares but specifically to a late-seventeenth-century use of enamels spotted onto biscuit in a more or less random manner, known as Hu P'i. The name is also given to eighteenth-century salt-glaze of the "crawled color" variety and could be applied to a number of highly decorative surfaces obtained by modern studio potters specializing in salt-glaze. See example under **Salt-glaze.**

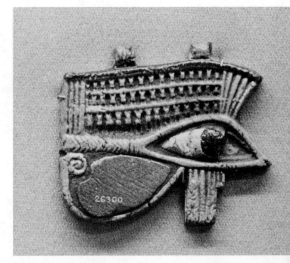

This striking Ancient Egyptian "Eye of Osiris" was probably inset into wood or other ceramics and used like a tile for wall decoration.

Tile Decoration

The Egyptians made glazed tiles using relief, inlay, and incising covered with turquoise and other bright-colored glazes. Some were of a mosaic-like character. Flora, fauna, and scenes of human activity were depicted on them. The Cretans made plaques, sometimes rather crudely constructed, though their architectural ceramics were more advanced than the Egyptians'. Nebuchadnezzar's Tower of Babel used glazed-faced bricks of quite startling colors for the period. Han China produced countless tiles, friezes, etc., that were often decorated with everyday scenes in splendidly drawn relief, giving a rare insight into the culture of the period. They were sometimes green-glazed. It was not, however, for another thousand years that the decorated tile became general in the Near East. The Greeks and Romans concentrated mainly on plain building tiles. The upsurge of activity from the ninth century resulted in a flood of tiles with involved star-shaped and other outlines, which were decorated with relief modeling, colored glazes, and painted designs. The mosques became scintillating bursts of colored abstract and repetitive patterns on walls and roofs, inside and out. The use of tiles on floors was a later Western fashion, since the Arabs traditionally used their equally brilliant carpets and rugs. Pigment, colored glazes, relief patterns, enamels, light-catching varicolored lusters—all played their part in the most dazzling houses of worship in the world.

The decorated tiles of Europe were more subdued but still striking en masse. The first alternately colored plain tiles soon gave way to stamping and inlay, buff on red.

An incised Norman English floor tile, probably part of a large design but complete in itself.

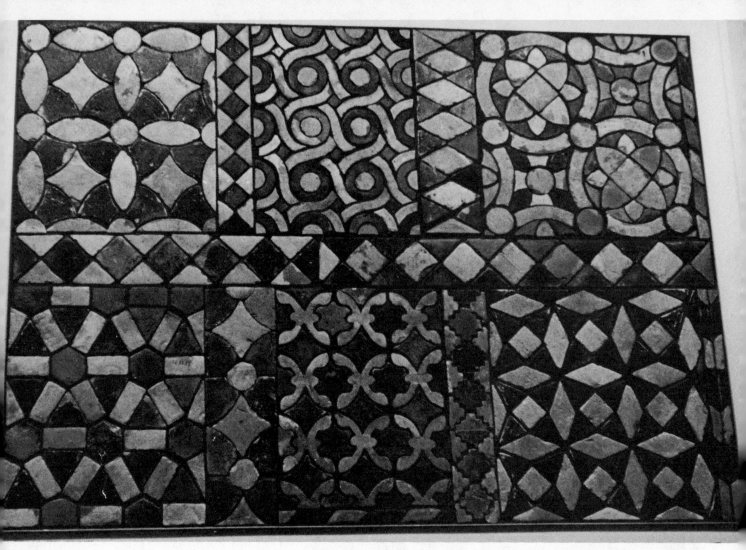

Probably preceding the inlaid type, plain mosaic tiles in colored clays were used to give interest to floors. Such intricate forms as are shown here are rare. From Rievaulx Abbey, Yorkshire, England.

These must have been made in vast numbers. Those that remain show great skill and variety of design. Both the painted and the inlaid tiles were designed to be both self-contained pictures or motifs and at the same time elements in a larger composition. Multi-tile compositions are most successful where the decoration is most stylized and patterned and least where a more figurative or "easel painting" style is attempted, as was done in tin-glaze. In the latter, the inevitable grouting between the tiles can be a disfigurement, and the genius of the early tilers was in covering great areas without this becoming evident. The spread of tin-glaze, majolica painting, and luster across Europe took the tile into Spain, Italy, France, and Holland, the last being supreme in numbers if not always in artistic merit—the ubiquitous Delft tile. The Dutch tile moved, rather surprisingly, from early polychrome to single-color blue or manganese during the seventeenth century. By then, what had been the prerogative of the church, the mosque, or the wealthy had permeated all sections of society and tiles assumed a more modest appearance. There were special techniques employing colored grounds, bianco-

Large relief tiles made in their hundreds of thousands for the decoration of mosques and other buildings in thirteenth-century Persia.

Very few decorated roof tiles have survived. This one is from thirteenth-century Yorkshire.

The style of intricately shaped and decorated tiles that were made in countless numbers in medieval Persia. Note that the drawing of "images," animals in this case, was general at the time and was only frowned upon by the more puritanical converted Turks of a later age.

sopra-bianco, etc., at Bristol and elsewhere, and enamels began to be used. But finally the all-conquering hard flint earthenwares swept from England across the world and tin-glaze lost supremacy. Printing, transfers, dry-pressing of tiles, which had the supreme advantage of side-stepping the problem of warping during drying, had served to turn the tile into a bland background object in spite of the fact that molded, mottled, imitation "encaustic" tiles, designs in a multitude of bright colors, tube-lining, barbotine, lusters, etc., were all turned out in mass-produced quantity. Some rooms and even

The natural wear and tear of time and use accelerated by wholesale ripping up of old tile pavements, meant that few whole patterns of medieval floors remained by the mid-nineteenth century. Efforts were made, however, somewhat belatedly, to repair or reconstruct the most striking of them, including that in the original Parliament Chamber in Westminster Abbey. Factory methods were developed to give excellent copies to fill in the many gaps. In this fine display of inlaid tiles, many are replicas. From the Royal Place at Clarendon, the King's private chapel, 1240–1244. Each row is shaped to fit the great circular design.

buildings entirely clad in flat and molded tiles still exist: at the York Railway Hotel, the incredible Woolworth building in New York, and many others. The British pub took to tilework equally for hygenic and decorative reasons, and there are still fine examples, though they are rapidly disappearing. There are also vast designs of floor tiles in many great houses. De Morgan used modern resources in often distant imitation of Islamic work. They were highly decorative but lacked the verve of the originals and were inevitably stamped with the style of his time. The industrial tile today is at a low ebb of invention and flair, and its main use is a not too obvious background to a bathroom, a kitchen, or an underpass.

A curious Dutch tin-glaze tile with a design resembling a gasometer. Painted in manganese.

A well-drawn example by Walter Crane in the typical style of the late nineteenth century, entitled "Aesthetic Maiden Reclining." A romantic classicism.

Rounded forms contrast with the square outline of the tile in graffiato design by Bernard Leach.

Perhaps the major development in hand-made or individually decorated modern tile work has been the extension from low relief to overt three-dimensional compositions, a movement paralleled in fabrics and other crafts in the late 1970s and the 1980s. These are more often wall sculptures than tiles. Among the well-known potters, Ruth Duckworth, Hans Coper, and Derek Davis have made large three-dimensional wall decorations. Artists like Miró and Artigas have remained closer to traditional techniques though the effect is very different. A successful and distinctive technique by Alan Wallwork is described under **Glaze over glaze.**

The mere shape of a tile can produce ornamental schemes: regular and infill patterns, crosses, stars, hexagonal and other geometric shapes have been used. For a

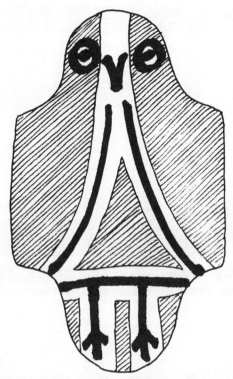

Painted by Picasso, an adaptation to the owl form of the shape of Spanish interlocking tiles.

A circular mosaic-tile table, the tesserae painted in oxides on tin-glaze. The shapes of the sections give form and definition to the design. By Mary Ball.

A multi-tile landscape by Bernard Leach in subdued stoneware colors.

279

"Cat Tryptich" by Alison Britton. Hanging tiles with amusing and original designs, engraved and filled with color.

An example of the three-dimensional type of wall decoration that has been popular over the last twenty years. This is a section of the entrance to a restaurant. By Peter Wright.

convincing finish the shapes must be precise and accurate. Because of its flat surface and simple geometric outline the traditional tile is at once the easiest ceramic to decorate and yet demanding because no help is available from formal qualities. The many methods of decoration are to be found under the appropriate headings, including **Cuenca, Cuerda seca, Glaze** (various headings), **Inlay, Lithophane, Photoceramic processes, Printing, Screen printing, Silkscreen, Transfers,** and others.

Tin Ash

Through the 800 years of the Islamic and European tin-glaze period, the roasting of tin ores with lead oxide was carried out to produce this vital glaze ingredient known as tin ash. It must have been highly injurious to health from the lead fumes, and many a majolica potter must have suffered from "potter's rot." Today the tin oxide is added to fritted lead compounds and other ingredients for tin-glaze wares.

Tin-Glaze

Tin oxide in an earthenware glaze will whiten, opacify, and render it more viscous—the three properties necessary to give clarity and brilliance to pottery colors. Because of its opacity it is confusingly called "tin enamel" by historians, especially if the glaze itself is colored with oxides. Although a comparatively rare metal, tin had long been used in the production of bronze before potters discovered that its oxide or "ash" could be used to provide bright colors. It was used on the Babylonian bricks that made up the great wall decorations in the first millennium B.C. It was then more or less abandoned for a thousand years until it burst again onto the pottery scene with the remarkable achievements, technical and aesthetic, of the Islamic world of the ninth to twelfth centuries. Until that time, any brightness of color had depended on light-colored clay or slip as a ground. The use of tin-glaze as a base for oxide and luster brush painting spread with the Arabs to Spain and thence all over Europe and northern Asia. Strangely, the great Islamic power of the sixteenth century onward, the Turks, returned to the white-slip ground with a clear glaze over, as of course did eighteenth- and nineteenth-century Europe with its improved white clays. The painted tin-glaze in Europe was variously known as Hispano-Moresque, majolica, faience, and Delft in its spread through Spain, Italy, France, Holland, and England, and it reigned supreme in ceramics for five centuries. In Spain the luster brush (or pen?) work, sometimes combined with cobalt blue, is described by Leach as probably the best European brushwork on ceramics. In Italy, work of unbelievable skill led to some excesses, to over-exuberance, to the slavish aping of oil paintings, but also to some great delights. The powerful stylishness of the Islamic-Christian melange in Spain was certainly never repeated. In each country the character of tin-glaze work changed: Spain and Italy have been mentioned; there was a more sophisticated and "classic" approach in France; charming simple brushwork, even when assisted by pouncing, in Holland; a certain naiveté in England, and so on. A tin-glaze ware was made in Liverpool on a body that was virtually a stoneware and is sometimes described as "tin-glaze porcelain."

All this refers to the traditional technique of painting with oxides onto the damp or dry surface of the unfired glaze, a method that necessitates the assured and rapid movement of a well-loaded brush. "Frequent reference is made by writers on ceramics to the difficulty of painting on the porous and friable surface of tin enamel; but it must be pointed out that this had a deterrent effect on niggling painters and was on the contrary a spur to the free use of the brush" (Leach). There are other ways of using tin-glaze. These are discussed later in this article and under **Tin-glaze over slip.**

A somewhat disgruntled (and exposed) Queen Mary on an English tin-glaze plate of 1692.

Typical English eighteenth-century painting on tin-glaze. A barber/surgeon's basin with the instruments of his craft depicted.

A Picasso excursion into painting on tin-glaze, "Simone as a Bride."

The biscuit for tin-glaze should be well fired but not, of course, approaching vitrification, and it must be free from dust and grease. A buff or pink body can subtly "warm" the glaze. The very properties that give brilliance and sharpness to colors also predispose the glaze to crawling. The precise thickness of the coating is therefore crucial, and this demands some experience. A minimum of clay in the recipe is recommended for the same reason. Any signs of cracking of the drying glaze are danger signals. Both crawling and crazing difficulties can be alleviated by firing to 1,100° C./2,010° F. or higher.

Colors are gound in water and used fairly thinly, as the unfired glaze will absorb them rapidly. Normally the oxides alone or as mixtures are used; the carbonates are useful for identification, but it must always be remembered that they are somewhat toxic. Chrome, which may react with tin at any temperature to produce a harsh pink, is best avoided. Longish brushes are needed to hold enough liquid for a free stroke, but all types can be used for special effects so long as they do not harm the glaze surface. Sponging and careful sgraffito through the color are possible.

Tin-glaze is at its most physically stable when damp and is less likely to bubble and drag when painted onto. Caiger-Smith, however, paints on dry glaze. Fritted glazes will be even more powdery. Rhodes suggests adding a fixative so that the painter can be free of the anxiety of lifting the glaze. He also suggests that the detailed painting of the high Italian period may have been done on a sintered surface. Underglaze commercial colors are sometimes used, but beware of chrome. Oxides themselves may be diluted with tin-glaze for painting.

As with all pottery painting, unevenness or touching-up of colors may be masked in the raw state but will show disastrously in the firing. The quality of the colors will vary with the type of glaze. A lead glaze is kinder than a leadless one. "A glaze deriving its alumina from china stone or feldspar is likely to have richer colors and carrying properties than one dependent on china clay" (Caiger-Smith). Tin itself is preferable to other opacifiers such as zircon, which is liable to give brasher colors. A mottle or speckling of the color may result from a high whiting content in the glaze.

Tin-glaze painting can be combined with a sgraffito through the glaze to the body, with greater effect over a redder than normal clay. This can quite alter the character of the technique. Colors will stain upward through a tin-glaze if adequately applied. See notes under **Transmutation of color** and **Underglaze colors.** This method has the advantage that the painting can be done on the raw clay, a much less hazardous proceeding. The normal addition of tin to the glaze is 10 percent, but up to 15 percent has been used in a high-lead glaze by Casson and others, giving bright blushes through from a red body. Tin-glaze is also, of course, a base for colored glazes.

Tin-Glaze Over Slip and Clay

Tin-glaze normally covers the underlying biscuit and is only marginally affected by it. But if the body is of a dark red clay or is covered by a pigment-bearing slip, this can produce varied and pleasant effects, especially, strangely enough, if glaze with a high tin content is used. Amounts of tin oxide below 8 percent of the recipe will give watery, indecisive colors, but the recipe used by Casson on his early pieces—a high-lead glaze with 15 percent tin—gave sharp, bold, and attractive breaks, from milky white to deep red-browns on edges and along the lines of sgraffito and modeling. Slips under tin-glaze need rather more than the average amount of pigment added. Manganese is the most rewarding, using 8–15 percent of manganese dioxide, giving brown-grays of various qualities and depths with sometimes a rose blush as a bonus. If cobalt is added to the slip, a colder gray will result. Copper will produce a watery green, cobalt alone strong but muted blues. In combination with engraving, sgraffito, and resist patterns, a wide variety of character is possible. A slightly softer glaze than normal is a help, as is a higher firing to help the color transmutation. My experience has been with tin as the opacifier, but titania is also recommended by some potters.

Tin Luster

The frequent iridescence on white raku glazes is caused by the rapid reduction of tin oxide.

Tin Oxide

Historically, this is the most commonly used and is still the most effective opacifier for glazes up to about 1,200° C. (cone 5). Being acidic in action, it will harden a glaze and is sometimes subject to crawling. Pigment oxides respond in a softer and more attractive way than with zirconia or titania. Unfortunately, it was never a cheap material, and its use has been curtailed in recent years by soaring cost. 10 percent is the normal addition in an earthenware glaze. See also **Tin-glaze** and **Tin-glaze over slip.**

Titanium

Used as titanium dioxide—titania. It acts as an opacifier, but by reason of its ability to act as a minute source of crystallization during cooling it will develop a more matt surface than will tin oxide, which simply fails to dissolve. Small amounts can brighten colors but larger additions—3 to 5 percent—begin to cause mottle, and still higher amounts create a crystalline surface. Titania-opacified glazes tend toward a cream

Detail of an earthenware plate. Black slip has been used over paper resist with some areas sgraffitod. The whole is covered with 12 percent of tin oxide in a lead/lime/potash glaze, giving a soft gray ground with black edges to the motifs and cuts.

color. See also **Rutile.** Glazes with titania and some rutile develop, according to Hamer, both phototrophy and thermotrophy. Titania can develop yellows with chrome and can turn iron green with 0.1 titania to 0.9 iron oxide (Parmalee).

Tool Decoration

See **Carving, Chatter, Combing, Engine turning, Engraving, Faceting, Fluting, Incising, Indentation, Roulette, Stamping,** etc.

Torn-Paper Resist

See **Paper resist.**

Torsade

A band of decoration in which two lines twine regularly around a row of circles.

Tortoiseshell

An effect produced by dusting oxides of manganese, copper, and sometimes cobalt onto a damp lead-glazed pot. In the eighteenth century, Thomas Wheildon "sprinkled . . . green ware . . . with powdered lead oxide and calcined flint mixed with a trace of manganese di-oxide" to produce a tortoiseshell effect (Hughes). Later, other colors were used on biscuit.

Tou-T'sai

A Chinese palette of opposed or contrasting colors. Delicate translucent over-glaze enamels filled areas outlined in underglaze blue.

Trail and Feather

See **Feathering.**

Trailed Glaze

See **Glaze trailing.**

Trailers

See **Slip trailers.**

Transfers, Decals

Transferred designs were first used on small metal pieces such as patch-boxes, and the method was adopted by the rising ceramic industry from the mid-eighteenth century. It is therefore a relatively modern industrial technique that can nevertheless be used with advantage on certain studio ceramics. Two men, John Sadler and John Brooks, claimed to be the inventors of the technique in the 1740s. Sadler went on to the mass-production of tiles, first from wood blocks and then from copper plates. The first transfers, however, appeared on porcelain and only later on earthenware. The printing was done on prepared paper and applied, printed side down, onto a glazed surface. The paper was later floated off. Most prints were in black, some in purple, blue, or manganese brown. At Battersea Enamel Works, three specialists perfected their manufacture: Janssen was the paper expert, Brooks oversaw the copper plates, and Delmain mixed enamels with printer's inks (Hughes). Outlines printed onto ceramics were filled in by hand from 1825. After 1764, transfers were used extensively on Wedgwood and later on all industrial wares. Some designs were washed over with a pale color. Bat printing was used from 1760 to 1825 and has been used in a modified form since.

Lithographic transfers were used from 1839 but tended to be rather dim, as only a small amount of color could be applied. Printing in gold and other pigments was developed through the ninteenth century, as were techniques for printing realistic pictures of birds, etc., in natural colors. The system was slowly taken up in Europe. Boger (1957) asserts that "transfer printing generally produces an inferior quality of decoration"—inferior, presumably, to painting, to which it is not strictly parallel. The danger was that since anything could be reproduced, anything was. The other side of the argument is summed up by Honey: printed designs are preferable on industrial wares to complement multiple casting. He describes the decal as the autographic work of an artist engraver multiplied mechanically. Today photographic techniques are widely used.

Transfers are now made on a water absorbent paper such as Simplex (thermo-flat paper for slide-off transfers) coated with a gum onto which the design is printed in ceramic color, often enamels, sometimes underglaze. The whole is covered with another layer known as the cover coat. After soaking in water until it has curled up and straightened out again, the print and cover coat will slide from the paper and the residue of the gum will assist it in adhering to the ceramic surface, which is usually glaze but can also be presized biscuit. The surface should be clinically clean, and if necessary wiped over with methylated spirits. The transfer will be wet enough to slide into position. Working over with cotton wool or a soft rubber kidney will perfect the all-over adhesion, which is essential if it is not to curl away in the firing. The paper should not be stored too long. Transfers can be made by lithographic or screen techniques, the latter giving a thicker layer of color. They are generally made by specialist printers, although the screened variety is somewhat easier for the potter himself to make. See **Silkscreen.** Printing onto paper from a copper plate has been done for many years. The decal is placed image down on the ware and the paper soaked off. Victorian blue printing was done in this way. It will be realized that the ceramic color is an oil-based one in these methods.

Firing must be slow in the initial stages, taking three to four hours to reach 200° C. in a clean well-ventilated kiln. It can then speed up until the optimum temperature is reached for the particular pigment. Underglaze printing onto biscuit will need a firing to fix the color. If several firings are needed for different colors, choose those least likely to fade for the earlier firings, for example, the blues.

Transfers can be used by the studio potter as images in themselves, or the original design can be cut and rearranged until its identity is lost in a new concept. Layers of images, fired separately, can also be formed. Transfer technique is not a simple system and there are numerous pitfalls—curling, blowing, fading, etc. One glaze will be found to take the color better than another. Decals are sometimes used by modern potters to achieve flat, sharply defined areas of color in a "graphics" style. Glenys Barton uses them in this way on her angular forms of "bisected tetrahedrons" (see *Ceramic Review 22* and Lane, 1980) and the like. Some professional printers have started to advertise in pottery magazines offering to make short runs of a design. One such is McLaggan Smith Prints of Scotland. Further illustrations of techniques are under **Decal** and **Photoceramic processes.**

A distinctive system is described by Conrad, whereby ceramic color can be trans-

Open and translucent holes give variety to this porcelain bowl by Emmanuel Cooper.

ferred from an existing relief pattern or texture by coating the relief with an oil medium using a hand roller. Waxed paper is pressed onto the oil and then applied to the ceramic to give a tacky pattern, which can then be dusted with color. The loose color can be brushed away when the oil is dry.

Translucency

The early Chinese porcelains were often fairly thick, and translucency was not a prime aim. Later and especially in Qing (Ch'ing) times it assumed much greater importance, and such techniques as **secret decoration** depend upon it. Much of Japanese porcelain and English bone china is glassily translucent. The Islamic potters achieved it to a small degree by using a clay/frit body, which seldom has the other qualities of fineness of grain, smoothness, and whiteness. Many potters today find the quality intriguing and make both "true" porcelain and bone china to illustrate its magic The technique of varying the degree of translucency by cutting away from or adding to the thickness of the clay wall of a pot or bowl is widely practiced today. Landscapes and other designs are cut right through the rims of bowls and other forms. See also **Applied decoration.**

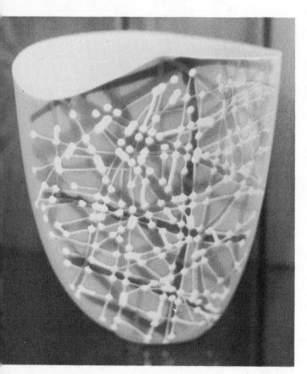

Drilled holes, scribed lines, and color enhance the natural translucency of cast bone china. By Angela Verdon.

A

B

An original system devised by Heather Anderson producing thin porcelain "windows" in a pot. A plaster impression of a linked rubber mat has been taken. This is brushed over with a fairly generous coat of porcelain slip (stained and therefore looking dark in the photograph). When the molded layer is leather-hard it is peeled from the plaster (B) and inserted into triangular apertures in the pot (C), increasing both its formal and visual interest.

C

Transmutation of Color

Some oxides will be transmitted through an opacified glaze so that painting on the raw clay or biscuit becomes color on the glaze surface. The color is generally more subdued than when pigment is used on the raw glaze surface (majolica). Titania is a better aid to transmutation than tin oxide, although the latter is quite effective with manganese, copper, and cobalt. Iron needs titania to show. Antimony does not transmit well through any glaze. Chrome may react in unwanted ways. See also **Tin-glaze over slip.** Copper and some other on-glaze lusters are called "transmutation colors" by Hamer.

Trompe L'oeil

In painting the term refers to a degree of realism designed to convince the eye that two dimensions are three. It is also used in ceramics for highly realistic and modeled pieces such as those made in the eighteenth century at Meissen and Strasbourg. It may also

The innovative French potter Palissy crowded his large dishes with realistic creatures and plants and attained a great control over his colors and clays. This is a typical example made at Saintes around 1560.

have had its origins in Italian Della Robbia wares or in the Pallisy ceramics of sixteenth-century France with their realistic creatures and plants on platters and dishes. The telephones and fried eggs in pottery of a few years ago exploited the same idea—to produce a minor surprise or double take. More recent decoration has stemmed from work in graphics or has attempted to confuse or reverse the dimensions. See also **Optical decoration.**

Tube Lining

An industrial system of slip trailing a tile or other piece at the biscuit stage and filling the outlined pattern with colored glazes. The design would have been pounced before trailing. Probably derived from the Spanish **cuenca** and **cuerda seca.** Tube lining is found on Victorian fireplace tiles, etc., although because of the time and expense of trailing many similar ones were stamped out with metal dies.

Tulip

While a general discussion of decorative motifs would take up a book in itself, the tulip has a rather special place in ceramics. According to Jacquemart's *Histoire de la Ceramique* (1875), the tulip symbolized love. "At the festival of the tulips the most curious varieties are shown in the interior of the Harem." The flower appears on Isnik ware and was introduced into Europe in the mid-sixteenth century. From Germany it spread to Vienna and England and appears on French pottery, often in sgraffito, in the late seventeenth century. An English blue-dash charger of 1682 signed "Richard Key" shows tulip and foliage in blue, yellow, orange, and green. It was in Germany, however, that tulip madness or "Tulpenwuth" took firmest hold, close-run by the Dutch. The Persian name "dulband" has continued in Germany as "dullaban." It also figured at Meissen and Dresden as well as on the less sophisticated peasant ware.

Tulip ware was widely made by the Pennsylvanian-German potters and by others in New England and in areas further south. Generally drawn in sgraffito, the flowers with their leaves arranged symmetrically, were accompanied by other motifs—animal, vegetable, and human—as well as many entertaining inscriptions.

Various stylizations of the tulip motif from nineteenth-century Pennsylvania and elsewhere.

Turned Decoration

Since the development of the throwing wheel, potters have used it to score and cut the surface of pots, if only as a discreet accentuation of the form at the base of the neck or on the shoulder. Turned ribbing or grooves are more common than deliberate throwing spirals. Han wine jars, imitating bronze forms, show double grooves; the Romans sharply incised beakers and pottery of all kinds on the wheel; Iron Age British pots are sometimes heavily turned. Though hard and mechanical in character, Greek pots are seldom ornamented with turned lines, painting being all-important. Similarly other cultures for whom painting was paramount tended to eschew turned ornament. The Chinese are something of an exception: the neck of a Kiangsi ewer, for instance, may have as many as five ridges, but the statement holds for most of the Islamic and the ensuing European tin-glaze periods as well. Early German salt-glazed and unglazed stonewares, on the other hand, can be heavily turned over most of their surfaces. It occurs, often delicately, on English lead-glazed ware, on jugs, and later on posset pots. Tin-glaze is very occasionally ridged or rilled as a dividing line between patterns. It does not often occur as a purely ornamental feature on industrial porcelain or creamware, which is unexpected since the introduction of lathe turning meant that most of the profile was, in fact, turned. The shaped stem and foot of some pieces may be consid-

Roughly turned grooves in the unglazed portion of this Han jar point to a difference in approach between the major periods of China. They would be unlikely to appear on Song (Sung) ware but are in keeping with the sturdy character of this piece.

The body of this eighteenth-century industrial teapot has been turned in sharp horizontal bands, softened to a degree by the twisted handle and modeled knob. The base and rim have been "beaded" with a roulette.

Like the Han pot above, the uncompromising turned grooves in this beaker emphasize its rugged quality. By Denise Wren.

ered as turned decoration. The associated engine turning and rouletting are more common. Many later styles, especially the early-twentieth-century Art Nouveau, reverted to smoother profiles.

The emphasis in studio pottery during the first sixty years of this century on direct and untouched throwing discounted the more mechanical but valid contribution of turning as an embellishment. If one takes Dora Billington's definition of turning as any wheel work that is not throwing, then the perfection of a rim and any circular mark counts as turning, and much tableware pottery gives an emphasis and interest to a simple form with turned grooves or ridges either in the wet clay or when leather-hard.

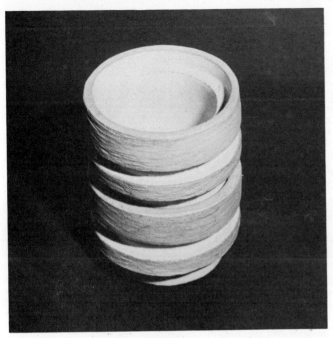

Deep grooving in a thick-walled cylinder enhanced by cleaning the glaze from the textured surface.

A boldly cut spiral in the lid of a porcelain box by Richard Batterham. Compare with similar treatment under **Salt-glaze***.*

Keith Murray designed an ivory-glazed vase for Wedgwood in 1936, the whole swelling form of which was cut with gradated turned grooves. It became well known but had few successors. Karen Karnes' pots often rely for emphasis on complicated turned profiles. In a freer style Richard Batterham's lids are turned in a lively, spiral ridge. The inner foot rings of some bowls and pots, notably the porcelain of David Leach, exhibit an almost voluptuous spiral finish. Scored grooves can define the boundaries of other decoration. Turned decoration can have great potential and is due for a revival.

Turquoise

A turquoise-blue glaze, colored with copper oxide, was almost certainly the first ceramic glaze to exist, the so-called Egyptian paste. It was used for three millennia, largely eclipsed by the Greek and Roman ascendancy, and rediscovered in brilliant variety by the Islamic potters of the ninth century onward. The chief chemical characteristics are that the glaze should be low in alumina and high in alkalis. The body needs to be siliceous for the best results. Because of its crazing tendencies and the preference for muted colors, it went out of fashion in recent times among studio potters but there is now some revival. Frits are practically essential in earthenware, though in stoneware glazes the color can be generated through the use of barium and dolomite with about 1.75 percent of copper carbonate or oxide. It can be very brilliant on porcelain. The color can be imitated by mixtures of cobalt and copper, these more often in enamels.

A Sussex, England, jar inlaid with stars and lettering, which have been impressed with printer's type. An effective minor technique used by country potters for the last 300 years.

More than usually elaborate type-impressed lettering, spelling out a medieval rhyme and signed M.C.–H.B.— The Winchcombe Pottery (1932). Michael Carew and Henry Burgen. The lettering has not been colored or inlaid and relies on the glaze breaking on the edges of the impressions for its clarity.

An interesting use of deeply impressed typefaces, probably wooden ones, for decorative purposes.

Type Impressions

Lettering by means of type pressed into soft clay has long been practiced, especially on eighteenth- and nineteenth-century flasks, bottles, and plates. On most salt-glazed pieces the simple impressions are considered sufficient, but other ware is often inlaid.

The asterisk and other printer's motifs were also used with attractive effect. The use of type is a painless way of overcoming the difficulties of brush lettering. Batches of out-of-use type can be picked up; the larger wooden letters can be used as decorative elements without actually spelling anything See also **Lettering** and **Printer's type.**

Umber

A natural iron earth. Used more as an easel painting color than for ceramics, but it can be employed as a pigment compound. It usually contains some manganese.

Underglaze Colors

Pottery colors, especially when used as oxides, fail to develop brilliance if applied to a buff or darker body; from very early times, pottery has been given a coat of white slip (in some places an imported rarity) or a white body has been developed. Thus the intense hues of Turkish Isnik are painted onto a white ground, itself laid onto a more dun-colored body. A variation using tin-glaze is discussed under **Tin-glaze over slip** and **Transmutation of color.**

The most stable of oxides for underglaze is cobalt, hence the ubiquitous blue-and-white. Although it is so reliable, it can also be crude and needs diluting with china stone, a glaze, or other oxides. Leach used as much as 98 parts of ocher to 2 of cobalt for a pale background wash. Manganese is an effective oxide, copper is watery, antimony needs handling with care, and iron is rather fugitive under a lead glaze. See **Oxide painting** and at the entries for the various coloring metals. Color can be painted onto the raw clay or biscuit. On the former, mistakes can be more easily rectified and sgraffito is possible. The Chinese blue-and-white was probably painted onto the clay, the Japanese onto biscuit. Normally water is used as the base, but in

Underglaze painting enlivened with sgraffito and surface cutting, by Kate Wickham.

A cobalt/manganese/iron mixture was used for the "24 Blackbirds" on this pie dish by Mary Ball. The crosshatching on the bodies of the birds lightens the central mass.

A gay mixture of underglaze and enamels on a slab bottle by Cris Coe.

One of Eric Melon's individual designs in iron and cobalt under an ash glaze (see text): "Theme of Tenderness."

Japan they prepare a boiled green-tea solution that, they claim, helps the brush to move smoothly and freely over the surface. In this connection Tomimoto used a technique by which the surface is covered with tea liquid, engraved when dry, and the whole brushed over with dilute cobalt. The coated area takes up less pigment and the design is retained or "printed" as a deeper color. Glycerine is sometimes used to assist the flow of color, and gums are added to prevent smearing. With oxides the addition of a little glaze or low-temperature flux can avoid the crawling of glaze on loose color. It will be realized that many colors develop only as silicates in the glaze, and in this connection commercially prepared underglaze pigments have the advantage of being stained to resemble the fired color. They are also stabilized by fritting but are essentially the familiar pigment oxides. Storr-Britz suggests the use of metal salts in solution with water, alcohol, or glycerine to give soft-edged effects.

Quality, character, and hue will be affected by the type of glaze used over underglaze colors. For prepared stains a recommended glaze is usually mentioned in the catalogue. The thickness of the coating (commercial colors are usually concentrated and applied sparingly); the thickness of the covering glaze; the speed of firing and degree of soaking; and other factors all count in the finished effect. One of the problems of prepared colors in the frequent presence of chrome often as a stabilizing agent (a count of one catalogue revealed ten out of seventeen hues), which can have unwanted effects in a mixed kiln. Underglaze is also made up as crayons or even

Ruth Dupre's distinctive use of underglaze color with enamel additions.

felt-tipped pens. The crayons can be used like chalks, the excess dust blown away, and the piece then glazed and fired (according to the makers). Color can also be sprayed on.

Mixtures of colors will not always give a "logical" result, and the hues will sometimes separate out under the glaze. Glazes containing zinc will spoil some colors, and each glaze will have its own particular effect. Reduction alters and even destroys colors, except for the ever-steady cobalt. Painting is normally done over stoneware glazes

An easel painter's approach to ceramic decoration with less concern for the actual shape of the brushstroke than with the image to be delineated. The result is wilder than most potters' decoration but is also stimulating. By John Piper.

except for ground washes, which may be underglaze. As with all pottery painting, the single unretouched brushstroke will always give the most satisfactory result. Underglaze colors always develop a certain degree of transparency, and a solid-looking block will look very different when glazed. Stippling, ground-lay, transfers, rubber and other stamps, printing, screening, and other techniques can be employed.

The great problem with all pottery painting is the softening and running of the colors. It is difficult to combine the quality and clear transparency of lead glazes with the viscosity needed to prevent flowing. The Persians soon found that many oxides were more stable under an alkaline glaze, and they accepted the almost inevitable crazing. Effective fluxing onto the biscuit can help, as will the addition of some clay to the color, but this may alter its character. The industrial system of high-fired biscuit and low-fired, thin, fritted glaze minimizes color movement. An object lesson on the great care that a professional potter will expend on this subject is the note on Eric Mellon in a catalogue of one of his exhibitions. He achieves his varied and subtle decorations with cobalt diluted with a little copper, as well as with iron oxides. His medium is stoneware, and the painting is covered with an ash glaze (escallonia ash in this particular case) compiled with the utmost care to retain and enhance the line and brushwork. To quote W. A. Ismay, "It is hard for the layman to comprehend the arduous complexity of the many permutations—of clays, glazes, and pigments which have to be tried out—in the search for a clay body and ash glaze combination which will not too often distort the drawing unacceptably rather than modulate it to added beauty."

Unfired Painting

Pottery and ceramic modeling have been embellished with unfired pigment throughout the ages. The tomb wares of China often show traces of once-bright pigment. A black pigment was used on Mochica stirrup pots. A few peasant wares have been painted after firing. Today many potters, especially in America, use emulsions and other types of house paint on ceramics. Presumably the ancient Chinese tomb figures were colored with unfired pigment for economic reasons, but today it is a state of mind that demands immediate effect, even though the object will long outlast the finish applied to it. There has always been "temporary art" about, but it was usually of a frivolous nature. It may be said that the modern house-painted pot is not a frivolous object but a reminder of the ever-imminent destruction of the world, with no future for any artifact. See also **Nonceramic surfaces.**

Unground Oxides

See **Inlay** and **Speckling.**

Uranium

This material, which has become so central to nuclear technology, was just another coloring oxide until the 1940s. It was mined in Saxony and Cornwall by the 1840s and used as a green-gold enamel and later to produce tangerine and red colors. It can still be purchased as "spent uranium" with low radioactivity. It can be used in glazes up to about 1,050° C. (cone 04). Yellows and oranges may be obtained. The glaze should be low in alumina. Commercial preparations of uranium as a trioxide also give greens.

Vanadium

A modern pottery color that gives rather weaker yellows than antimony but will survive higher temperatures. It is prepared with tin oxide as a yellow stain and with zircon for a blue hue. The stains are rather refractory and need a well-fluxed glassy glaze to give the full potential of the color. See also **Yellow.**

Varnish

See **Nonceramic surfaces.**

Venturine Glazes

See **Aventurine glazes.**

Volcanic Glazes

Many glazes go through an erupting stage during their firing, but most are allowed to settle down again to a smooth surface. The phenomenon, however, can be used as a rather violent form of embellishment. Crawling can also give a broken lava-looking effect, and glazes can be persuaded to crawl quite excessively on a black slip. Such a glaze can be compounded to have a high wet-dry shrinkage and a high viscosity, both obtainable from clay additions. Small craters or holes through a light glaze to a dark body can be elements of subtle and satisfying decoration. Robin Welch, Lucie Rie, and others use glazes in this way. See also **Crawled glazes.**

A glaze (by Lucie Rie) that has erupted and run but is sufficiently fired to have softened and smoothed over while still retaining some of its volcanic nature.

The other kind of volcanic glaze with broken craters can be caused by the addition of a fairly coarse silicon carbide, or of sulphates such as barium sulphate. Lepidolite is sometimes used. Trial firings are needed to find the point at which the craters are still apparent, but their sharpness has softened in a partial melt. Maija Grotell, working in the United States, used Albany slip under a Bristol glaze to achieve a crater effect. Small amounts of silicon carbide can be incorporated into the body to cause some glazes to pinhole and erupt into an overall volcanic effect. This has been done in porcelain by Sally Bowen Prange (see illustrations in Lane, 1980).

Wax

A number of types of wax, including beeswax, have been recommended for wax resist, but a plain white candle (Price's candles in England) will work as well as or better than any. Wax needs heating, of course, and also diluting or thinning. In England the brand name "3-in-1," a penetrating and lubricating oil, is excellent for this purpose, but any thin oil is suitable. It is less inflammable and smoother in use than kerosene (paraffin), which is most commonly used as a thinner. Oil will also allow more time for a brushstroke before the mixture sets. A double saucepan is essential.

Wax Emulsion

There are a number of proprietary brands of wax/water emulsion that can be painted cold onto ceramic surfaces and that dry to a waxy film. Apart from the advantage of no heat being required, brushes can be washed out in water, but the emulsion generally takes a little time to dry. Some potters prefer the quality and thicker coating of the wax/oil mixtures mentioned under **Wax.**

Wax Resist

See **Wax** and **Wax emulsion** for discussion of the materials used in wax resist. An old-fashioned glue pot is useful for melting the wax mixture, and there are sophisticated heat-regulated electric saucepans. The wax/oil proportions are roughly 50:50. Test on a shard with the slip, glaze, or color to be used. Many potters consider wax

Wax painting between glazes in characteristically bold shapes by Shoji Hamada.

An overall pattern built up of short strokes of a wax brushed over with color. The effect is of a great shoal of fish.

Wax resist used equally as a design element and for the practical purpose of leaving the holes unencumbered by glaze. Hand-built salt and pepper pots by Sheila Fournier.

less versatile than latex, especially for sprayed materials, which tend to hang on wax in tiny droplets. Because of the more cohesive nature of slips or high-clay glazes, they do not readily break over wax unless fairly thin or, possibly, deflocculated. Dribbles of wax can be scraped and rubbed with spirit, but badly spoiled pieces need refiring.

The wax coating can itself be cut through to form finer patterns that will take color brushed over, the reverse of the usual effect. The resist in stonewares can be through to the biscuit or between glazes. Other more complicated methods are also used.

At first glance this dish by John Maltby has the appearance of paper resist, but it was, in fact, decorated by means of cold wax emulsion using cut synthetic sponge as a "brush" to obtain square-ended lines. The dots were applied with the end of his finger.

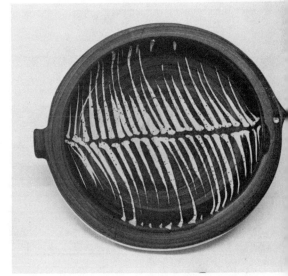

Free and varied wax strokes on a subtly designed "fish" plate by Sheila Fournier.

*Sheila Fournier using wax resist on raw glaze: A. Applying the wax (note the permanently bent-over brush; see text under **Brushwork**), where free and rapid strokes are essential. B. and C. Covering the glaze and wax on a spinning wheel with different thicknesses of pigment.*

Brigitta Appleby uses wax resist and on-glaze brushwork in a unique combination. David Leach frequently uses wax for slip and glaze resist. An early teapot by Peter Voulkos gives interest to the blank resisted areas by using a body with an extensive bleed-through of flecks and spots. On a more mundane level, bases and lid channels are often waxed to give a sharp, clean line to the glaze coverage. An unusual variation is to wax a raw glaze, wash off the unwaxed areas, and then reglaze in another color. A broad pattern is recommended for this technique. Although commonly used today, wax resist is not very evident in the history of pottery.

Wax need not always be used with a brush. Candles, shaped or pointed, can be used directly on biscuit or fired glaze, and wax crayons can also be used. This is of value mainly as a pigment resist. It would hardly be thick enough to resist slip or glaze. Cuerda seca is an associated wax technique. The use of wax with tin-glaze is a modern innovation. Wax resist on earthenware had a vogue in the 1950s, and Picasso used it in his casual way.

An original use of wax as a protective coating rather than a resist is described by Shafer. A design is painted in wax onto a damp, slipped surface and the uncovered areas gently scrubbed so that the slip is washed away to leave the design in slight relief. A simpler variant is used by Caiger-Smith, who paints with a pigment-stained wax and then covers the whole with a darker color, giving a light-on-dark effect.

Welsh Ware

A term used for a high-quality English slipware, usually with a pale body and combed decoration, of the seventeenth century on. See also **Slip trailers.**

Wet-Clay Decoration

The rapid and direct scoring or manipulation of the pot on the wheel are often sufficient decoration. Reeding or grooves near the neck and base are popular embellishments, emphasized as they are by most stoneware glazes. If the pot is not to be turned, the natural or an applied thick slip can be manipulated on the outside walls to give character to the surface, but the method needs skill and a rapid reaction.

Wire Cutting

The shell-like pattern made by drawing a twisted wire through clay is normally

It is possible to develop an interesting surface from stiff slip either by using a brush as in the illustration or by applying it to a pot on the wheel and throwing ridges and swirls, which may also drip to give vertical variations.

Shell-like coarsely-twisted wire cuts constitute the sole decoration on these flowing forms by Deborah Acott.

confined to the base of a pot, where the piece is cut from the wheel, but it has also been used to give pattern and texture to clay surfaces in the building of slab pots and other forms, especially raku-fired pieces. Thicker wires with coarser and deeper striations can be useful. Thin, wire-cut slabs can be applied to the surface in the manner of sprigs. An effective example by the Australian Heroe Swen is shown in Lane (1980).

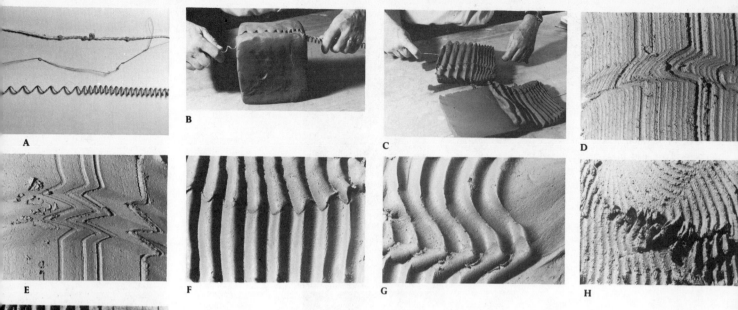

A series showing the result of experiments using various materials to produce wire-cut slabs, which can be used on other surfaces or built up themselves into various forms. A. Knotted, coarse string, loosely knotted fine twisted wire, and an electric kiln element with stretched and close coils. These were all used on a block of clay as in B. C. From the cut block slabs can be sliced with the normal potter's wire. D. Patterns and textures obtained by cutting with the "tools" shown in the first picture. In each case the cut was made with one or more sideways movements to add interest. D. The knotted string. The effect of the knots was to increase the depth of the striations caused by the twist of the string itself. E. The shallower effect of the knotted wire. F. G. The "positive and negative" of a cut with the stretched section of the element; a smooth pattern resembling the effect of waves on sand. H. and I. The same element but more closely wound (on the right of A). This has ploughed and broken the line and has given a completely different effect to the same coil stretched.

White, White Painting

True white is rarely found in pottery decoration. The effect of some near-white slips was emphasized by being placed on a dark ground as early as pre-Dynastic Egypt. Pipe clays are almost pure white. Painting with tin oxide over a slightly tinted ground was practiced in sixteenth-century Italy and elsewhere. See **Bianco-sopra-bianco.** The ground of Isnik painted ware is a brilliant white slip, possibly with tin oxide additions, against which the colors are vivid. Flint and china clay are used in bodies to increase whiteness, as in bone china, possibly the whitest pottery of all. See also **Opacifiers** and **Tin-glaze.**

Window Dip

See **Bib.**

Yellow

Antimony, used as a pigment to produce yellow with lead (in the absence of lead oxide it is simply an opacifier), was known at least as early as the first millennium B.C. and probably before then. Iron will give an ocher-yellow "when bleached in a lime-matt glaze or restricted by titania" (Hamer). Yellow spots from iron can appear on the

302

surface of a high-iron ash glaze in oxidation. Antimony yellow—"Naples yellow"—reappears on Italian majolica of the fifteenth and sixteenth centuries. Lusters from silver in Islam and Spain were golden-yellow in hue. The Italian yellows tended toward orange or ocher, but the later antimony enamels were of a bright lemon-yellow. Enamels in K'ang H'si China were used on biscuit and glazed porcelain in a great variety of hues, from lemon to mustard and primrose, the "imperial yellows." In modern times, low-fired lead/soda glazes have been made to produce a bright yellow with 1 percent of chrome. Iron in a high-barium glaze can give subdued yellows in oxidation at high temperatures. Crocus martis, an iron salt, is reputed to give soft colors in a lead glaze. Uranium has been used, and there exists a rather unstable cadmium yellow. Chrome with titania, and the rare-earth praseodymium with zircon, are compounded as pigments or stains. Vanadium as ammonium metavanadate can be used up to 1,280° C. (cone 9).

The term *yellow ware* is used in the United States for buff clays under a clear glaze, and also appears as a synonym for slipware in England.

Yellow Ocher

See **Ocher.**

Ying Ch'ing Glaze

A pale blue or blue-green stoneware or porcelain glaze of the celadon family, using only about 0.5 percent of iron oxide in reduction. Very suitable for fluted and engraved or incised porcelain.

Zaffre

A now almost obsolete glass or glaze pigment variously described as an impure cobalt arsenate or a calcined mixture of cobalt ore, sand, and a flux. More or less synonymous with **smalt,** but originally a less finely prepared material. See also **Cobalt.**

Zinc

A color-affecting mineral used in glazes, deadening some pigments, altering others, and sometimes causing mottle. Even small amounts will affect many prepared colors. Cobalt and copper react most favorably, but its use should always be preceded by trials. It is also an ingredient in crystalline glazes, forming crystals of two molecules of zinc oxide with one of silica.

Zirconium

Zirconia, the oxide, can replace tin oxide but creates a shinier and less sympathetic surface. It will stand higher temperatures than tin without dissolving. It is not liable to pink flushes from chrome, but there is a zirconium-iron pink compound. Also used as zirconium silicate.

Bibliography

Adkins, Lesley, and Adkins, Roy. *A Thesaurus of British Archaeology*. London and Newton Abbot: David & Charles, 1982.

Austwick, Jill, and Austwick, Brian. *The Decorated Tile*. London: Pitman, 1980.

Barber, Edwin Atlee. *Tulip Ware of the Pennsylvania-German Potters*. New York: Dover, 1970.

Barton, K. *Pottery in England 3500 B.C.–1730 A.D.* Newton Abbot: David & Charles, 1975.

Beard, Geoffrey. *Modern Ceramics*. New York: Dutton; London: Studio Vista, 1969.

Billington, Dora. *Technique of Pottery*. London: Batsford, 1962; rev. ed. 1974.

Birks, Tony. *The Art of the Modern Potter*. London: Country Life, 1967.

———. *The Potter's Companion*. London: Collins, 1974.

Boger, Louise Ade. *Dictionary of World Pottery and Porcelain*. London: Black, 1971.

———. and Boger, H. Batterson. *Dictionary of Antiques and Decorative Arts*. New York: Scribners, 1957; rev. eds. 1967 and 1979.

Bray, Warwick. *Gold of Eldorado*. London: Times Newspapers, 1978.

———. and Trump, David. *Penguin Dictionary of Archeology*. Harmondsworth: Penguin Books, 1970.

Brears, Peter C. *The Collector's Book of English Country Pottery*. London and Newton Abbot: David & Charles, 1974.

Caiger-Smith, Alan. *Tin-Glaze Pottery in Europe and the Islamic World*. London: Faber & Faber, 1973.

Cameron, Elisabeth, and Lewis, Philippa. *Potters on Pottery*. London: Evans, 1976.

Cardew, Michael. *Pioneer Pottery*. London: Longman, 1969; New York: St. Martin's Press, 1976.

Casson, Michael. *Pottery in Britain Today*. London: Tiranti, 1967.

Charleston, Robert J. *World Ceramics*. London: Hamlyn, 1968.

Chiera, Edward. *They Wrote on Clay*. Chicago: University of Chicago Press, 1938.

Clark, Garth. *American Potters: The Work of Twenty Modern Masters*. New York: Watson-Guptill, 1981.

———. and Hughto, Margie. *A Century of Ceramics in the United States 1879–1979*. New York: Dutton, 1979.

Clark, Kenneth. *Pottery and Ceramics*. London: Studio Books, 1964.

———. *The Potter's Manual*. London: Macdonald, 1983.

Colbeck, John. *Techniques of Decoration*. London: Batsford, 1983.

Conrad, John W. *Contemporary Ceramic Techniques*. Englewood Cliffs: Prentice-Hall, 1979.

Cooper, Emmanuel. *World Pottery*. London: Batsford, 1972; rev. ed. 1983.

———. *The Potter's Book of Glaze Recipes*. London: Batsford, 1980.

———. and Lewenstein, Eileen, eds. *Ceramic Review*. London: Craftsmen Potters Association (CPA), February 1970–.

———. *Potters: An Illustrated Directory of the Work of Full Members of the Craftsmen Potters Association of Great Britain*. London: CPA, 5th ed. 1980.

————. *Studio Ceramics Today.* Catalogue of Victoria and Albert Museum Exhibition and Directory of CPA Members. London: CPA, 1983.

Cunningham-Smith, Judy, and Herbert, Mollie. *Self-Sufficient Pottery.* Newton Abbot: David & Charles, 1979.

Dickerson, John. *Pottery Making.* London: Thomas Nelson, 1974.

Dodd. A. E. *Dictionary of Ceramics.* London: Newnes, 1967.

Eames, Elizabeth S. *Medieval Tiles.* London: Trustees of the British Museum, 1968.

Fournier, Robert. *Illustrated Dictionary of Practical Pottery.* New York and London: Van Nostrand Reinhold, rev. ed. 1977.

————. *Illustrated Dictionary of Pottery Form.* New York: Van Nostrand Reinhold, 1981.

Fujioka, Ryoichi. *Shino and Oribe Ceramics.* Tokyo and New York: Kodansha International, 1977.

Garner, E. H., ed. *English Delftware.* London: Faber & Faber, 1947.

Green, David. *Experimenting with Pottery.* London: Faber & Faber, 1971.

Guilland, Harold F. *Early American Folk Pottery.* New York: Chilton, 1971.

Hamer, Frank. *The Potter's Dictionary of Materials and Techniques.* London: Pitman; New York: Watson-Guptill, 1975.

Hamilton, David. *Pottery and Ceramics.* London: Thames & Hudson, 1974.

————. *Architectural Ceramics.* London: Thames & Hudson, 1978.

Hawkes, Jacquetta, and Wooley, Sir Leonard. *Prehistory and the Beginnings of Civilisation.* London: Allen & Unwin, 1962.

Hobson, R. C. *Guide to Islamic Pottery of the Near East.* London: British Museum, 1932.

Hogben, Carol, ed. *The Art of Bernard Leach.* London: Faber & Faber, 1978.

Honey, W. B. *Art of the Potter.* London: Faber & Faber, 1976.

Hughes, G. Bernard. *Collector's Pocket Book of China.* New York: Hawthorn Books, 1966.

Johns, Catherine. *Arrentine and Samian Pottery.* London: British Museum, 1971.

Lane, Arthur. *Greek Pottery.* London: Faber & Faber, 1948.

————. *Style in Pottery.* London: Faber & Faber, 1948.

————. *Hispano-Moresque Pottery.* London: H. M. Stationery Office, 1957.

Lane, Peter. *Studio Porcelain.* London: Pitman, 1980.

————. *Studio Ceramics.* London: Collins, 1983.

Leach, Bernard. *A Potter's Book.* London: Faber & Faber, 1940.

————. *A Potter's Work.* Tokyo: Kodansha International; London: Evelyn, Adams, and Mackay, 1967.

————. *Hamada, Potter.* London: Thames & Hudson, 1975.

Lewis, J. M. *Welsh Medieval Tiles.* Cardiff: National Museum of Wales, 1976.

Litto, Gertrude. *South American Folk Pottery.* New York: Watson-Guptill, 1976.

McTwigan, Michael, ed. *American Ceramics.* New York: American Ceramics. Quarterly, Winter 1982–.

Medley, Margaret. *The Chinese Potter.* Oxford: Phaidon, 1976.

————. *Handbook of Chinese Art.* London: G. Bell & Sons, 1977.

Memmott, Harry. *The Art of Making Pottery.* London: Hamlyn, 1971.

Mikami, Tsugio. *The Art of Japanese Ceramics*. Tokyo: Heibonsha; New York: Wetherhill, 1972.

Miki, Fumio. *Haniwa*. Arts of Japan, Number 8. Tokyo: Heibonsha; New York: Wetherhill, 1974.

Moorey, P. R. *Ancient Egypt*. Oxford: Ashmolean Museum, 1970.

Oswald, Adrian; Hildyard, R. J. C.; and Hughes, R. G. *English Brown Stoneware 1670–1900*. London: Faber & Faber, 1982.

Parmalee, Cullen. *Ceramic Glazes*. Chicago: Industrial Publications, 1951.

Piepenburg, Robert. *Raku Pottery*. New York: Macmillan, 1972.

Piggot, Stuart. *Ancient Europe*. Edinburgh: University of Edinburgh, 1965.

Pollex, John. *Slip Ware*. Ceramic Skill Books. London: Pitman, 1979.

Primmer, Laurie. *Pottery Made Simple*. London: Allen & Unwin, 1974.

Rackham, Bernard. *Medieval English Pottery*. London: Faber & Faber, 1972.

Rawson, Philip. *Ceramics*. London: Oxford, 1971.

Rhodes, Daniel. *Stoneware and Porcelain: The Art of High-Fired Pottery*. London: Pitman, 1960.

———. *Clay and Glazes for the Potter*. London: Pitman; New York: Chilton, 1969.

Riegger, Hal. *Raku Art and Technique*. London: Studio Vista; New York: Van Nostrand Reinhold, 1970.

Rose, Muriel. *Artist Potters in England*. London: Faber & Faber, 1955; rev. ed. 1970.

Ruscoe, William. *Manual for the Potter*. London: Scopas Academy Editions; New York: St. Martin's Press, 1973.

Sanders, Herbert H. *The World of Japanese Ceramics*. Tokyo: Kodansha International, 1967.

Saraswati, Baidyanath. *Pottery-Making Cultures and Indian Civilization*. New Delhi: Abhinav Publications, 1978.

Schweitzer, Bernard. *Greek Geometric Art*. London: Phaidon, 1971.

Scott-Taggart, John. *Italian Majolica*. London: Hamlyn, 1972.

Shafer, Thomas. *Pottery Decoration*. London: Pitman; New York: Watson-Guptill, 1976.

Simpson, Penny, and Sodeoka, Kanji. *Japanese Pottery Handbook*. London: Phaidon, 1980.

Storr-Britz, Hildegard. *Ornaments and Surfaces on Ceramics*. Dortmund: Kunst und Handwerk. Verlagsanstalt Handwerk, 1977.

Thorp, Harold. *Basic Pottery for the Student*. London: Tiranti, 1969.

Watson, William. *The Genius of China*. London: Times Newspapers, 1983.

Williams, Gerry; Sabin, Peter; and Bodine, Sarah, eds. *Studio Potter Book*. New York: Van Nostrand Reinhold, 1979.

Winkley, David. *Pottery*. London: Pelham, 1974.